The School Board Primer
A Guide for School Board Members

Jon Wiles

Joseph Bondi

Allyn and Bacon, Inc.

Boston   London   Sydney   Toronto

Library of Congress Cataloging in Publication Data

Wiles, Jon.
   The school board primer.

   Includes index.
   1. School boards—United States—Handbooks, manuals,
etc. I. Bondi, Joseph. II. Title.
LB2831.W54   1985   379.1'531'0973   84-15858
ISBN 0-205-08331-5

Printed in the United States of America.

10 9 8 7 6 5 4 3 2 1   89 88 87 86 85 84

This book is dedicated to the thousands of school board members throughout the United States who so selflessly give of their time and energy to improve this nation's schools.

We also dedicate this book to our wives and children who understand and appreciate the many hours of effort that go into the making of each book.

Contents

Chapter 3
School Law and the Board Member   65

Chapter 4
Personnel Matters   101

Chapter 5
What Are Schools All About?   127

Chapter 6
Financing Schools   165

Chapter 7
Business Aspects of a School System   195

Chapter 8
Dealing with Interest Groups   215

Chapter 9
Making a Difference—Improving School Systems   235

Chapter 10
Getting Through to People—Leadership and Public
Relations   263

Preface

Serving as a member of a school board is one of the oldest and most cherished traditions in our American democracy. You have been selected by your fellow citizens to provide leadership for the schools in your district. Leadership means more than just a willingness to serve in public office. It means you must study and think. It means you must possess the knowledge and skills to make the best educational decisions possible.

The School Board Primer is intended to provide you with knowledge about the authority of the board; information about major roles of the board and staff members; knowledge about school organization and programs; and understanding about the budget process and business aspects of a school system. It will provide you also with the skills necessary to work with the administrative officers of the school district, parents, students, the press, and community groups, and, finally, it will provide skills needed in assessing school leadership and school programs.

The School Board Primer will serve as an excellent orientation tool for all new board members and a handy reference for all experienced board members. It is easy to read and full of useful information.

Good reading, and good luck during your term of office.

J.W.
J.B.

CHAPTER 1

Welcome to the School Board

Local government is the cornerstone of American democracy. As a school board member you are a part of a rich tradition of dedicated citizens serving in public office. Membership on a Board of Education is a high public trust.

School board members are often the forgotten persons in American public life. Every workday, in communities across America, men and women leave home to attend a school board meeting in a hall or room prepared for them by school administrators.

Your board exists because the legislature of your state has seen fit to establish the school district in which you serve. The legislature can give and take away—that is, it can create or abolish school districts.

SCHOOL DISTRICTS

There are about 14,500 school districts in the country, each represented by a school board. Nearly ninety thousand men and women serve on Boards of Education today representing all ages, races, incomes, and vocations.

There are six types of school districts found in the fifty states:

State Districts.   Hawaii is the only state that has only one school district for the entire state. The only other state approaching the Hawaii single-district model is Alaska. In that state, District One, geographically the largest school district in the country, contains all of the schools in the state except for those in a few cities and villages controlled partially by city councils.

County School Districts. In most of the states in the Southeast and in Nevada, Utah, and Louisiana, the county is the operating unit for both elementary and secondary school districts. Florida, for example, has sixty-seven counties and sixty-seven school districts.

Common School Districts. Most of the Western states and New York, Ohio, Michigan, South Carolina, and Mississippi have common school districts. The common districts are often small and found in rural areas. A recent trend has been for such districts to combine into larger units.

City School Districts. Many states permit large cities to operate their own school systems because larger cities present unique problems of organization and governance.

Town and Township School Units. Many school districts in New England, Indiana, New Jersey, and Pennsylvania are organized on a town or township basis. "Towns" usually comprise a village and the rural area surrounding it while townships are often less than logical natural units.

Regional School Districts. California, Illinois, New Jersey, and New York have local school districts that have been combined to form regional high school districts while continuing to operate separate elementary schools. A parent can have two children attending two separate school districts. In a few areas of the country a superintendent may be the superintendent of an elementary and high school district at the same time and have to deal with two separate school boards.

Some states, e.g., Pennsylvania, Massachusetts, and Connecticut, have organized school units that are called Intermediate Units (I.U.). The I.U. is governed by an appointed school superintendent and a school board along with superintendents of the member school districts it serves. The I.U. serves as a resource unit for special programs for exceptional children and as a source for inservice training of teachers and administrators. Although it does not operate any schools, it does provide special teachers, materials, and even bus service to students in the districts it serves.

Other states, such as New York, Nebraska, Michigan, Washington, and Wisconsin, have established special purpose or supplementary service districts which serve a number of local school districts. In many instances, these new units were created to administer vocational educational programs and other state-mandated educational services. Connecticut, Maine, New Hampshire, and Vermont have set up mid-level administrative units that are called "supervisory unions."

Regional agencies may exercise authority over local school districts on some matters but for others may be subject to the decisions of local districts.

Decline in Number of School Districts

During the past forty years the number of local public school systems in the United States has declined precipitously. The movement to reduce the number of school districts has been encouraged by state governments to provide better programs to school youth and to take better advantage of the taxable wealth.

The number of school districts in the United States reached a peak of almost 127,000 in the 1930s, that number being reduced to approximately 80,000 by 1950. During the 1950s and 60s major reorganizations took place in such states as New York and Illinois. Illinois, for example, reduced the number of school districts between 1945 and 1955 from 12,000 to 2,300.

Between 1950 and 1982 the number of school districts experienced a dramatic decline. In 1983 the number of school districts was only 14,500. That number represents a reduction of almost 65,000 school districts since 1950! During the 1980s a continued decline in school enrollment and resources will likely continue the trend toward combining smaller school districts into larger units. (See Figure 1.1)

There is also a vast difference in the sizes of school systems between today and forty years ago. In 1945–46 the 101,400 systems enrolled 23.3 million students with an enrollment per school system of approximately 230 pupils. By 1983, there were approximately forty-two million students enrolled in 14,500 school systems. Hence the average enrollment in 1983 was about 2,700 students.

LEGAL AND HISTORICAL PRECEDENTS FOR LOCAL SCHOOL BOARDS

Every state organizes school districts in ways it deems best. There is no common pattern of school district organization. Some districts have the same geographic boundaries as towns or counties while others don't. Most are "unified" school districts in that they manage both elementary and secondary schools. Some are "independent" in that they are free of local government control while others are dependent upon a city or county government. One must not lose sight of the fact that the state has full and complete power over school districts by virtue of the fact that education is a state function.

Figure 1.1   Number of Local Public School Systems: United States, 1945–46 to 1984–85

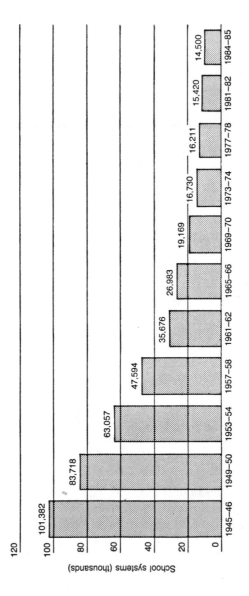

Sources: U.S. Department of Health, Education, and Welfare, National Center for Education Statistics, *Statistics of State School Systems;* and *Statistics of Public Elementary and Secondary Day Schools, Fall 1977.* (Updated by authors to include 1979–84.)

Legally, all authority over public school matters not delegated to boards of education resides in the state. However, for efficient administration, much power of the states is delegated to local school districts. States differ, however, in the degree of delegation of power to local districts and how that power is delegated. The local school district is a quasi-municipal corporation and also a civil subdivision of the state with boundaries and procedures for altering those boundaries determined by school law.

School Boards: An American Invention

School boards were first established in the eighteenth century and were outgrowths of school committees appointed by town councils to supervise schools. In colonial times government and religious affairs often interrelated. Members of school committees were responsible for such tasks as teacher appointments and supervision of schools. Ministers were often responsible for selecting teachers and overseeing schools. As the population increased and civil affairs became more complicated, Horace Mann, "the father of American public education," led a movement to make public schools nonsectarian. The function of supervising schools became a more secular function, left almost entirely to elected or appointed School Boards.

During the nineteenth century school boards became more independent of municipal government and more congruent with a natural community. School boards until the first half of the nineteenth century administered the schools and supervised the instructional program. By the mid-1800s school administration had become so complex that superintendents began to assume the administrative duties formerly performed by the Board of Education. By the beginning of the twentieth century all major cities had superintendents. In the twentieth century most districts have allocated executive functions to the school superintendent with policy decisions carried out by the school board. Since few members of school boards have the training or time to carry out administrative, supervisory duties, or business functions, those duties have been delegated to professional staff.

The authority of a local Board of Education lies in the board as a corporate body. Since school boards have no existence except as dictated by constitutional or statutory enactment, their powers and duties are essentially those possessed by the school district.

There are five sources of control over local school boards. Each of these sources both gives the school board authority to act in specific situations and limits the independent action of the board.

1. Constitutional provisions. These are usually quite broad and the establishment of specific laws is generally considered a legislative function. Any constitutional provision (such as relating to individual rights) takes precedence over statutory provisions.
2. Legislative enactments. School boards are responsible to legislative control and can exact no powers outside of the provisions of the statutes. The state legislature can determine the degree of control which it exerts over the local school districts. Hawaii and Alaska represent examples of strong state control. The state of New York, on the other hand, has a legislature which provides a much broader definition of school board powers.
3. Rules and regulations of the state Board of Education. State legislatures usually consider it their function to establish the broad outlines for operation of public education and to leave specific details to a state educational agency or local school board. Operating under the commissioner of education or state superintendent for public instruction, the state Board of Education has powers narrowly described by the legislature. The Board of Education can establish rules and regulations, prescribe courses of study, and prescribe standards to be met.
4. Legal interpretation. Legal interpretation of statutes affecting the operation of schools is done by two agencies. The first, in most states, is the state attorney general. The other agency is the courts, which may decide on suits brought either by other agencies of the state or by private citizens. These cases may involve the proper legal definition of the authority of school boards. Legal definition of school board authority is necessary particularly because of the doctrine of implied powers. The courts generally allow a school board to exercise the following powers and no other: (1) those powers expressly granted in the statutes; (2) those that are fairly implied in or incidental to the power expressly granted; and (3) those essential to the accomplishment of the schools' objectives.
5. Societal demands. In recent years society has demanded more and more of the schools. Functions formerly carried on by such agencies as the home or church are now considered to be the responsibility of the schools. As a result of increased pressures to extend the school program, school boards have either expanded the school program and justified their actions on the basis of implied powers, or the legislatures have extended the boards' powers.

BOARD MEMBERS

Most school board members are elected and serve for specified amounts of time, typically two to six years. Most of the members are elected in nonpartisan elections. The average length of service is slightly more than five years. About seventy percent of school boards have either five or seven members; the range is from three to twelve members. As late as 1905, the upper limit was over five hundred members! A majority are male although increasing numbers of women have been selected or elected to school boards in recent years. An increasing number of board members are college graduates. Although minority representation on boards has increased in the past twenty years, the percent of minority board members is still small.

HOW BOARDS OPERATE

School boards all operate differently, but most have designated meeting times (e.g., the first Tuesday each month), schedule work sessions and public meetings, and follow a published agenda. Since school board members are state officers and act as a corporate body, they are bound by certain state regulations such as "sunshine laws" (meetings open to the public) where such regulations or laws exist.

An example of how a school board operates can be found in the public relations documents of the Upper Darby, Pennsylvania, School Board that follow in Figures 1.2, 1.3, and 1.4. The Upper Darby School District, founded in 1834, is the oldest school district in Pennsylvania. Upper Darby, with approximately 5,800 students, has a long tradition of excellent school boards and school administration.

FUNCTIONS OF A SCHOOL BOARD

The functions of a school board include policy and decision making, developing programs, recruiting personnel, financing and housing the educational program, provisions for educationally related services, and interaction with the community.

Major Duties of Board Members

Board members have many duties. Among them are the following:

1. The selection of the superintendent of schools, the chief school administrator.
2. The establishment of procedures and policies in accord with which the educational services are administered and a range of programs is developed.
3. The establishment of policies relating to planning improvements and accountability.

Figure 1.2 Upper Darby, Pennsylvania School Board—Functions

ABOUT YOUR SCHOOL BOARD

BOARD OF SCHOOL DIRECTORS

TERESA F. FUREY, President
NICHOLAS A. PANGOPLOS, Vice President

RICHARD J. GENTILE
JANET A. HENEGHEN
L. ROBERT JUCKETT

THEODORE N. KOUKOS
HARRY J. PATTERSON
WALTER M. SENKOW

W. L. MICHAEL MAINES, Acting Superintendent

WHAT IS A SCHOOL BOARD?

The Board of School Directors is the planning and policy-making authority for the Upper Darby School District. In this responsibility, the Board operates in accordance with the School Laws of the Commonwealth of Pennsylvania. These laws relate primarily to administrative organization, general procedures, and instructional (curriculum) and financial matters.

The Upper Darby School Board is composed of nine residents. School Directors are elected for four-year terms. Members are elected at large and may seek reelection to successive terms. When vacancies occur mid-term, the Board names an appointee who serves until a successor is elected at the next municipal election. School Directors are not paid for their service to the District.

WHAT HAPPENS AT BOARD MEETINGS?

Meetings of the School Board are held for a number of purposes. The School Directors act (vote) on recommendations of the Superintendent of Schools and Board committees. These recommendations cover matters ranging from personnel, curriculum and instruction, to building maintenance, property and supplies. The Directors also authorize spending of all monies according to an operating budget prepared and adopted by the Board.

Almost any items related to the operation of the schools can come before the Board, although most problems are routinely handled through administrative channels.

WHEN ARE THE BOARD MEETINGS?

The Upper Darby Board of School Directors meets for its executive work sessions on the first Monday of each month, and for its regular business session on the second Monday of the month unless otherwise announced.

Special business meetings of the Board may be called by the President when there is need to conduct additional business. These meetings are advertised and open to the public. Meetings are held in the Administrative Building, Lansdowne Avenue and School Lane, Upper Darby, at 8:00 p.m. (unless otherwise advertised). The presiding Board Chairperson, on his or her own action or upon request of any School Director, may designate agenda items to be discussed in closed session. All voting and official Board action must take place only at regular or special (public) business meetings of the Board.

WHAT ABOUT PUBLIC PARTICIPATION AT MEETINGS?

The board provides two opportunities during business sessions for the public to speak. First, following the presentation of each committee report and prior to a Board vote on the report, the public may comment on any items in that report. Copies of the committee reports, as well as other information items for distribution, are available to the public on a table in the Board Room. Following the business portion of the meetings, time is set aside for public input on any other items of concern. The Board encourages the public to make comments and/or ask questions, but asks that remarks be brief and to the point.

WHAT IS THE ROLE OF THE SUPERINTENDENT OF SCHOOLS?

The Superintendent, as the educational leader in the school system, is charged with the direct responsibility of carrying out the policies adopted by the Board of School Directors. He must provide the Board with essential information, guidance, advice and recommendations so that the Board can determine what policies will maintain and improve the educational program for this community's students. At the same time, he must direct the use of staff and facilities so that the educational program will be the best effort possible consistent with Board policy.

DID YOU KNOW THAT . . .

— Upper Darby's School Board members average between 20–30 hours of service, all unpaid, to the District each month

— For the past three years, the Board has received a letter of commendation from the Pennsylvania Auditor General concerning State audits of District financial statements and procedures

— Through a strict energy conservation program effected by the School Board, the District, over the past four years, has reduced its fuel oil consumption by 29% and use of electricity by 41%

— More than 1500 senior citizens have picked up Golden Age cards made available by the Board. These cards entitle the bearer to free admission to School District activities.

Source: Courtesy of Upper Darby School District, Upper Darby, Pa.

Figure 1.3 Upper Darby, Pennsylvania School Board—
Organization

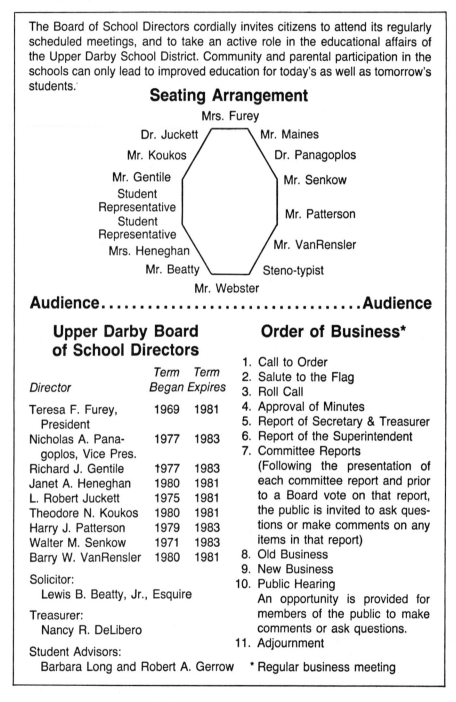

The Board of School Directors cordially invites citizens to attend its regularly scheduled meetings, and to take an active role in the educational affairs of the Upper Darby School District. Community and parental participation in the schools can only lead to improved education for today's as well as tomorrow's students.

Seating Arrangement

Mrs. Furey

Dr. Juckett   Mr. Maines

Mr. Koukos   Dr. Panagoplos

Mr. Gentile   Mr. Senkow
Student
Representative
Student   Mr. Patterson
Representative
Mrs. Heneghan   Mr. VanRensler

Mr. Beatty   Steno-typist

Mr. Webster

Audience. . . . . Audience

Upper Darby Board of School Directors

Director	Term Began	Term Expires
Teresa F. Furey, President	1969	1981
Nicholas A. Panagoplos, Vice Pres.	1977	1983
Richard J. Gentile	1977	1983
Janet A. Heneghan	1980	1981
L. Robert Juckett	1975	1981
Theodore N. Koukos	1980	1981
Harry J. Patterson	1979	1983
Walter M. Senkow	1971	1983
Barry W. VanRensler	1980	1981

Solicitor:
  Lewis B. Beatty, Jr., Esquire

Treasurer:
  Nancy R. DeLibero

Student Advisors:
  Barbara Long and Robert A. Gerrow

Order of Business*

1. Call to Order
2. Salute to the Flag
3. Roll Call
4. Approval of Minutes
5. Report of Secretary & Treasurer
6. Report of the Superintendent
7. Committee Reports
   (Following the presentation of each committee report and prior to a Board vote on that report, the public is invited to ask questions or make comments on any items in that report)
8. Old Business
9. New Business
10. Public Hearing
    An opportunity is provided for members of the public to make comments or ask questions.
11. Adjournment

* Regular business meeting

District Administrative Staff*

W. L. Michael Maines, Acting Superintendent
Michael H. Zolos, Assistant Superintendent
Charles E. Webster, Director of Business Management
and Secretary to the Board
A. Patricia Ramsdell, Director of Curriculum
Robert F. Lewis, Acting Director of Pupil Services
Mary K. Sweet, Supervisor of Language Arts
and Social Studies
Joseph P. Batory, Director of Communications
Maurice J. Matteson, Purchasing Agent
Nancy R. DeLibero, Administrative Assistant
to the Director of Business Management

Committees

INSTRUCTION CURRICULUM
Nicholas A. Panagoplos,
Chairperson
Barry W. VanRensler
Administrative Contact
W. L. Michael Maines
A. Patricia Ramsdell

PERSONNEL
Richard J. Gentile, Chairperson
Theodore N. Koukos
Administrative Contact
W. L. Michael Maines

AGENDA ACTION PLANNING
Teresa F. Furey, Chairperson
Nicholas A. Panagoplos
W. L. Michael Maines

RENOVATIONS TO BUILDINGS AND GROUNDS
All improvements to property
and buildings over $25,000
Walter M. Senkow, Chairperson
All members of the Board
Administrative Contact
Charles E. Webster
W. L. Michael Maines

FINANCE BUDGET
L. Robert Juckett, Chairperson
Theodore N. Koukos
Administrative Contact
Charles E. Webster
W. L. Michael Maines

PROPERTY, BUILDINGS AND GROUNDS
Theodore N. Koukos
Chairperson
Barry W. VanRensler
Administrative Contact
Charles E. Webster
Charles DeMonde

SUPPLIES
Harry J. Patterson, Chairperson
Janet A. Heneghan
Administrative Contact
Charles E. Webster
Maurice J. Matteson

POLICY MANUAL
Janet A. Heneghan, Chairperson
Nicholas A. Panagoplos
Administrative Contact
W. I. Michael Maines

Figure 1.3 *(Continued)*

Other Assignments

District County Intermediate Unit Board
Walter M. Senkow
Vocational Technical Operating Advisory Committee
Barry W. VanRensler, Representative
Nicholas A. Panagoplos, Alternate
Community College Liaison/Appointing Committee
Harry J. Patterson, Representative
Janet A. Heneghan, Alternate
Deleware County School Boards Legislative Council
Janet A. Heneghan, Representative
Teresa F. Furey, Alternate
SPOTLIGHT Committee
Teresa F. Furey
Meet & Discuss – U.D.E.A
Teresa F. Furey
Richard J. Gentile
Nicholas A. Panagoplos
Upper Darby Township Council Liaison Committee
Harry J. Patterson
Nicholas A. Panagoplos

* Usually present at meetings.

Source: Courtesy of Upper Darby School District, Upper Darby, PA.

Figure 1.4 Upper Darby, Pennsylvania—Budget Information

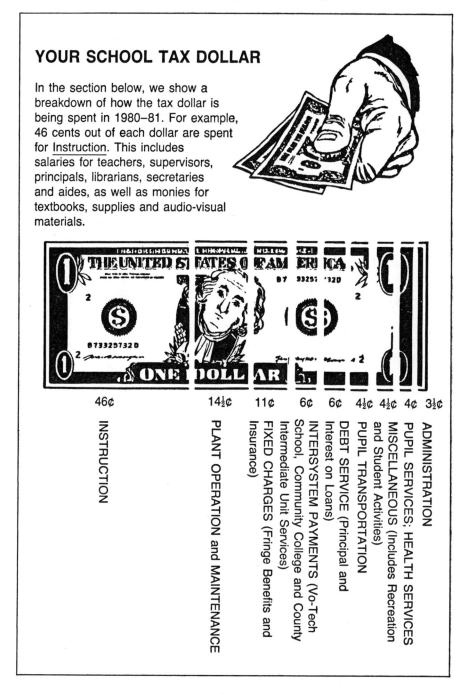

YOUR SCHOOL TAX DOLLAR

In the section below, we show a breakdown of how the tax dollar is being spent in 1980–81. For example, 46 cents out of each dollar are spent for Instruction. This includes salaries for teachers, supervisors, principals, librarians, secretaries and aides, as well as monies for textbooks, supplies and audio-visual materials.

46¢	14½¢	11¢	6¢	6¢	4½¢	4½¢	4¢	3½¢
INSTRUCTION	PLANT OPERATION and MAINTENANCE	FIXED CHARGES (Fringe Benefits and Insurance)	INTERSYSTEM PAYMENTS (Vo-Tech School, Community College and County Intermediate Unit Services)	DEBT SERVICE (Principal and Interest on Loans)	PUPIL TRANSPORTATION	MISCELLANEOUS (Includes Recreation and Student Activities)	PUPIL SERVICES; HEALTH SERVICES	ADMINISTRATION

Figure 1.4 *(Continued)*

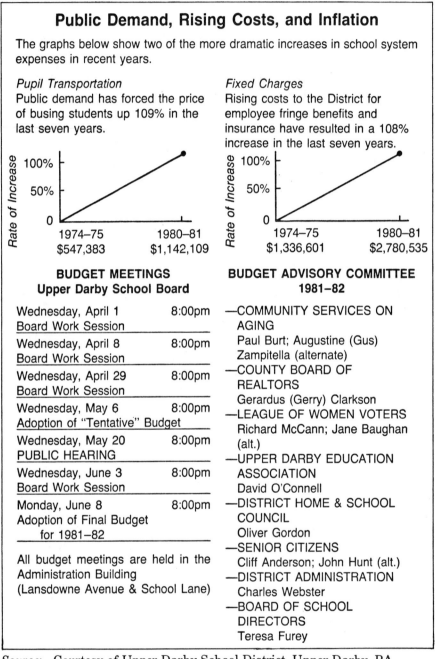

Public Demand, Rising Costs, and Inflation

The graphs below show two of the more dramatic increases in school system expenses in recent years.

Pupil Transportation
Public demand has forced the price of busing students up 109% in the last seven years.

Fixed Charges
Rising costs to the District for employee fringe benefits and insurance have resulted in a 108% increase in the last seven years.

	1974–75	1980–81
Pupil Transportation	$547,383	$1,142,109
Fixed Charges	$1,336,601	$2,780,535

BUDGET MEETINGS
Upper Darby School Board

Wednesday, April 1	8:00pm
Board Work Session	

Wednesday, April 8	8:00pm
Board Work Session	

Wednesday, April 29	8:00pm
Board Work Session	

Wednesday, May 6	8:00pm
Adoption of "Tentative" Budget	

Wednesday, May 20	8:00pm
PUBLIC HEARING	

Wednesday, June 3	8:00pm
Board Work Session	

Monday, June 8	8:00pm
Adoption of Final Budget for 1981–82	

All budget meetings are held in the Administration Building (Lansdowne Avenue & School Lane)

BUDGET ADVISORY COMMITTEE
1981–82

—COMMUNITY SERVICES ON AGING
  Paul Burt; Augustine (Gus) Zampitella (alternate)
—COUNTY BOARD OF REALTORS
  Gerardus (Gerry) Clarkson
—LEAGUE OF WOMEN VOTERS
  Richard McCann; Jane Baughan (alt.)
—UPPER DARBY EDUCATION ASSOCIATION
  David O'Connell
—DISTRICT HOME & SCHOOL COUNCIL
  Oliver Gordon
—SENIOR CITIZENS
  Cliff Anderson; John Hunt (alt.)
—DISTRICT ADMINISTRATION
  Charles Webster
—BOARD OF SCHOOL DIRECTORS
  Teresa Furey

Source: Courtesy of Upper Darby School District, Upper Darby, PA.

4. The acquisition and development of properties and the provision of supplies.
5. The enactment of provisions for financing schools and the adoption of a budget.
6. The adoption of personnel policies relating to appointment of instructional and noninstructional staff.
7. The appraisal of the work of the schools and adoption of plans for improvement.

AMERICAN EDUCATION AND THE MODERN BOARD MEMBER

In this guidebook you will be able to examine the role of the modern school board member in determining policies, developing budgets, dealing with school district personnel and business matters, and working with the public. You will also become knowledgeable about school programs, federal, state, and local laws pertaining to schools, and school finance. Finally, you will learn that the role of a board member is a complex one and demands high levels of leadership in a number of different situations. And what of the future? What lies ahead for board members in the last two decades of the twentieth century?

It is difficult to project ahead in a world of uncertainty but there are conditions in American education today that, if analyzed, can help us make better decisions for the future.

School leaders know that skills for a successful practice are determined by the situation and the task. School leaders in the 1960s, for instance, were operating out of an environment of surplus resources and were expected to be both visionary and innovative. In the 1970s school administrators were experiencing the slow recognition that a resource crisis was ahead. Still, they were expected to promote desired change with a constrained and businesslike operation. In the 1980s expectations for schools have changed dramatically, and many school leaders have been traumatized by the new expectations for their performance. Rather than being visionary or businesslike, board members and school administrators have been asked to work miracles in an era of decline. In this section we will examine the conditions of scarce resources and declining enrollments because these conditions are expected to remain in the public sector for at least another decade and perhaps longer.

Some liken the present state of education in American public schools to a declining industry. Industries, it is said, evolve through three predictable stages of development: a period of growth, a period of conflict, and a period of neglect. The period of growth in public school education continued unchecked until the early 1970s in the United States. This condition was characterized by rising enrollments, an expanding curriculum, and a widespread belief that schools were a positive medium to problem resolution. For the most part, schools were able to meet expectations prior to 1970 by expanding programs and retaining public confidence. This expansion was made possible by the generous allotment of resources to the public school mission.

Early in the 1970s three conditions came into play that pushed schools into a period of conflict. First Vietnam and Watergate left the American public with a deep distrust of all governmental officials. Second, the economy of the nation became strained by an unprecedented inflationary spiral. Because support for schools came from property taxes, the tolerance of the public was rapidly exceeded in terms of contributions to support schools. A third event, and perhaps a larger problem, was that at the same time the mission of public education became clouded. Civil rights and individual rights became issues that were expressed in school settings (community control, student rights, ethnic studies, etc.), and for the first time a national consensus for education was lacking. By 1974, expectations for education "crossed" declining resources and schools could no longer satisfy all demands for performance.

The third stage, the period of neglect, took hold in the late 1970s and continues to date. The period of neglect is characterized by excessive expectations where the capabilities of schools fall short of performance goals. It is also characterized by stagnation, increased political activity, and widespread indifference. Under such conditions, schools react to dominant pressures without consideration of the long-term implications for daily decision making and policy.

Whether this analogy is correct or is overdrawn, it does contribute to our understanding of the problems that school board members face in this decade. With the expectation of limited areas of population increase (notably the suburban sun-belt cities), most boards will be addressing a phased-in scheduling of reduction and redesign of educational programs during the 1980s and 1990s. A review of these conditions and tasks will assist you as a board member in determining how school leaders can best respond to promote successful practice.

CONDITIONS FACING BOARD MEMBERS TODAY

The conditions confronting board members and school administrators today are challenging to say the least. Among the conditions that call for high degrees of leadership skills are the following: general suburban decay, inflation as a way of life, rising salaries and fixed costs, rising transportation demands, declining enrollment, an aging and highly unionized staff, facilities decay, negotiation as a communication medium, a shrinking curriculum, and excessive administrative turnover. While all of these factors are intertwined, a review of each condition separately will aid in understanding the issues and problems to be administered.

General Suburban Decay

The period from 1940 to 1970 in America was dominated by the mass exodus of population from our cities to our suburban areas. A desire for living space, relief from high taxation, and the availability of cheap fuel for transportation aided this outward migration from the cities. During the 1960s and 1970s a constant inflationary spiral pushed up suburban property values and taxes, resulting in homes too expensive for young couples. With fixed land boundaries and little or no new construction, suburban townships soon found themselves facing the same problems as did the cities in the 1960s: low mobility, a middle-aged population, rising taxes, declining enrollments, and some outward migration by those most able to contribute financially. In the 1980s a stabilizing of market values for housing due to slow real estate sales has produced the dilemma of rising costs and no option but to increase property taxes.

Inflation as a Way of Life

Inflation has always been with us in the United States in this century, but the rate of inflation since the post-Vietnam era has alarmed economists of all stripes. At a modest estimate of 12 percent per year, schools would need to double their revenue every eight years just to remain constant in dollar purchasing power. Obviously, schools have not been able to do so and the results are beginning to show. In many school districts financial crises are common. In others, deferred decisions have led to poorly maintained buildings, desperate teacher strikes, and curricula reduced to the barest levels of service. In particular, school budgets have been eroded by two expenses that show no product: transportation and teacher salaries. With bonding an unpopular subject, taxpayer revolts gaining support, and high interest rates, the effects of inflation are proving devastating.

Salaries and Fixed Costs

Salaries and fixed costs (such as retirement obligations) represent a significant proportion of any school budget. Collectively, these items can account for 85–90 percent of a local district's budget. From year to year the base of these items (what was spent last year) is nonnegotiable unless a reduction-in-force is implemented. In addition, salary increases to meet inflation are always the number one demand in any modern negotiation session between teachers and the school board.

Transportation and Fuel Costs

Bussing school children to public schools is nearly as old as the automobile in the United States. However, since the onset of court-ordered integration plans in the 1960s, bus purchasing and maintenance has become a major budget item for most school districts. Beyond procuring and maintaining these buses, school districts must purchase gasoline to run them, and this single factor has done a great deal to direct new monies away from instruction. During the first fuel shortages of 1973, for instance, school districts were faced with a major reassessment of discretionary monies as fuel prices doubled during the year. Since 1973, the cost of transporting pupils has continued to rise. Coupled with fuel for transportation was a parallel rise in the cost of oil for heating school buildings. These costs are now fixed in many districts but absorbed major portions of new school revenue between 1970 and 1980.

Declining Enrollments

In the period 1970–1980 elementary school enrollments in public schools fell a full 18 percent. Secondary school enrollments, during the same period, declined 25 percent in the public schools. A corresponding decline was found in the ratio between teachers and pupils. Between 1955 and 1974 the elementary teacher-pupil ratio fell from 1:30.2 to 1:22.7. Secondary teacher-pupil ratios in the same period declined from 1:21.7 to 1:18.7. Since 1974, these ratios have fallen even further, testing a widely circulated argument by teachers in the 1950s that "quality of instruction will go up if teacher-pupil ratios go down." Finally, even with declining enrollments and decreasing teacher-pupil ratios, the cost per pupil has risen steadily, reflecting both inflation and a greater real investment in the education of each student.

An Aging and Unionized Staff

Another changing condition faced by board members and school administrators in the 1980s is a highly unionized teaching faculty. The 1970s saw a revolution in teacher organization with the number of states recognizing the right of collective bargaining rising from eleven (1966) to thirty (1977) in a decade. During that period union membership rose at a corresponding rate so that by 1977 the National Education Association claimed 1.8 million members and the American Federation of Teachers a half million members.

With the rapid decline in student enrollment in the late 1970s not only did the percentage of teachers unionized increase but also their age and degree of seniority. Since few new teachers are entering many school systems, the aging process continues today and will continue throughout the coming decade.

Facilities Decay

The 1960s and early 1970s were a time of vigorous school construction as new curricula and selected population growth encouraged expansive facilities planning. As the reality of a long-term decline in enrollment took effect, however, school construction diminished and a period of neglect set in. If there were budget deficits, school leaders reasoned, deferment of maintenance or construction was surely a logical way to save money. After nearly ten years of cutting corners with facilities, schools today are saddled with aging and poorly maintained plants. In addition to making hard decisions about closing schools, many districts will worry about saving neglected buildings in the 1980s and beyond.

Negotiation as a Medium of Communication

The rapid spread of unionism in public schools in the 1970s meant the introduction of negotiation as an annual task for chief school officers. In addition to a new and highly complex process, negotiation of teacher contracts has also bedeviled budget-making processes since negotiation processes are usually lengthy. During the past ten years the scope of such bargaining has expanded from extrinsic issues (pay and work conditions) to educational issues (inservice patterns and an essential core of courses). The formality of this communication medium between superintendents and teachers has emphasized differences rather than commonality.

Shrinking Curricula

The period from 1920 to 1970 in American education was one of expansion as the school curriculum reflected a widening clientele. In the mid-1970s, however, school leaders were confronted with a declining resource base and a steady, if not declining, enrollment. The response to these conditions was to "manage" schools more for fiscal efficiency, including a major curriculum reform movement called "back to the basics."

The "basics" movement originated in the late 1960s as educators sought goal clarity. The trend toward behavioral objectives, early performance contracting, criterion-referenced evaluation, and competency testing have all reflected the sharpening of curricular focus. Since 1975, however, most of the emphasis for a return to the basics has been economic. School leaders in the next two decades will be asked to assess the relative merit of various components in the curriculum and eliminate those that cannot be supported.

Administrative Turnover

Finally, a condition that reflects all other conditions is the high degree of administrative turnover among school administrators in the United States. The average survival time for large city superintendents is estimated to be two to three years and the overall survival average of superintendents is less than four years. These stark figures indicate that few school leaders are able to juggle successfully so many pressing conditions for long. For one thing, few new administrators can even conceptualize the degree of change about them or develop a logical way to confront the conditions. Additionally, too few school leaders today possess the skills for dealing with the predictable tasks of the 1980s and beyond. The next section addresses those new tasks.

Your district may or may not now be experiencing the conditions mentioned in the previous sections, but there is a good chance one or more of these conditions will surface during your term of office. Knowing what happened to other boards may help your board deal with the same problems.

MAJOR LEADERSHIP TASKS AND ISSUES

Because of the conditions outlined in the previous section, school leaders are facing new tasks in the 1980s. Many of these tasks are direct responsibilities of school board members and are central to providing quality education for school children. Four tasks are representative of the new challenges of school leaders in an era of decline: negotiation of employee contracts, closing school buildings, maneuvering budgets, and conducting a reduction-in-force of the instructional staff.

Negotiation of Employee Contracts

In addition to a dramatic rise in union membership, the 1970s may well be remembered for the increased degree of teacher militancy across the nation. In seeking to upgrade their profession, teachers have become more vocal and have sought to use traditional labor methods to achieve results: strikes, grievances, sanctions, and collective bargaining. These moves by teachers have forced administrators to assume a more traditional "management" posture, and many school leaders have experienced difficulty with such a role. In a human organization such as a school, with an intangible product such as the education and nurturing of children, adopting traditional labor perspectives has not come easily.

While strikes and grievances have grabbed the attention of the press and the public, professional negotiation has been far more important in determining the leadership of school administration. It is through professional negotiation, in the 1980s, that the School Board communicates with teachers and addresses the important issues of education.

The question of what is negotiated is a local issue, but it can safely be observed that the scope of issues has expanded during the last decade. A sample list might be the following:

Teacher salaries	Curriculum
Teacher assignments	Class load formulas
Transfers and promotions	Inservice education
Recruitment of teachers	Personnel policy
Grievance procedures	Non-Salary benefits
Sabbatical and leave policies	Collateral duties

This list might be extended indefinitely. For example, it is not uncommon for a large city teacher union to negotiate 35 to 45 items in a given session. Figure 1.5 illustrates the issues of negotiation in one school district with about five thousand students.

Closing School Buildings

A second major task ahead for school leaders is the selective reduction of physical facilities used to educate children. From the data presented in Figure 1.6 it can be seen that public school enrollment will continue to decline through 1990, with the major impact after 1985 being felt at the secondary level. This means that many school districts, and particularly those in older and more established suburban areas, will experience rapid declines in junior and senior high school populations. A natural response to this condition will be to consolidate programs and close unnecessary buildings.

Figure 1.5   Issues of Negotiation

The issues: Teachers have a master contract that expires June 30. The board and the teachers have been working for the last several months to arrive at language for a new contract.

Disagreement over language for this new contract is partly responsible for the teachers' strike that started May 11.

At least two issues—contract clauses dealing with mill-levy contingencies and evaluation of teachers—are no longer sticking points in the negotiations.

At recent talks, the teachers dropped most of their objections to the district's proposal for teacher evaluations.

And the 1981–82 mill-levy for the high school district has already been approved, so the levy contingency is no longer an issue in current negotiations. But the clause remains a concern and will likely be an issue in the future.

The district wants a contract that specifically allows them to reopen negotiations if any levy fails.

Here is a look at some of the more significant issues that continue to keep the board and the teachers from settling the dispute.

	Current contract	Teacher proposal	Board position
Involuntary transfers	Involuntary transfers are a "management right" and no specific procedures are outlined for transferring a teacher to other schools against his or her will.	Teachers would be transferred based on specific criteria, including the number of years worked in the district and the academic area in which that teacher is certified. Teachers' proposal sets up a procedure for notifying affected teachers, and allows transfer decisions to be reviewed under union grievance procedures.	Same as current contract. The teachers' proposal takes away management's right to move teachers from school to school to best use staff members' training and expertise, according to district officials.
Layoffs	If the levy fails or the enrollment declines and the district must cut its teaching staff, teachers are laid off	In the case of layoffs, teacher seniority would be calculated on a districtwide basis, not a department-by-	Essentially the same as the current contract. Seniority is of primary importance, and administrators should

	Current contract	Teacher proposal	Board position
	on the basis of their seniority among other members of their departments. Administrators are not included on the seniority list.	department basis. A teacher's certification would also be a criterion for layoff. Administrators would not be included on seniority lists.	be included on the seniority list. Consideration should also be given to "needs of the total program and recent teaching experience" in the teacher's area of certification.
Representation fee	Teachers who are not members of the teachers union are not required to pay a fee to the union, which represents them in salary and contract negotiations.	Teachers must either belong to the teachers union or pay a representation fee equivalent to union dues, currently $185 a year. Teachers say they want the fee because the union, by law, must negotiate contracts and protect the rights of union and non-union members alike.	Same as the current contract. The district does not feel that a teacher must, as a condition of employment, be required to join a union, pay union dues or pay a representation fee.
Lunch duty	Teachers may choose an uninterrupted, duty-free lunch one class-period long. (This item was put into the contract when class periods were 35 minutes long. Classes last 65 minutes now.)	Teachers prefer existing contract. If asked to supervise the cafeteria during lunch hour, teachers should be paid $9 hour. Teachers say the board's proposal cuts down on voluntary teacher-student contact time while increasing obligatory teacher-student contact time.	The board thinks the 65-minute lunch period is too long and wants to reduce the lunch period to 45 minutes. Teachers are not being asked to help supervise the cafeteria.
No-strike clause	Current contract says teachers may not engage in a strike while the contract is in effect. However, the board recently waived that no-strike provision for the remainder of the current contract.	Teachers want the option of calling a strike when all other avenues of settling disputes have been exhausted and no agreement can be reached— or when there are no established procedures for settling a dispute.	Wants to keep the language in current contract, which prohibits strikes and other concerted activity while the contract is in effect.

Figure 1.5 *(Continued)*

	Current contract	Teacher proposal	Board position
Teacher discipline	District has the authority to discipline (reprimand, suspend, reduce in ranks or pay, transfer, dismiss or terminate) teachers for "cause." Teachers may appeal decisions through union grievance procedures or through procedures established by law.	Teachers want to replace the word "cause" with "just cause" in the contract. Teachers also want to keep "termination," "dismissal," and "transfer" in this part of the contract.	Agrees that discipline may only be imposed for "just" cause. But the transfer of teachers is a management right and the district need not show just cause. Also, decisions to terminate or dismiss a teacher should be reviewed through procedures set by law, not through union grievance procedures and arbitration.
1980—81 salaries	Under the 1979-80 contract (the contract teachers have worked under pending settlement of 1980-81 salaries), a beginning teacher makes $11,020 for 187 days; a teacher with a master's degree and seven years experience makes $15,340; and the highest-paid teacher makes $22,950. Average salary for MCHS teachers is $16,039. District pays $921.60 a year for health and dental insurance for each teacher and his/her family.	Proposed cost-of-living increase is 7.2 percent, applied to each teacher's current salary. Most teachers would also get additional money for gaining one more year of experience and some would receive more money for earning additional college credits. Cost to the district: about an 11 percent increase in salaries over the 1979-80 year. District continues to pay health and dental insurance of $936 a year for each teacher.	Proposed cost-of-living increase is about 6 percent, applied to each teacher's salary. Most teachers would also get additional money for gaining a year's experience and/or for earning additional college credits. Cost to the district: about a 10.6 percent increase in salaries over the 1979-80 year and about 1 percent more than was budgeted. District would pay health and dental insurance of $936 a year for each teacher.
1981-82	Does not apply.	All teachers should receive the same cost-of-living increase and no flat, across-the-board dollar raises, which teachers say will skew the salary schedule. Proposed cost-of-living increase is 12 percent for	The district wants to combine a cost-of-living increase with a flat, across-the-board dollar increase for all teachers. Strict percentage increases benefit higher-paid teachers and not younger teachers, according

Current contract	Teacher proposal	Board position
	each teacher. Most teachers would also receive addition-al increases for gain-ing another year's experience and some would receive more money for earning ad-ditional college credits. Cost to the district: about 15.4 percent over teachers' pro-posed salaries for 1980–81. District pays health and insur-ance benefits of $1,429.32 a year for each teacher.	to the district. This approach to dis-tributing the money makes computing the cost-of-living in-crease difficult be-cause the increase varies. Cost to the district: 12.1 per-cent over the board's proposed salaries for the 1980–81 year, or about 2 percent more than is now budgeted for salaries. District would pay health and dental insurance as in teachers' proposal.

This chart was prepared before negotiations late Saturday night. Offers and counteroffers may change some of the listings.

Source:　The *Missoulian*, Missoula, Montana, 1981. Used with permission.

School budgets are dominated by fixed costs that allow flexibil-ity for cost reduction in only three areas: educational programming, personnel, and facilities. Forced to find ways to reduce spending, most administrators will select facilities as the area least sensitive to change. While facility closings may seem promising, the experience of school districts in the 1970s and early 1980s would suggest that caution is needed in proposing and administering such a reduction. For one thing, rationalizing the closing of a school can only be accom-plished when enrollment has declined significantly over a relatively long period of time. Second, savings from such a closing are not likely to show up immediately on the ledger sheets. Finally, with the excep-tion of certain school activities (sports), school buildings are the most visible symbol of public education in a community. Community iden-tity is often tied closely to a structure in the neighborhood.

While it would seem reasonable that closing a school building would save significant amounts of money, sometimes real savings are minuscule. For one thing, certain costs such as insurance continue even after the building is closed. Second, abandoned buildings are more susceptible to physical deterioration. Finally, security measures for fire and vandalism are often costly. Usually, in building closings, there are no personnel savings since teachers and staff are transferred to other sites. The money saved in janitorial services and consumables

Figure 1.6 Projected Enrollments in Grades K–12 in the United States for Selected Years, 1974–1990[1]

Grade	Enrollment in Year (in thousands)			
	1974	1980	1985	1990
K	2,672	2,431	2,950	3,172
1	3,527	3,179	3,783	4,200
2	3,540	3,194	3,579	4,095
3	3,691	3,416	3,462	4,074
4	3,793	3,546	3,250	3,902
5	4,036	3,611	3,226	3,879
6	4,045	3,485	3,124	3,677
7	4,092	3,447	3,181	3,519
8	4,108	3,487	3,330	3,353
Total, K–8	33,504[2]	29,796	29,885	33,871
9	4,034	3,552	3,480	3,191
10	3,964	3,657	3,409	3,050
11	3,653	3,501	3,083	2,765
12	3,669	3,619	3,108	2,870
Total, 9–12	15,320[2]	14,329	13,080	11,876

[1]Estimated on the basis of Series II projections of the U. S. Bureau of the Census and age-grade ratios from the U. S. Census of 1970. Series II is one of three Bureau of the Census population projection series. It is considered the most reasonable choice at this time.

[2]In the fall of 1974 there were an estimated 34.4 million enrollees in K–8 and 15.6 million in grades 9–12. See National Center for Education Statistics, *Digest of Educational Statistics* (Washington, D.C.: U. S. Government Printing Office, 1975), Table 1.

Sources: U.S. Bureau of the Census, *Current Population Reports*, Series P-25, No. 601, "Projections of the Population of the United States, 1975 to 2050" (Washington, D.C.: U. S. Government Printing Office, 1975); and U. S. Bureau of the Census, *Census of Population: 1970,* Subject Reports, Final Report PC(2)-5A, "School Enrollment" (Washington, D.C.: U. S. Government Printing Office, 1973), p. 119.

not used is simply not impressive on a year-to-year basis. Without concurrent board decisions to reduce staff and other costs, simply closing schools is not enough to reduce school budgets substantially.

The issue of closing school sites also has a political dimension that often surprises board members. School buildings represent stability to local neighborhoods, particularly in terms of real estate values. When a proposal to close a local school becomes public, the reactions of the neighborhood around that school range from denial of need to irrational self-serving arguments (anti-bussing). It behooves the board member, therefore, to approach closing of a school building only after considerable research. The following items are suggested for study:

Operational Efficiency of Schools

In determining which buildings in the district are most efficient to operate, board members should look at items such as needed capital outlays (new roof, heating plant), annual cost of heating/cooling the plant, use of electricity, annual insurance costs, custodial costs, and general facility condition. A related variable that may prove of importance in closing a building would be the overall safety of the structure in terms of fire, earthquake, or structural (load-bearing) stability.

Performance Capability of Schools

Among the variables to consider in this category are the previous achievement record of the school (is it known for academic excellence?) and the general cohesiveness of the parents at the school. In cases where a school is reputed to be "one of the better schools" in the district, or where parents are formed into an active political coalition, it will be difficult and perhaps not cost-effective to close the building. Such a move will be resisted by influential parents and can lead to an exodus of support for the public schools in the community.

Possible Alternatives for the Schools under Consideration

A third category to consider, and probably the most important, is other possibilities for the targeted structures. During the past decade it has been found that the real amount to be saved by closing a school building is determined by its alternative use. In this case, there are a number of possibilities depending upon the geography of the school site and the construction of the facility itself.

Among considerations of geography are the location of the site in relation to environmental growth patterns, the zoning of the site (it is easier to reuse a building near a commercial area), transportation to the site, building costs in the area, and physical barriers that might be a disadvantage for schools but a plus for business (railways, freeways, airports).

Among those factors related to the facility itself would be age, soundness of structure, special facilities on site, loading and unloading access points, and possibilities for conversion. As board members study possible school closings, they must see them as structures other than schools. Does the location make the school desirable for an outright sale? Can the school site be converted for office or storage space? Can the building be leased? Could part of the building be rented to other agencies? Experience would suggest that seeking professional advice from architects and city planners will pay dividends for educators who must project and implement building closings.

Maneuvering School Budgets

A third important task for board members in an era of decline is to maneuver school budgets in such a way that the real objectives of education are accomplished. Many new board members feel uncomfortable with budgets, believing that budgets are something for which a business officer or school superintendent is responsible. Nothing could be further from the truth, for in the struggle over preferences "the budget records the outcome of the struggle."

An initial observation about budgets is that they are governed by either choice or conflict resolution. Stated another way, budgets reflect values about the priorities of education. While words are plentiful, the allocation of scarce resources to fund certain activities in the 1980s will reflect the true priorities of school districts.

A beginning point for the development of any budget, then, comes from the assessment of needs in the district and a consensus on the mission of the organization. A needs assessment, which seeks to determine what the district *is* accomplishing through its programming, should be comprehensive in nature. Such a general overview increases the odds of an integrated plan for education. The value of a needs assessment, for budget, is that it moves the level of communication about budget items from philosophy to data.

The critical job for school administrators is to translate abstract budget concepts (for example, allocations for facilities maintenance) into practical realities *before* budget issues are decided. School boards today are dependent upon school administrators providing clear and adequate information to them so that they can make important educational decisions. Administrators can assist such decision making by projecting educational implications of the budget in terms of day-to-day operations and quality control.

It follows that in the 1980s and 1990s a rational budget plan simply may not reflect political realities. School leaders involved in budget projection and preparation must sometimes "maneuver" budget items in order to best "advocate" for school children. Also, long-range planning can help support certain items. Where budget items are tied to a comprehensive and long-range plan rather than an isolated program, their chances for survival are maximized.

Reductions in Force (RIF)

Without question, the toughest task facing board members in the 1980s and beyond is the reduction of the teaching force to maintain some degree of reason in school budgeting. A reduction of force (RIF) almost always comes following easier solutions. First, equipment and supplies are cut back. Then, materials are not ordered. Third, school buildings are closed. Finally, when there is no other possible source of savings, the possibility of reducing the teaching staff is considered. Since teacher salaries are the largest single item in any district budget, and since salaries must increase by 8–12 percent per year to parallel inflation, most school districts in the 1980s will eventually arrive at the point where some tough decisions have to be made.

In the late 1970s and early 1980s many school districts found themselves without a plan for reducing teaching staff. Using attrition as the major response, some superintendents and boards slipped into a pattern of staffing that resulted in an out-of-balance curriculum. Such districts experienced a shortage of math and science teachers and an abundance of social studies and foreign language teachers. Given this rapid and surprising development, the districts took dramatic and often depressing actions to rebalance the instructional staff pattern. In the long run, court challenges, grievances, and lawsuits did much to negate projected savings from such reductions.

The dilemma confronting many boards is that they are faced with experienced and aging staffs that represent higher unit costs for instruction. While qualified and competent, these teachers have no outlets for growth and soon focus solely on extrinsic benefits through aggressive union activity. The public, seeing a declining pupil-teacher ratio, push board and administrators into a "conflict management" role. From such a situation school leaders must find both reasonable solutions and quality control measures. This is no small order!

A number of steps may be taken prior to the outright dumping of excess teachers. One natural step is to cease hiring new teachers and begin retraining those already on tenured contracts to fill available positions. This is more difficult and stressful than it is expensive, due to the seniority of many of today's teachers and the natural resistance of any individual to change.

Another possibility is to furlough teachers (without pay) or to move toward providing teachers with part-time work (work sharing). While this could be a satisfactory arrangement for some individuals, it is an unrealistic approach for those who are family providers. A disturbing trend in the early 1980s is for the school district simply to start school late and have a shortened school year as one means of forcing a furlough situation.

Yet another common move is to encourage an "early retirement" by most senior teachers. This is a good idea in theory since the same teachers are the highest cost units in the staff. However, recent court rulings extending the mandatory work age, plus the general anxiety about the national social security system, has undermined this approach. In some of the more creative districts early retirement incentive plans (ERIP) have included a provision to use senior teachers as consultants for a guaranteed number of days per year.

Another variation of this same idea is to use retrenched teachers in a role of permanent substitute. Such a move guarantees the district a competent pool of substitute teachers while providing employment to those who would otherwise be released.

Finally, a great deal has been written about, and some things done about, expanding the clientele of public schools. Prospects for new students include child care centers, early childhood/kindergarten education, adult or senior citizen education, and long-term roles with teacher interns. Unfortunately, rhetoric has outstripped performance in this area.

Boards may find themselves an ultimate target for savings in the supervisory and administrative substructure in the district office. Ultimately, teachers can claim that the roles performed by subject supervisors, guidance counselors, building level (and, perhaps district level) administrators *could* be performed by teachers-in-the-field. While this *may* be true, the timing of such arguments usually suggests a self-serving motivation. Long before this step is reached, boards should have a plan that identifies targeted reductions.

During the 1970s and early 1980s some boards sought to curtail curriculum programs and extracurricular activities as a means of reaching fiscal stability. While eliminating football or the music programs may save dollars in the short run, it appears that these types of school-sponsored activities are lifelines to the community. As such, they do not represent a viable means of addressing the problems of an era of decline.

In addition to facing a hostile teacher union and an excited taxpaying public, school boards can also expect to spend considerable time in hearings related to affirmative action and minority discrimination during the 1980s. These legal factors will hinge upon the existence or absence of a reduction-in-force plan which spells out precisely the procedure and rationale for cuts in staff. Few board members can expect to withstand pressures from all of the various forces.

Boards must also understand that rapid drawdowns of faculty may not result in immediately visible savings to the district. Firing junior faculty, while maintaining a fixed pupil-teacher ratio, will only result in a higher expenditure per pupil. The lag time from making cuts to seeing expenditures come down is beyond the control of the board without a plan.

In conclusion, a reduction-in-force is an extremely complex task with many alternatives. Such a task is much easier in a calm environment than during the demanding routine of the day-to-day. Addressing changes by dollars saved or simply taking out the least-protected segments of the school program cannot be considered a satisfactory solution. Such an approach will only compound problems and fails to address the bottom line of educational leadership: the quality of the educational experience for students. The skills needed for serving as a school board member in an era of decline are additional to the more traditional leadership qualities for board members which have evolved during this century.

It should be obvious that serving in an era of decline will call for close communication with the public about the difficult choices to be made. Modern board members must study the issues and develop alternatives that are best for all school children if they are to be effective in today's world of expectations higher than resources.

CHAPTER 2

How Boards Operate

BOARD POLICIES

As stated in the previous section, the authority of a local school board lies in the board as a corporate body. Such a corporate body must operate by the policies it establishes. Board policies include general policy statements, rules, and regulations. The remaining sections in this chapter contain a description of board policies and the roles of board members. A study of those policies and roles will give you the understanding you need of how boards operate.

Authorization

The authorization for existence of your board and any special classification, i.e., metropolitan school district, intermediate district, special service district, should be clearly delineated in the first policy statement found in board rules.

An example of such a statement follows:

TITLE: AUTHORIZATION FOR EXISTENCE OF BOARD OF
EDUCATION

The Board of Education of the City of _____ is a body corporate created and existing pursuant to 162.521 R.S. for the purpose of supervising and governing the public schools and public school property of the _____ School District. The _____ School District is classified by law as a metropolitan school district.

Read carefully the state statute authorizing the existence of your school board. Know how your district is classified and what limitations of authority exist.

MEETING THE CHALLENGE

Sometimes reality can be discouraging. Modern school board members can sit back and ask: Why?—or ask: Why not? The enthusiasm experienced by board members as they first take office must not be lost in a plethora of regulations, decline in revenues, court cases, and bitter union negotiations. The challenge, therefore, is to remain alive, alert, and ready to take on the problems of the day no matter how complex they prove to be.

Studying the great leaders of the world, one can see that most certainly the times made the person, but also that the person rose to the occasion. The 1980s and beyond will be the greatest challenge to school boards ever experienced in this country. We can't forget that the school board is the real cornerstone of American democracy because it represents the agency of government closest to the people and determines what our future society will be like.

Again, welcome to the school board and to the challenge of leadership. We hope *The School Board Primer* will be a handy reference for you as you serve as a member of the school board in your community.

You are a part of a rich tradition in serving on the school board. Read, study, ask questions about how boards operate. Be aware of the legal and historical precedents for local school districts and school boards.

Know the difference between policy and administration. You sit on the board to make policy and insure that policy is carried out. You are not an administrator. You hire administrators to carry out board policies and must not interfere with their duties. A good board establishes policy and the administration implements policy. That separation should be maintained.

Compensation for Board Members

Compensation for members of the board may range from no compensation to as high as twenty to thirty thousand dollars a year. In some states, compensation is determined by the number of school children in a district. In other districts, the board itself may set its own rate of compensation.

Historically, service on a school board has been viewed as a public service with no salary or only expenses for travel paid board members. Persons serving on boards usually were financially secure and could spare time away from their jobs. As the running of schools became more complex in the latter half of the twentieth century, more and more time was required of board members, particularly in large school districts. After 1950, many boards began to view service on the board as an important political position, especially where members were elected and not appointed. What began as a part-time position on a board for many evolved into an almost full-time position demanding thirty to forty hours a week. Salaried employees or business persons who had to leave work for board meetings soon began to withdraw from service on boards. The move to compensate members was aimed at keeping those persons on boards.

A particular problem exists when compensation reaches such a high point that school board positions become attractive to those seeking a full-time job. The politicizing of school boards through competition for high-paying jobs serves to further discourage those truly interested in public service from seeking election to Boards of Education.

A policy statement such as the following should be found in your board's policy book:

TITLE: COMPENSATION FOR BOARD MEMBERS

Pursuant to Section 162.581, no compensation shall be paid to members of the Board. However, Board members may, on authorization or approval of the Board of Education, be paid for actual, reasonable, and necessary expenses incurred in the performance of their official duties as Board members.

Review carefully the policy relating to compensation for service on your board. Talk to other board members, past and present, and school officials about the tradition of compensating or not compensating members. If you want to change the rate of compensation for board members, do your homework. Find out what the legal procedures are for changing the compensation rate, outline the responsibilities and time required for service on the board, find examples of compensation rates for other districts of similar size, and, finally, have support for changing the rate of compensation from other board members, the superintendent, and from the community.

Number of Members — Length of Time

Board sizes vary from five members to as many as thirty members who may hold office for two years to as long as six years. Terms are usually staggered so that a majority of the board does not stand for election or appointment at one time.

You already know the number of board members and the length of terms since you have been elected or appointed to the board. You may want to propose changes in the length of terms or possibly shorten or lengthen terms. Find out what procedures you must take to change either the number of members or the length of terms. Since boards are created by the state, you will have to seek help from your legislators or assembly members to make those changes. Since this would be a very sensitive political issue, it would pay to seek considerable public support, as well as the support of a majority of your fellow board members, before you attempt changes in the number of members or length of terms. Then, again, you may be faced by outside pressure groups and local members of the state assembly or legislature who want to make changes you don't desire in the composition of the board. When that happens, be ready with a plan and supporting evidence to maintain present rules relating to length of time and number of members.

Qualifications of Board Members

Qualifications for board members may vary from district to district. There may be age, residency, and citizenship requirements. As with other political offices, persons serving on a school board may not hold any other office except that of notary public. Board members also are prohibited from engaging in any contract work with the board.

Obviously you know the qualifications for the office you hold or you wouldn't hold that office. However, you may want to seek changes in the qualifications for board members and should be aware of requirements for holding office for other boards.

Election Procedures

Election procedures for members of the board are governed by state statutes. Rules for the nomination and election of board members are regulated by the local Supervisor of Elections or Election Board.

The majority of board members are elected by popular vote and most are not sponsored by political parties. Some board members are elected by district or ward but all represent the district as a whole.

Again, you would not be serving on the board had you not followed election procedures. You are a member of the board but must keep abreast of any changes in procedures in the future. Each year, ask the superintendent and school board attorney to furnish the board with any changes in procedures or regulations for nomination and election of board members.

Vacancies on the Board

When a member leaves before his or her term of office is up, the vacancy must be filled by means of an established procedure governing vacancies or resignations. For instance, the member resigning should address a formal letter to the board chairman, mayor, or the governor (or all three in some cases). Certification of the fact that a vacancy exists should come from the Secretary of the board (or Chairman) to the person who will appoint a new member or call a special election. The vacancy may be filled by a special election or by appointment of the mayor if a city school district, appointment by the governor, or by the board itself.

Be aware of rules relating to vacancies on the board. A power shift could occur and the philosophy of the board could change dramatically with the resignation of one person. While you would not get involved directly with the nomination or appointment of a new member, you have a vested interest in the board and may want to speak out about the direction the board should take in the future on certain issues. By speaking to issues you might influence the selection of a person holding similar views.

POWERS AND DUTIES OF THE BOARD

Boards are empowered with general and supervisory control over the government and management of the schools and school property in the district. A board has all of the powers of school boards in other school districts under the laws of the state. Where city school districts exist, additional duties may be required to meet the laws of the city.

A board may appoint any officers, agents, and employees it deems necessary and proper and may fix their compensation. The board has the following powers:

1. To make, amend, and repeal rules and laws for its meetings and proceedings, for the regulation and management of the schools and school property within the district, for the transaction of its business and for the examination, qualification, and employment of teachers, administrators, and other employees (unless other employees are governed by civil service). Boards are legally bound by the rules and procedures until they are formally repealed.
2. Fix the time and place of meeting.
3. Provide for special and standing committees.
4. Levy taxes authorized by law for school purposes.
5. Invest the funds of the district.
6. Purchase and hold property, both real and personal, deemed necessary for the purposes of education.
7. Build and construct improvements for such purposes and sell the same.
8. Provide for the gratuitous transportation of pupils to and from schools in cases where by reason of special circumstance pupils are required to attend schools at unusual distances from their residences.

Transportation

Transportation is a major cost factor in many districts. In many school districts desegregation orders have led to phenomenal costs for transportation. Free transportation is usually furnished students living more than two miles from their schools. In some cases the board may establish shorter or longer distances. By federal and state laws, special needs students are exempt from distance factors. Those students must receive free transportation.

In certain city districts it has been found cheaper to transport by cab certain students isolated from normal school bus routes. Some students may also be furnished tokens for transportation to and from school in city buses or subways.

As a board member, ask for comparison costs and advantages of owning or leasing school buses. Ask too about fuel, maintenance, and other cost factors involved in transportation.

Read carefully the section of state statutes that sets out the powers and duties of your board. Do any of the powers and duties differ from those listed above?

Your board may have a policy against standing committees. Standing committees sometimes stray into administration and thus violate the rule that board members should engage only in policy decisions and not get involved in administrative matters.

Note, too, the legal responsibilities a board has relating to levying taxes and investing funds. Be aware that you must not be involved directly or indirectly in any firm doing business with the board (banking, investment, real estate, or construction). If you are unsure about a possible conflict of interest involving an item to come before the board, consult the board attorney and ask him or her to solicit an opinion from the state's attorney. See the example of a Board Policy Statement regarding conflict of interest at the end of this section.

Conflict of Interest

All boards should have a strong policy regarding conflict of interest. Conflict of interest is dealt with in policy statements such as the following:

> Members of the Board may not become interested in any contract with or claim against the Board, directly or indirectly, or as an agent or employee of any individual, firm, or corporation which is so interested.

In addition to the prohibition found in policy statements, members of the board are subject to certain portions of statewide conflict-of-interest statutes. The statutes prohibit such conduct as:

1. A board member (or a business in which a board member owns a substantial interest) performing services for the district for compensation;
2. A board member (or a business in which a board member owns a substantial interest) selling, renting, or leasing property to the district and receiving payment therefor;
3. A board member attempting to influence a decision of the board by reason of a payment, promise to pay, or receipt of anything of value;
4. A board member using or disclosing to others confidential information obtained in an official capacity for personal financial gain;
5. A board member performing services for any person or business for

compensation, either while a board member or during a one-year period following termination in office, by which performance such board member attempts to influence a decision of the board;

6. A board member participating in any matter, directly or indirectly, in which the board member attempts to influence any decision when the board member knows that the result of such decision may be the acceptance of the performance of a service or the sale or rental of any property to the district for consideration to the board member, the board member's spouse, a dependent child, or any business with which a board member is associated.

The foregoing represents only a general statement of prohibited activities and is described for informational purposes only. Board members are governed by the exact offenses that are contained in their state statutes.

BOARD POLICIES, RULES, AND REGULATIONS

Board *policies* are general principles which give the board and administration direction in managing the school system. Board *rules* generally refer to the structure of the board itself and the way it operates as well as describing general duties of certain administrative officers. Board *regulations* generally involve certain guidelines and procedures for the governance of the school system.

Board rules and regulations are spelled out in documents in a codified form. Both rules and regulations contain board policy.

Board policies, rules, and regulations must be consistent with the statutory powers invested in the board and the local school system. They cannot infringe upon that statutory authority in any way. Where any policy, rule, or regulation purports to restrict the Board of Education's power to act, that provision shall be deemed void and of no effect.

Board rules and regulations may be repealed or amended by a percentage of the vote of the entire board (usually three-fourths or two-thirds) or may be revised in their entirety. Procedures for repeal or amendment of board rules and regulations should include provisions for having all proposals in writing and checked by legal counsel to see if changes are consistent with state laws.

You should receive a code book outlining each adopted board policy, rule, and regulation. Read carefully that document. If a board member violates board policy, ignorance cannot be an excuse. If any officers of the board or any employees of the board violate any policies, rules, or regulations, a board member should immediately call that action to the attention of the full board.

   Board rules and regulations should be completely reviewed periodically and revisions, additions, and deletions made. Usually, the board will assign that task to one of its officers who, with help from the administration, will present a recodified form to the board for adoption. Procedures for revising board rules should be adopted to allow for input from board members, administrators, and teachers, and from the public.

OFFICERS OF THE BOARD

The officers of the board usually consist of a president or chairman, vice-president or vice-chairman, and secretary. Most terms are for a period of one year. A rotation system is often used with seniority on the board determining who the officers are in a given year.

   Boards have procedures for removing board officers. Removing an officer usually takes more than a simple majority, i.e., three-fourths or two-thirds of the entire board. A board may remove an officer at any time during that officer's term of office.

   Board officers are elected at a set time, e.g., first regular meeting in October. Any vacancy in a board office is filled immediately by the board. Election of officers is held at a regularly scheduled meeting or at an adjourned session of the regular meeting for that purpose. Officers are elected by majority of the entire board.

Be familiar with board rules regarding election of officers. Resist efforts by any members to deviate from normal rotational systems of electing officers or to politicize the election process for selecting officers.

Duties of Board Officers

The president or chairman of the board is responsible for presiding at all board meetings, preserving order, enforcing rules, and signing all agreements, letters, bonds, deeds, or leases ordered executed by the board. The president or chairman shall also appoint the members and chairperson(s) of all committees.

The president or chairman of the board may also act as an ex-officio member of other boards such as the Library Board, Museum Board, or Council of Governments Board.

The board president or chairman may also have other duties such as notifying the state treasurer or collector of revenue to make payment of funds to a certain depository selected by the board.

The vice-president or vice-chairman shall perform all duties of the president or chairman in the case of absence, resignation, or disability of the chief officer. If both the president and vice-president (chairman and vice-chairman) of the board are unable to serve, the board may select one of its members to chair or have a rule where the secretary or past-president or past-chairman will assume a vacancy in the offices of the president and vice-president (chairman and vice-chairman).

If a board has a secretary, that person has custody of the Books of Record of board proceedings and may also perform such other duties as the law requires. The secretary also furnishes copies of all communications directed to the board to each board member.

Some boards have a treasurer or secretary-treasurer who signs documents along with the president (chairman) and superintendent. A facsimile of that person's signature usually appears on checks issued by the board.

Where the office of secretary does not exist, the work of the board secretary is carried out many times by the superintendent who serves as executive secretary of the board. In reality, it is the superintendent's secretary who serves as the board secretary. That person is responsible for communications, duplicating the agenda, and recording minutes of board meetings.

MEETING PROCEDURES

The location and time of regular meetings of the board shall be set by the board and published in board rules, e.g., "The Board will meet at 8:00 p.m. on the second Tuesday of each month at the Board of Education Building, 1812 E. Main Street." Boards may choose not to meet for regular sessions in certain months, e.g., the month of July. A board may adjourn its meeting to some other time before the next regular session, and at such adjourned regular session it shall have the powers it has at its regular session.

Special meetings of the board may be called at any time by the president (chairman) of the board or by the secretary upon written request of a majority of the board. Special meetings of the board (unless executive sessions dealing with legal or personnel matters or regulations) are open to the public. Such meetings are usually held at the same time of day (usually evening) as regular meetings.

Special meetings usually contain safeguards for the public, e.g., special meetings may not be held without forty-eight hours' written notice stating the time, place, and business to be considered. In emergencies, the forty-eight-hour notice requirement (some districts have a twenty-four-hour requirement) may be waived upon oral or written request of the board (usually three-fourths or two-thirds of the board must agree). Any oral waiver can be reduced to writing and executed as soon as possible.

A board may not carry on business at a regular or special meeting unless there is a quorum. A quorum consists of a majority of the entire board unless stipulated otherwise in board policy. A smaller number may adjourn from day to day or to a day certain.

Agenda

The president or chairman, upon taking the chair, shall call the meeting to order on the appearance of a quorum. The order of business usually follows the following agenda form:

1. Roll call
2. Appearances before board by members of public
3. Minutes of previous session
4. Reading of letters and communications by their title
   If reading in full is requested, the president may direct that this be done as new business.
5. Reading of motions or resolutions for reference without debate
6. Reports in the following order:
   a. Superintendent of Schools
   b. Board President
   c. Standing committees
   d. Special committees
7. Unfinished business
8. New business
9. Motions to reconsider
10. Adjournment

Rules of Order

Motions concerning matters other than procedure are reduced to writing at the request of any member of the board.

Meetings of the board and committee meetings are always open to the public unless, as indicated earlier, legal, personnel, or negotiation matters are to be discussed. Those matters can be held in private sessions. Where there are "sunshine" or "open meeting" laws, board members should read carefully the provisions of those laws.

Interested persons are allowed to appear before the board or its committees at open meetings to address the board on board business. Usually, a time limit is imposed, e.g., thirty minutes at the beginning of each meeting to allow interested persons to address the board. The reasoning behind the time limit is to allow the board time to carry on its normal business and not be "filibustered" by one or two persons with narrow interests. Boards have allowed citizens to speak early in the agenda to keep those persons from having to sit through long hours of board business before being allowed to speak. Board presidents or chairmen may solicit comments from members of the audience on matters before the board but are careful not to allow persons to interject opinions indiscriminately while the board is in session.

Those desiring to speak before your board should comply with the following rules of order:

1. Persons desiring to speak before the board should appear at least one-half hour before the start of the meeting. Most boards require those persons to sign a roster so that names, addresses, and the nature of their business can be accurately transcribed into the public record.
2. Each presentation before the board should not exceed five minutes in length.
3. Each presentation shall be in consonance with good taste and decorum befitting the occasion and dignity of the assembly. Shouting, loud statements, threats, name calling, offensive personal references, or other improper conduct are strictly forbidden.
4. At all meetings, regular or special, comments from interested persons shall be limited to the agenda items.

In all meetings of the board procedural matters not covered by the rules of the board shall be governed by the manual known as *Robert's Rules of Order Newly Revised.*

A rule of order may be suspended during a board meeting by action of three-fourths, two-thirds, or other percentage of all the members present. Those occasions should be few in number and should be made to allow more rather than less discussion on a matter, i.e., allowing extensive discussion on a matter *before* rather than after a motion is made.

Media Coverage

Media coverage of board meetings may include radio, television, and newspaper. The president or chairman should clear any requests for reporting proceedings of regular meetings from the floor of the meeting room. Good press relations are important and full coverage of meetings should be encouraged. Boards often install t.v. lights in the board room to assist television coverage. Because meetings are often held at night, items of interest to the media may be moved up in the agenda to allow taping for late evening television news programs. With modern equipment, some television stations carry proceedings live if held during the newscast.

Study carefully the format of the agenda. Although your agenda may differ slightly, the items on the sample agenda in this section are found in most board agenda. As a newly elected board member you may find that the business before the board moves so fast that the meeting is over while you're still on agenda item three or four. That is common during the first months of service, but soon you will be able to keep up and not feel you are just a spectator.

The president or chairman is the key figure in maintaining order. If the person in the chair is strong and fair, meetings will proceed in an orderly and professional manner. As a board member, it is incumbent upon you to treat everyone with respect even if those persons don't do the same. Don't be drawn into a "personality contest" with fellow board members or with persons appearing before the board. Those who violate rules of good conduct soon become isolated with little or no support.

If you feel your board is beginning to slip into personal attacks, ask for an open discussion of the rules relating to board decorum.

Remember, also, that the press has a job to do. Don't "play to the press" or "play up to the press." As an individual board member you may have certain opinions and feelings but always remember that you have just one vote and cannot speak for the board, only for yourself.

Attendance at Meetings

Your board should have established rules for attendance at board meetings. Some boards establish a limit on the number of meetings that can be missed, e.g., three consecutive regular meetings unless excused by the board for reasons satisfactory to the board, before a member will be deemed to have vacated his or her seat. Once a member vacates a seat, the mayor, or governor, or appointing officer or group should immediately fill the seat.

Board members should always obtain permission of the president or chairman of the board in order to leave the meeting before the close of the meeting.

Holding a public office is a public trust. If you find that you have consistently to miss meetings, resign your seat on the board. If you have a temporary problem, illness, or work that prevents your full participation, discuss your problem openly with the board and make arrangements to read board materials and to be present for important votes.

Official Minutes

At all regular and special meetings a person designated by the board shall be responsible for the taking and preparation of official minutes of board meetings. The official minutes should contain a concise record of what was done but should not contain a verbatim transcript of what board members say at the meeting. A board member may wish to submit a written summary or verbatim text of his or her address on a special issue and have that printed in the text exactly as written. However, any board member and the superintendent may also attach responsive statements to be included in the official minutes. Any written reports submitted to the board should be printed exactly as submitted.

Official minutes of all board meetings shall be printed and published. Minutes of closed meetings (those exempt under the sunshine law) are not published. Excerpts from a board meeting are presented in Figure 2.1.

Figure 2.1

Excerpt of Official Board Minutes

February 8, 1982

A Regular Meeting of the Board of School Directors of the Upper Darby School District was held in the Administration Building, Lansdowne Avenue & School Lane, Upper Darby, Pennsylvania, on Monday, February 8, 1982, at 8:15 p.m., appropriate public notice of which was given as required by law.

Present: Dr. Nicholas A. Penagopios, Rosalie Gallo, Walter M. Senkow, William J. Buchanan, Barry W. Van Rensier, Josephine T. Sorrentino, and Teresa F. Furey

Absent: Richard J. Gentile and Harry J. Patterson

Also present: Charles E. Webster, Secretary; Lewis B. Beatty, Jr., Solicitor; W. L. Michael Maines, Superintendent; and Student Representatives Barbara Loper and Sue Clark

The meeting was called to order by President Furey, followed by the Flag Salute–Pledge of Allegiance.

President: The Secretary will mark the roll; all Board members are present with the exception of Mr. Gentile and Mr. Patterson. Both gentlemen are involved in business commitments.

We have two sets of minutes to be approved: the meeting of December 1, 1981, and December 7, 1981. What is your pleasure, please?

Motion was made by Dr. Panagopios, seconded by Mr. Van Rensier, that the minutes be approved as received. Voice vote taken, all members present voting Aye. Motion carried.

President: The Report of the Secretary, what is your pleasure, please?

Motion was made by Dr. Panagopios, seconded by Mrs. Gallo, that the Report of the Secretary be received and made part of the record. Voice vote taken, all members present voting Aye. Motion carried.

President: The Report of the Treasurer, please, what is your pleasure?

Motion was made by Dr. Panagopios, seconded by Mr. Senkow, that the Report of the Treasurer be received and made part of the record. Voice vote taken, all members present voting Aye. Motion carried.

President: The Report of the Superintendent, Mr. Maines, please.

Mr. Maines: Madam President, the first thing I would like to call to the Board's attention is the report of enrollment which shows a decline of 300 students as compared to the same period last year.

It is my pleasure this evening to present Mr. Conte from the High School faculty who has our Band and Orchestra, to present a short concert.

(Musical presentation)

Source: Courtesy of Upper Darby School District, Upper Darby, PA.

In addition to the official report of board minutes, the board may also print up a brief outline of board actions for interested parties. Figure 2.2 is an example of such a document:

Figure 2.2

St. Louis Public Schools
Board Briefs

Board Actions – February 9, 1982

Attending: Donald Williams (president); Penelope Alcott (vice president); Nathaniel Johnson (secretary); Gordon Benson; Raymond Decker; Betty Klinefelter; Lawrence Nicholson; Daniel Schesch; Dorothy Springer; Joyce Thomas and Marjorie Weir.

The following reports were presented to the Board for action:

I. Office of Instruction - no report

Figure 2.2 *(Continued)*

II.   Administrative Support Services - approved
      Items of special interest included: 1) contracting for radio-dispatched bus-
      es to transport students between various city locations and county schools;
      2) rejection of a bid by Checker/Manchester Cab for transportation of
      city-to-county and county-to-city (emergency use of this cab service in
      January has shown it to be inadequate in meeting Board specifications);
      3) appropriation of $2,000,000 made from the supplementary balance of
      the Textbook 1982-83 Fund to Budget Function (00). This action allows
      for encumbrance of funds for delivery of books after July 1, 1982.

III. Financial and Budgetary Support Services - approved

IV.   Personnel - approved

V.   Superintendent's Report - approved
      The Board approved administrative modifications and improvements
      which call for the establishment of a Human Resources Development Clus-
      ter and an Occupational/Lifelong Learning Center. Each unit will be ad-
      ministered by an associate superintendent. The Human Resources Devel-
      opment unit will include Instructional and Program Development, Staff
      Development, Evaluation and Research, State and Federal Programs, Spe-
      cial Education and Special Services. Occupational/Lifelong Learning will
      include Vocational Education (O'Fallon Technical Center; Business, Man-
      agement & Finance Center; Health Careers High School and Arthur J.
      Kennedy Skills Center), Career Development (Partnership Programs;
      Career Education; Work Study/Coop/Distributive Education Programs,
      and Jobs for Missouri Graduates), Community Education (Community
      Schools and Adult Education). This unit will also be responsible for the
      Metro Coordinating Committee (Voc/Ed), Corporate Advisory Committee
      (Career Ed.), and the Community Education Advisory Council (Com-
      munity Education).

VI.   President's Report - approved

VII. Governmental Affairs
      The Board did not approve a phase-in process for election of Board mem-
      bers by sub-district since legislation now before the Missouri General
      Assembly will affect this procedure.

VIII. Instruction Committee - approved
      Items of special interest included approval of a Leadership Development
      and Exchange Program; agreements between the Board and Camp Wy-
      man; Young Audiences, Inc.; Theater Project Company; Young Audiences/
      Missouri Perspective on French Influence in Dance and Music, and Janet
      White Architects; and proposals for Law at Work, Urban Consumer Educa-
      tion Project, Juvenile Problems and Law, and Project Opportunity. The
      Board also voted to discontinue contractual negotiations with Radio Sta-
      tion KWMU.

IX.   Management Committee - approved
      Items of special interest included approval of Budget Priorities and Guide-
      lines for 1982-83 and the Desegregation Budget for Year 3, and purchase
      of LRA-owned lots adjacent to Marquette School.

X.   Unfinished Business - Revision of Rule 1045 - Official Minutes of Meeting -
      approved

XI. New Business - Revision of Rule 1208 - Superintendent - Authority to Sign Contracts - referred to attorney
Revision of Regulation 5035 - Contracts for Teachers and New Regulation 5279 - Defense of Criminal Charges - approved.

Source: Courtesy of St. Louis School District, St. Louis, Missouri.

As a board member you should read carefully the official minutes of board meetings before you vote to approve those minutes. Be prepared to amend the minutes to correct errors, especially if they relate to your vote on an issue.

BOARD COMMITTEES—FUNCTIONS AND DUITIES

As noted in earlier sections, a board may or may not have standing committees. Many boards do create and maintain standing committees as well as special committees which it deems necessary. It must be pointed out that the board cannot delegate the powers granted it under state statutes to such committees.

If standing committees exist, the chairpersons and members of those committees are usually appointed annually by the board president or chairman. Chairpersons of standing committees are also appointed by the president or chairman. Special committees may be established at any time.

Committee meetings must be held in the open or "sunshine" and must follow the same rules of order as regular meetings. Committees shall regularly report their recommendations to the board for final action. As noted earlier in this section in the sample agenda, reports of standing committees have a regular place on the agenda. Meetings of standing committees are held at regular times as are regular board meetings, e.g., Instruction Committee will meet on the first Wednesday of the month, Budget Committee on second Wednesday, etc.

Examples of duties of four standing committees follow:

TITLE: BUDGET COMMITTEE—DUTIES

The Budget Committee shall hold public budget hearings, recommend to the Board a balanced budget each July, develop policy to provide for the accountability and operation of the budget, monitor each month the rolling budget including local, state, and federal funds, and this committee shall perform any other functions that may be assigned by the President on behalf of the Board.

TITLE: INSTRUCTION COMMITTEE—DUTIES

The Instruction Committee shall review existing educational policy, develop and recommend policy to provide equal educational opportunities, recommend to the Board amendments to existing policy or the establishment of new policy which maximize the accountability and operation of the instructional support services area. This Committee shall perform any other functions that may be assigned by the President on behalf of the Board.

TITLE: LEGISLATIVE/ADMINISTRATIVE SUPPORT COMMITTEE—DUTIES

The Legislative/Administrative Support Committee shall, in cooperation with administration, staff, the community and legislative representatives, develop and recommend to the Board legislation—local, state and federal—that provides for a more effective and efficient accomplishment of the responsibilities of the Board of Education. In addition, this Committee shall review existing policy, recommend to the Board of Education any amendment to existing policy or establishment of new policy affecting the accountability and operation of the administrative and operational departments under the supervision of the Associate Superintendent—Administrative Support Services (Commissioner of School Buildings), Data Processing, Community and Public Relations. This committee shall perform any other functions that may be assigned by the President on behalf of the Board.

TITLE: PERSONNEL/EMPLOYEE CONCERNS COMMITTEE—DUTIES

The Personnel/Employee Concerns Committee shall review current personnel policies, equal employment opportunity policies, affirmative action guidelines; and shall recommend to the Board of Education any amendment to existing policy or establishment of new policy that affects employees; and shall meet, confer, and discuss with employees and their representatives or through Board-designated representatives concerns that may be brought to the attention of the Committee. This committee shall perform any other functions that may be assigned by the President on behalf of the Board.

Study the committee structure of your board. Talk to the president or chairman about the committee(s) in which you have a special interest. If you have a particular talent, e.g., finance, ask to be placed on the appropriate committee. Always remember that committees, whether regular or special, do not act for the board but serve as a resource for the board. Committees allow for in-depth study of issues and free up regular board meetings for more decisions to be made. Where trust and good feelings exist among board members, committee reports and recommendations are routinely approved by the full board at its regular meeting.

If committees are ever split in making recommendations on an issue, that issue should be left for the full board to discuss and vote on in a regular meeting.

If you serve on a committee where members are not working in harmony, ask that the president or chairman mediate. Do your part to make the group process work by being a good listener and a positive thinker.

RESPONSIBILITIES OF THE SUPERINTENDENT

The superintendent of schools is the chief administrative officer in the school district.

The superintendent of schools is either elected or appointed by the board or by the mayor with confirmation by the board. When appointment is made by the board or confirmed by the board, each member has a particular responsibility to choose the very best person available for the position.

Terms of the superintendent are set by the board during which term compensation cannot be reduced. The written contract for the superintendent should specify his or her total compensation for each of the years in his/her term of office.

Perhaps the most important task, where there is an appointed superintendent, is the selection of the school superintendent. Daniel Griffiths suggests the following steps in the selection of the chief school officer (some steps may be omitted by individual boards according to local needs):

1. The board meets with a person who can give advice on selection procedures, standards, and criteria; helps in screening applicants; suggests questions to be asked in the interviews; and works with the board in other ways.
2. The board establishes the mechanics of selection, including the setting of deadlines for each step, deciding on criteria for selection, agreeing on a salary, and informing the public that the superin-

tendency is open. A brochure is prepared describing the school district and the qualifications desired of candidates; this is sent to college and university placement officers.

3. All applications and credentials are screened.
4. A standard interview procedure is developed and a guide given to each board member for each candidate.
5. The board selects an agreed-upon number (usually three) of top candidates who are invited to come to the district for interviews.
6. Two or more board members visit the communities of the top candidates to learn more about them.
7. The leading candidates may be invited back for further interviews, with their wives.
8. The new superintendent is selected, every effort being made to obtain a unanimous vote.
9. Before being appointed, the candidate selected is asked to undergo a complete physical examination and to submit a report to the board.
10. After the candidate has accepted the superintendency, a public announcement of the appointment is made.

Duties of the superintendent of schools include the general supervision of the school system, including its various departments, physical properties, instructional program, and personnel. All of those duties are subject to the board's control.

Appointments, transfers, and promotions of teachers and administrators are made by the superintendent with the approval of the board. Appointment of teachers is made subject to teachers meeting state certification and other requirements for employment. Appointment of both teachers and administrators should be upon the basis of merit. Examinations for appointment should be conducted by the superintendent under regulations set by the board. The superintendent should make regular reports to the board on appointments.

The superintendent shall have general supervision (again subject to approval of the board) of all buildings, equipment, school grounds, construction, repair, installation, and maintenance; the purchasing of supplies and equipment, operation of school lunchrooms; the administration of examinations for promotions of all employees in the school system; and the preparation and administration of the annual budget for the school system. The superintendent, with approval of the board, can appoint as many employees as necessary for the proper performance of his or her duties. The superintendent has the authority to suspend with or without salary any certified or non-certified employee pending a hearing of formal charges by the board, following civil service requirements where they exist. The superintendent can terminate the services of any non-certified employee whose work is unsatisfactory.

Most school districts require the superintendent to reside within the school district.

The superintendent or his designated representative must attend all sessions of the Board of Education unless excused by the board. He or she should submit in writing all reports of the superintendent requiring board action prior to the meeting of the board at which they will be presented.

The superintendent has the authority to sign all contracts (new or renewal of existing contract(s) on behalf of the board that have been approved in advance by the board at a regular or special meeting.

As you can see, the superintendent is the agent of the board in carrying out policies set by the board. Note that every action of the superintendent is carried out with the approval of the board.

One area that often causes confusion with board members is the appointment of administrators. Examinations, interviews, and selection of administrators under the superintendent is an administrative action. The board can and should develop policy statements regarding the appointment of administrators but should stay out of the selection process. Where there is an appointed superintendent and board members continue to disagree on appointment of administrators, the board has recourse to the superintendent. If appointments result in overall poor administration of schools, the board can remove the superintendent.

SELECTION AND DUTIES OF THE LEGAL COUNSEL

The board should select and employ legal counsel at such times and in such manner as it deems necessary. Most boards have an attorney who serves on retainer and is present at all board meetings.

Legal counsel shall advise the board, superintendent, and superintendent's staff on Board of Education legal matters. Legal counsel represents the board in all legal proceedings and litigation in which the board is involved. Legal counsel represents the superintendent in employee and student disciplinary hearings and performs any other legal duties assigned by the board and superintendent.

DUTIES OF THE TREASURER

Where the office of treasurer exists in a school district, duties should be spelled out clearly in board rules.

The treasurer exercises general supervision over the fiscal affairs of the school district. That includes collecting and paying of funds to school depositories of the board. The treasurer should see that no liability is incurred or expenditure made without due authority of law, shall be custodian of all interest property of the board as well as all documents, books of record (other than books of record of board proceedings), and sureties, documents, and other title papers. The treasurer is the general accountant of the board and should preserve in his/her office all accounts, contracts, and works pertaining to school affairs. The treasurer is responsible for examining and auditing all accounts and demands against the board and certifying their correctness. Finally, the treasurer shall keep all accounts and make available budget and cost information as requested by the superintendent and board.

Ask the superintendent to arrange a seminar conducted by the treasurer for you and other interested board members so that you can become familiar with how the fiscal affairs are carried out in the district. Learn the terminology of the budget and how to interpret the reports of the treasurer. Insist on a reporting format from the treasurer that is simple and consistent.

BUSINESS PROCEDURES AND POLICIES

School boards are protected from liability by having clear policies relating to fiscal management and business practices. Some of the important policies follow:

1. No assignment (transfer) of wages or salary, earned or unearned, of any employee should be allowed.
2. No payment or expenditure should be made unless the treasurer certifies there is sufficient money in the proper fund at the time of payment or expenditure. All claims and bills against the board and board expenditures should be made by check drawn by the treasurer on the banking institution having the board's deposits. All payments or expenditures should be made only upon order of payment issued by the treasurer (and controller if one exists).
3. Every claim or bill against the board should be certified as proper and accurate by the head of the department or office from which the claim or bill is received.

4. The treasurer should keep a complete copy of all contracts entered into by or on behalf of the board.
5. Board resolutions authorizing expenditure of funds should specify the fund and specific appropriation to which the expenditure is charged, and should be accompanied by the certificate of the treasurer showing that there is a sufficient balance in the fund from which the proposed expenditure is to be made.
6. Contingency funds may be established for the superintendent and certain designated administrators to draw upon but such funds should be closely monitored by the board.
7. Revolving expense funds should be authorized for each department office to pay for cash purchases, not exceeding a pre-authorized amount. Procedures should be established relating to how revolving expense funds are used.
8. Audit of all operations and departments should be authorized by the board at the times and manner deemed necessary by the board. At the close of each fiscal year, the board (or mayor) should appoint one or more expert accountants (or accounting firm) to examine the books, accounts, and vouchers of the district and make a report thereof to the board (and mayor in city school districts).
9. The treasurer should keep a "Bond Record Log" open to public inspection, which should exhibit the name of every surety company on any bond running to the board, either for the board's benefit or that of third parties; the name of the principal therein, and the amount of liability. A performance bond should be in effect until the obligation secured by that bond is satisfactorily fulfilled. When a bonded contract has been properly and satisfactorily performed by the contractor, the person in charge of overseeing the performance of the contract should notify the treasurer. The board should only accept bonds from surety companies approved by the state.
10. Performance bonds should be required of contractors insuring faithful performance in the furnishing of supplies, making of repairs, or construction of facilities. If emergencies dictate waiving of performance bonds, rules should be established for those situations.
11. Contracts should only be drawn and executed on proper forms adopted by the board. The board attorney shall approve all contracts executed by the board.
12. Nondiscrimination clauses may be included in board contracts for the construction, alteration, or repair of school buildings. Such clauses include agreements by contractor not to discriminate against employees or applicants for employment because of race, sex, or national origin.

13. Execution of contracts approved by the board should include signatures of the president or chairman and any other officers the board authorizes. Facsimiles of certain signatures may be authorized by the board.
14. Purchases of supplies and materials usually are authorized up to a certain amount (usually $1,000) without public bidding being required. Where costs exceed a designated amount, there must be an invitation for bids maintaining all procedures relating to public bidding.

Before plans are made to construct, alter, or repair buildings, the superintendent should seek approval of the board.

The board may use its own employees to maintain and repair school buildings, equipment, and grounds without the letting of contracts when the total cost of labor does not exceed a certain figure, e.g., $20,000 or $30,000.

When property is to be purchased or sold, the person in charge of buildings should employ competent appraisers and a title company to examine the title of the property. Compensation for those services should be no more than is customary.

The board may also be involved in the leasing of real property owned by the board or may lease property from the private sector. All such leases should be handled by the person in charge of buildings and descriptions of those leases provided the board. The associate superintendent, building commissioner, or person designated to oversee buildings should exercise general supervision over the tenants of the board.

Boards will authorize the sale of real property that has been declared surplus to their needs. In recent years declining enrollment has precipitated the sale of school buildings. The following procedures are suggested to be followed in the sale of real property:[1]

1. Unless the sale is to a public governmental body of the city or state or any agency thereof, or to a not-for-profit organization approved by the Board of Education, the district shall conduct a public auction sale of such real property, to be held at the main offices of the board, upon receipt of a bona fide offer to purchase, accompanied by an earnest money deposit of five percent of the amount of the offer. Notice of the proposed sale shall be given by publication in a newspaper of general circulation in the district, for three consecu-

---

[1]It must be noted here that each board must follow its state law regarding sale of real property. There may be provisions for sale of real property other than public auction.

tive days, the last publication to be at least three days prior to the date of the public auction.

The results of the public auction shall be promptly reported to the board, which shall accept the offer of the highest bidder, provided, however, that the board has the right to reject any and all bids.

2. Real property may be sold to a public governmental body or the city or state, or any agency thereof, or to a not-for-profit organization approved by the Board of Education, at such sum as may be agreed upon between the parties.

3. The deed of conveyance shall be executed by the president of the board and the proceeds of the sale, after payment of expenses incident to the sale, shall be placed to the credit of the building fund.

In Review . . . . .

Let's stop here and examine the previous section on business practices. Perhaps only the instructional program will draw more attention of the board than the business operations of the school district. Sound fiscal management and business practices are essential to any business, and the school system is a big business in your community. (See Chapter 7 of this guide for thorough descriptions of the business aspects of a school system.)

What can you as a board member do to insure that good business practices are followed?

1. Hold your superintendent and his associates absolutely responsible for establishing and monitoring sound business practices. You and the board are legally responsible for balancing the budget of your school district and for insuring that the taxpayers' dollars are wisely spent. If the board feels sound business policies and/or practices are lacking, don't wait until the end of the school year to make necessary changes. If necessary, hire outside consultants and accountants to correct any practices your administrators are unable to correct themselves. Then hire administrators who are able to institute sound business practices.

2. The treasurer or other designated person in charge of paying and receiving funds in the district is a key person. "Second best" is not good enough when hiring such a person.

3. Insist on an accounting and reporting system to the board that is simple and easy to read. A report to the board that requires a Certified Public Accountant to help you interpret it, is not what you need.

Check carefully the policies in your district relating to contracting with persons and businesses in the private sector. If policies and procedures are not clear, they can only cause dissension and distrust in the business community and ultimately cast doubts in the community about your competence.

MAJOR POLICY DECISIONS FACING BOARD MEMBERS

Closing Buildings

The closing of school buildings today is causing considerable grief in many communities. School buildings have historically been the heart of a community—a place to vote, to hold meetings, a temporary home for churches, and even shelters in times of emergency. Many districts are selling school buildings outright while others are holding on to such buildings, modifying them, and leasing them to private and governmental agencies.

Still an uncertainty about future trends in enrollment exists. Although all signs point to continued declining enrollment in most areas, the situation could turn around in future years. Districts that have disposed of school buildings would find that they would have to replace them at a staggering increase in costs both in construction and financing.

Closing buildings in one section of the district may have implications in terms of greatly increased costs of transportation and in integration patterns. Some districts have responded with such patterns as one-grade school centers or in combined middle-high schools. Organizational patterns and school programs may suffer if wrong decisions are made.

Insist that school closings (and construction of new buildings for that matter) not occur piecemeal. Ask that the district administration provide the board with a long-range comprehensive plan that will tie together building utilization, program development, and staff development.

Naming Schools

As a board member you may one day vote on naming a new school or renaming an existing school. What seems a pleasurable task may evolve into an unwanted controversy. By having a clear-cut policy on naming schools, boards can eliminate problems when naming schools.

Review the policy for naming a school in your district. If the policy is not clear, ask that the policy statement be rewritten.

Regulation of School Activities

A number of activities involving students, teachers, administrators, parents, and community persons take place in schools. Most of the activities can be classified as instructional but some may be considered noneducational. Most boards have a clear policy statement related to noninstructional activities such as the following:

"The sole purpose of the _____ Public School System is to provide quality education to students. The schools are not permitted to take part in activities not directly related to the educational programs of the Board, unless authorized by the Superintendent or his designee."

Other school-related activities should be regulated by board policy. Some boards try to anticipate those that seem to be found in most schools including solicitation or sale of commercial articles, taking of photographs, collections, and use of public school property for public purposes. Invariably, there will be some activity for which the board lacks a policy. Rather than reacting directly to a pressure group asking the board to allow such an activity, the board should direct the superintendent and his staff to recommend a policy relating to the activity and follow that recommendation.

Perhaps the two areas of greatest concern to board members relating to school activities is the solicitation or sale of commercial articles in schools and the use of public school property for public purposes. A clear policy statement outlining exact procedures for solicitation or sale of commercial articles in schools should be in your policy book.

When examining its policy relating to use of public school property for public use, the board should have a separate policy relating to the use of school buildings by employee organizations in schools. Such groups as teacher organizations and other employee groups should be allowed to use school buildings for meetings, banquets, etc. with an understanding that all legal requirements are met.

Because school buildings are centers for community activities, numerous groups will ask to use school buildings. The board should have a direct policy relating to the use of buildings that spells out requirements for use of buildings but also allows the board the flexibility to deny requests when the use is not in the best interest of the school district.

Don't be "steamrollered" in a board meeting by an individual or group demanding use of school buildings. Make sure your policy statement is clear and don't hesitate to vote to turn down an individual or group request if you feel the use of a school building is not in the best interest of the school system.

Textbooks

The adoption of textbooks is regulated by the state with extensive adoption procedures followed at the state level. However, the approved adoption list may include a number of different textbook series. The sale of textbooks is a big business and representatives of textbook companies will descend on your district at adoption time. It is important that you have clear policy statements relating both to the adoption and use of textbooks in the district. Both policies should also include statements relating to the adoption and use of educational materials and supplies other than required textbooks. Where computers are used in the instructional program, policy statements should also be drafted on the purchase and/or lease of machines and software.

Textbooks and necessary supplies and materials required for use in schools should be provided free to all students by the board. Only textbooks authorized by the board should be used in the schools. All textbooks and materials used in the school should remain the property of the board.

Textbooks and materials used in schools must be covered in board policy. The board should closely monitor the procedures used in textbook adoption at the district level, insuring that necessary input from teachers is received. Procedures should be developed to allow parents and community persons to review proposed textbook adoptions and also library purchases. By being protective in involving parents and community persons in the selection process, textbook and library book controversies can be averted.

Student Rights

Court decisions and legislation, both state and federal, have affected greatly the rights of students in the last twenty years. In Chapter 3 of this guide you will be able to learn about those various court and legislative decisions. In this section we will focus on board policy and how the board should deal with student rights.

Every district should have a clear-cut policy statement relating to the admission and assignment of students. That policy statement should include provisions for residency requirements, health requirements, i.e., immunization, attendance zones, and special needs students. Under residency requirements, provisions should be made to charge tuition fees for students attending from outside the school district. The superintendent or his/her designee may be given the power to waive such fees under certain conditions, i.e., trade-off for equal number of district students attending in another district. Care should be taken that satisfactory evidence of residence within the district is provided before a child is enrolled.

Every school district should have a *Handbook on Student Rights and Responsibilities* that is read by every student and parent. That *Handbook* should contain many of the policies, rules, and regulations pertaining to students in the district. Local schools should also be encouraged to develop their own rules and requirements for their students in addition to those found in the district *Handbook*.

A sensitive and potentially legal issue is the reporting of child abuse and/or neglect. A board policy should hold the superintendent responsible for developing and implementing guidelines for the reporting of suspected cases of child abuse and/or neglect to the proper agency(s) as required by state law.

Employee Rights

The school board is an employer that must follow the letter of the law in dealing with its employees. As governmental employees, school board employees are protected by provisions of a number of such statutes. As with other legislation relating to schools, board policy must never conflict with state law.

Clear policy statements must exist relating to employee hearings. Teachers and principals whose appointments have become permanent should have a right to a hearing before the board prior to dismissal or demotion. Certain non-certified personnel who are dismissed, demoted, or otherwise disciplined, may have rights under state statutes and/or board policy to a hearing before the board. In some instances, the board may appoint a Personnel Committee to conduct a preliminary hearing. The board may also be under the jurisdiction of civil service laws relating to the rights of employees. When a hearing is granted an employee, the policy relating to such hearing should be strictly followed. Procedures for hearings usually include three steps.

First, the employee in question shall be notified in writing of the charges on which his proposed discharge is based, of the date, time, and place of the hearing of the charges, of the employee's right to be present at the hearing and to have counsel or other representative of his choice, and of his right to testify and to offer testimony of witnesses as well as other evidence in his defense, to cross-examine adverse witnesses, and generally to conduct a defense.

Second, a Board Hearing Committee of not less than three (3) members of the board shall hear and consider the evidence and statements that the parties present at the hearing. The board shall employ a stenographer who shall make a full record of the proceedings of the hearing and shall furnish the board members who did not personally hear the evidence with the transcript of record. The full board shall, by majority vote, decide the matter and no board member may vote unless he/she has either reviewed the transcript or heard the evidence.

Third, a copy of the board's decision, together with a copy of its findings of fact and conclusions of law, shall be given to the employee or to the employee's representative.

Use of Subpoenas by the Board

Each board should seek by legislation (if not already granted that power) the authority in contested areas, such as student expulsions or employee dismissals, to issue subpoenas requiring witnesses to appear and give testimony at hearings. The board should also have the right to issue subpoenas requiring persons who have possession or control of pertinent documents to produce such documents at hearings. The president or chairman of the board should be authorized by the board to issue subpoenas as necessary.

In today's world no person is exempt from a lawsuit and that includes members of the board. In addition to having good legal counsel, each board member should read carefully not only board policy statements relating to employee rights but also pertinent state statutes. Again, don't hesitate to request that the board attorney conduct a seminar on legal responsibilities of board members relating to employee rights.

PREPARING NEW MEMBERS

Inexperienced board members often feel frustration when first joining the school board. They find they can't make decisions that make a difference in their children's education which is why they wanted to serve on the board in the first place. All too often, the board reaches decisions that don't make sense to the individual member. The decision makers seem to be the courts, unions, or special interest groups. Demands are made of a board member's time that he or she never anticipated.

All of these factors may affect the smoothness with which the board operates and create an atmosphere of distrust between members and the board and superintendent.

The superintendent is the key person in helping new board members succeed. He or she can do the following to make life easier for new and experienced board members alike.

1. Discuss with the board the respective rules of the board and administrative officers of the district including the specific relationship of the superintendent and board.
2. Develop long-range comprehensive plans for the school district that give guidance and direction to educational decision making. (See Part Seven for an understanding of long-range comprehensive planning.)
3. Work with the board to keep clear channels of communication.
4. Work with new board members to help them understand policies and how they are carried out. Alert new members to areas of controversy.
5. Never have any surprises for board members (new or old). Make sure each member has a packet of materials and agenda delivered to him or her several days before each meeting. Never add items to the agenda under new business that board members are unprepared for during the meeting.
6. Meet with new members before they take office. Ask the president or chairman to assign an experienced board member to work with each new member. A "buddy system" can help new members understand what is going on during the first several meetings of the board. Ask retired members to be available the first month or two of new terms to assist new board members.
7. As soon as a new member is chosen, provide him or her with a packet of information about the school system. Provide other sources of information (*The School Board Primer*) for board members to review.
8. Arrange seminars for new members by the chairman or president of the board, the superintendent, the board attorney, and key ad-

ministrative officers such as the budget director and director of instruction.
9. Schedule tours of schools and school facilities.

Insist that board policies are clearly written and easily understood by all those who are affected by them. Ask that all policies be periodically reviewed and updated.

A good board establishes policy deliberately, avoiding making new policy in reaction to pressures of the moment.

Know how your board operates. Study the rules that guide the way the board itself operates and the rules and regulations that govern all the elements of the school district.

No matter how you were chosen as a board member, you were elected to represent the district as a whole.

A board member has no legal status when the board is not in session.

A good board acts legally, checking the legality of its actions and decisions.

A good board avoids misuse of the board by individual members. No "grandstanding" should be allowed.

A board member has no legal right to allocate board funds except when he or she is participating in the deliberations of the board.

Always remember as a board member that we act collectively as a voting body. Individual members hold no power. Only the board as a whole makes decisions.

CHAPTER 3

School Law and the Board Member

Unlike most countries, the United States has no national system of education. Furthermore, we have no national curriculum, no uniform testing program, and no uniform national standards. Under the Constitution the control of education rests with the respective states. Legally, a school board, as distinguished from a general function unit such as a city or county, is an agent of the state, responsible for the state function of public school education within a geographic boundary.

A school board is a corporate body and a quasi-municipal corporation, but is limited to the sole purpose of administering the state's system of public education. It follows from the concept of education as a state function that board members are state officers, as distinguished from local officers. This is true no matter how school board members are elected. State court cases have consistently upheld the right of a state to require that local school boards levy and collect taxes for schools.

In large part, the legal provisions for education are based on a conceptual design for education that is an expression of the values and beliefs of our citizens. The goals of our schools reflect the aspirations of the people and the democratic ideals of American society. In the early history of our nation there were few laws relating to education. States provided for education through broad statements found in state constitutions and state statutes. These statements, reflecting beliefs and attitudes, later were statutorily sanctioned. Some were the result of, or resulted in, state and federal court decisions.

Today we find more and more standards for education set by courts —in particular, the United States Supreme Court. In addition, the Congress of the United States, through funding programs for "the general welfare of the people," has become a major partner with states in determining what schools do.

Today's school board member must not only be aware of how boards operate, but must be knowledgeable of school law. In this chapter you will learn about the sources of school law, gain knowledge of state and national legislation and mandates regulating board actions, and examine closely major state and federal court decisions affecting education. Administrator, teacher, and student rights will be examined. You will also review the topic of liability of board members and examine the role of the school board attorney.

Request the board attorney to furnish you with a copy of your state legislative and constitutional provisions for education.

Ask the board attorney and superintendent to furnish you with updates of federal and state court decisions affecting schools.

Ask to attend seminars on school law and request the school board attorney to conduct regular seminars on legal implications of court decisions and legislation.

SOURCES OF SCHOOL LAW

Because the people of the United States believed strongly in universal education at public expense, states were able to obtain parents' permission to pass statutes requiring compulsory attendance of students and compulsory taxation for schools. Compulsory attendance and taxation preempted some of the personal liberties of individuals, but legislative bodies were able to accomplish that intrusion on rights because of the widespread belief that the American way depended on an enlightened citizenry. Thus states controlled those aspects of education until 1954 when the United States Supreme Court embarked on a wave of decisions that would bring a better balance between the responsibilities assumed by the states and the individual freedoms guaranteed under the Constitution. Prior to 1954, the courts hesitated to intervene to support individual rights in education as long as school boards had not acted outside their legal powers in an arbitrary or capricious manner.

Boards today are affected by both federal and state legislation, court decisions, and administrative mandates. In the next sections we examine the impact of both federal and state involvement in education and highlight federal and state court decisions affecting local boards.

FEDERAL RULES AND COURT DECISIONS

Federal involvement in education has been extensive, especially in the last thirty years. In the federal constitution adopted in 1788 schooling was not mentioned. In the drafting of the Constitution all powers not specifically identified were reserved to the states. The "enumerated powers" delegated to the federal government included such roles as raising taxes, the common defense, and collecting duties. Education, because it was not enumerated, was reserved for the states or the people. Two sections of the Constitution clearly establish this relationship:

Article I, Section 8, authorizes Congress "to lay and collect Taxes, Duties, Imports, and Excises and to pay the Debts and provide for the common defense and the general welfare of the United States."

Amendment X states that "powers not delegated to the United States by the Constitution, nor prohibited by it to the States, are reserved to the States respectively, or to the people."

While these provisions were acceptable in the 1780s, events such as industrialization, urbanization, wars, depression, and better transportation facilities changed the composition and nature of the nation. The original concept of "dual governments" outlined in the Constitution (federal and states) evolved to the concept of "national federalism." Under national federalism government interrelationships were overlapping rather than stratified—a marble cake as opposed to a layer cake. The catchall phrase, "general welfare," was stretched to expand federal influence on education. In particular, the addition of the Fourteenth Amendment to the Constitution legitimized and rationalized a federal role in education: ". . . no state shall . . . deprive any person of life, liberty, or property without due process of law."

The Expanding Federal Influence in Education

During the twentieth century the role of the federal government in educational activities has expanded dramatically. Economic, political, and security concerns have set the scene for legislation and court rulings which have altered traditional federal, state, and local government relationships in the provision of public and private education.

Following World War I, Congress passed the Smith-Hughes Act of 1917 to encourage the development of vocational education in the schools. This bill provided monies to pay teachers' salaries, prepare teachers in the areas of agriculture, trade, and industrial subjects, and to conduct investigations that would lead to improved programs of vocational education. The Smith-Hughes Act represented a first major inroad by the federal government for support of specified programs or curricula in the schools.

The 1950s witnessed an even greater acceleration of federal influence in education. Major activities included the establishment of the National Science Foundation, the formation of the Department of Health, Education, and Welfare (HEW), Public Law 531 for cooperative research between HEW and universities, and the passage of the National Defense Education Act.

The formation of the Department of Health, Education, and Welfare in 1953 represented an elevation of status for education in the federal bureaucracy. Prior to that time, the U. S. Office of Education had been placed in such unlikely departments as the Department of Interior and the Federal Security Agency. The direct appointment of the Commissioner of Education by the President of the United States, and the formality of the U. S. Office of Education as a major component of HEW, gave education a new visibility within the federal government.

The 1960s proved a watershed decade in the degree of federal influence in education. During the 1960s dozens of pieces of legislation increased the role of the federal government in the operation of schools, and appropriations for education managed by the federal government grew enormous. Among the laws and programs that most heavily influenced the role of the federal government were the following: Manpower and Training Act (1962), Vocational Education Act (1963), Civil Rights Act (1964), Economic Opportunity Act (1964), Higher Education Act (1965), Elementary and Secondary Education Act (1965), and the Education Professions Development Act (1967).

The granddaddy of federal legislation in the 1960s was the Elementary and Secondary Education Act (ESEA) in 1965. The scale of this act, both in funding and logistics, served to make the federal government a *major* partner in American education. In one program alone, Title I, some nine million school children from low-income families were given assistance.

ESEA programs, as they are known to practitioners in the field, were organized around various planks or "titles" of the sections of legislation. Title I, for instance, directed federal attention to the education of children from low-income families.

By far the most dramatic example of specificity in federal mandates for educational programs occurred in 1975 when Congress passed Public Law 94-142, a bill "to insure that handicapped children have available to them . . . a free appropriate public education which emphasizes special education and related services designed to meet their unique needs." Requiring twenty-three pages of the U. S. Code Book to spell out the details of implementation, Public Law 94-142 has come to symbolize federal control of local policy making for many educators.

Public Law 94-142 represents a new dimension of federal control over categorical aid. There are, in the law, new levels of specificity and regulations for implementation. The law, like the sex discrimination regulations of Title IX and the 1976 amendments to Public Law 94-482 (vocational education), establishes powerful regulating bodies called "advisory committees" at the state and local levels. Membership on these committees and councils is controlled to insure a watchful public. Finally, Public Law 94-142 clearly links compliance to the civil rights of those being served:

> No qualified handicapped individual in the United States . . . shall, solely by reason of his handicap, be excluded from participation in, be denied the benefits of, or be subjected to discrimination under any program receiving federal assistance.

This last provision, the discrimination clause, clearly gives redress to those who feel they are not being properly served, and establishes the services under the law as a "right." Hence, a new level of accountability is established for all school districts receiving federal funds to establish programs to meet the law of the land.

What should be the federal role in education? On the positive side, it can be observed that the federal government has produced and delivered many significant social and community needs programs in areas where little was being accomplished by local agencies. The federal government has also enriched school programs and upgraded the quality of professional education through the numerous acts and laws passed in this century. In particular, curriculum materials have been improved, basic skill programs and literacy upgraded, libraries improved, education delivery individualized, evaluation processes clarified, and critical issues highlighted as a result of federal participation in American education.

On the negative side, it can be stated that the federal government has substituted regulation for policy in extending its influence into the classroom. Changes that have been mandated or encouraged have rarely reflected local input or discretion, and the recent use of legal agencies such as the Justice Department to insure compliance with regulation has cast the federal role in education in a negative light.

In the future, without clarification of the federal role in education, lies the possibility of numerous confrontations between federal, state, and local education agencies. What will happen, for instance, if the federal government develops national criterion-referenced tests in basic skills? The only thing that can be said with certainty is that a significant federal presence will remain in American education and continue to influence local school operations in the foreseeable future.

Federal Court Cases Affecting Local Boards

Even though most of the important federal court cases affecting education occurred after 1954 (45 cases involving education to a significant degree reached the U. S. Supreme Court prior to 1954 . . . 33 education cases came before the Warren Court between 1953 and 1969), several cases before that date had important implications for local school boards. The following list summarizes some of the most important pre- and post-1954 federal court cases that every board member should know:

Brown v. Board of Education of Topeka, 3347 U. S. 483 (Kans. 1954). Established the controlling legal principle that racial discrimination in the public schools is a violation of provisions of the Constitution.

Tinker v. Des Moines School Board, 393 U. S. 503 (Iowa, 1969). Extended the 1967 Gault case *In re: Gault, 387 U. S. 1 (Ariz. 1967)* involving student rights which held that states could not maintain two legal standards, one for adults and another for children. Due process was guaranteed all students regardless of juvenile codes to the contrary.

San Antonio Independent School District v. Rodriguez, 411 U. S. 1 (1973). Upheld Minimum Foundation Program of financing public schools which requires all districts to provide a minimum educational offering in every school in the state but allows richer districts to raise additional monies to support their schools. Poor and minority students living in districts with a low tax base (and consequently receiving minimum state funding) unsuccessfully challenged the validity of the funding system.

Abington School District v. Schempp, Murray Curlett, 374 U. S. (1963). Struck down law requiring a prayer at the beginning of each school day or the reading of Bible verses—citing First and Fourteenth Amendments to the U. S. Constitution which requires a state to be neutral to religion and prohibits establishment of religion.

Zykan v. Warsaw Community School Corporation, U. S. District Court (December 1979). Upheld school board authority in making curricular decisions about use of textbooks.

Now that you've read the section on federal involvement and influence in education, you should understand how the federal government has gradually evolved into a major partner in educational decision making. Rather than blaming the "Feds" for certain policies, be informed about the rationale or purpose of certain federal laws, court decisions, or administrative mandates and be able to share those with fellow board members and persons appearing before the board. You may not agree with those laws, decisions, or mandates but you are committed as a citizen and board member to carrying them out.

Publications such as School Law News, The American School Board Journal, Law and Education Center Footnotes *published by the Education Commission of States, and others will keep you updated on new federal and state court decisions and legislation. Ask your board attorney also to keep you informed. A board that is not informed about legislation, mandates, and court decisions can make costly and embarrassing decisions.*

STATE GOVERNMENT AND LOCAL SCHOOL BOARDS

Board members must carry out the mandates of the state but still try to be responsive to the desires of local citizens. In a legal sense a local school board has both mandated and implied powers. Local boards can determine policies involving contracts, minimum standards, and the expenditure of certain funds, but must carry out specific state duties involving appointing personnel, providing for handling of district funds, keeping records, and following school calendars.

As opposed to the gradual evolvement of the role of the federal government in public education, the states have always assumed a major role in developing and implementing policies affecting schools.

Long before the adoption of the federal Constitution, states were heavily involved in education.

Early Precedents for State Authority in Education

Precedents were established early in the history of our country for the exercise of state legislative authority in educational matters. As early as 1642 the colonies were enacting legislation concerning educational matters. The colonial assembly of Massachusetts enacted compulsory education laws in 1642 and 1647. The 1647 legislation compelled communities above a certain size to set up and maintain grammar schools.

Massachusetts led the nation in establishing progressive educational legislation. In 1852 compulsory public education was enacted as law. As early as 1820 thirteen of the twenty-three states had constitutional provisions for education, seventeen had statutory provisions, and nine had both. Later, as more territories achieved statehood, they were required to include provisions in their constitutions for establishing and supporting schools.

Whatever the nature of constitutional provisions in states for education today, all states have supplemental educational statutes enacted by their legislatures.

Legal Basis of State Authority in Education

The legal grounds for state control of education are based on precedents set early in our nation's development.

Since education is reserved to the states, it is an inherent power of state government. While the U. S. Congress must find constitutional authority for every educational act, a state legislature may enact any educational legislation not expressly or by implication forbidden by fundamental law.

The authority of a state to provide for educational activities may or may not be found in the state constitution. Certain educational activities and obligations may be mandated in a state constitution, but the exclusive grant of state power is not found in the state constitution. The state legislature has plenary power and establishes educational policy. The constitution of a state is a restraining instrument that prohibits the legislature from enacting laws that are at variance with state constitutional provisions. It is obvious that state legislatures have absolute power over educational matters including school property.

States not only have the right and power to provide educational programs but must do so at public expense.

Legislatures have chosen to delegate the administration of schools to other agencies. Legislatures may not, however, delegate legislative authority to other agencies. The state legislature may direct another agency to carry out certain tasks but must establish standards, guidelines, and directions for the discharge of those tasks. When establishing such guideposts, the courts have held that administrative, not legislative, functions have been delegated. The degree of direction required does vary from state to state, the major issue still being whether legislative authority has or has not been delegated.

STATE ORGANIZATIONS

School boards are responsible for carrying out state laws originating in the legislative body of the state and from the state constitution. Substance and direction for those state laws comes not directly from the legislature but from some type of central educational agency. The usual state agency includes a state board of education, a state department of education, and a chief state school officer. Intermediate units also assist in administering educational programs. The modern board member should be knowledgeable about educational agencies and officers in his/her state.

Boards of Education

Forty-nine states have a state board of education charged with the general supervision of public schools within the state. Wisconsin is the only state not having a state board of education.

Many state boards are composed of lay citizens rather than professional educators. Some state boards are appointed by the governor, some are elected by popular ballot, other boards of education are composed of ex officio state cabinet officials who hold other titles.

State boards are in reality administrative agencies of the state that give direction to elementary and secondary schools in the state. In a few cases the state board is given some jurisdiction over higher education.

Although some state boards may be delegated some policy-making power by the legislature, most state boards simply carry out policy recommendations of the chief state officer and exercise little policy initiative.

State boards of education enforce minimum standards or regulations imposed by statute or by state board action. Although most of the enforcement duties are carried out by the state department of education and other agencies, the state board is often a "court of last resort." For instance, certification for teachers may be administered by the state department of education while the state board serves as the agency that makes the final ruling on revocation of teaching certificates.

Understanding the role of state boards of education is often confused by the existence of other education boards at the state level that have responsibility for certain educational activities. Examples are a state board of vocational education and a state board for higher education. State boards vary in number from three in Delaware to twenty-four in Texas. The state board is usually composed of from five to nine members. The trend in recent years has been toward reducing the number of separate boards and vesting the responsibility for all aspects of the elementary-secondary educational system in a single board of education.

Departments of Education

State departments of education have been established by constitutional or statutory provisions in thirty-four states. In the remaining sixteen states the department is not mentioned in law.

The state board of education determines educational policies and the chief state school officer helps carry them out. The execution of policies in a complex educational environment calls for the activities of many professionals. The state department of education has been created to perform the functions that the state board, acting through its chief school officer, determines to be important to the educational welfare of the citizens.

FUNCTIONS OF STATE DEPARTMENTS OF EDUCATION

State departments of education are responsible for a number of important functions. Usually the functions are carried out by various divisions of the department, each of which is headed by a director. The major divisions of the state department are often further divided into branches or bureaus. The following are suggested as major functions of state departments of education:

Gathering, Compiling, and Publishing of Statistics

State departments of education gather and publish detailed information about people and programs in education. Much of the data are used to determine funding of programs. The most familiar data source for funding is the average daily attendance of students (A.D.A.). Through the use of a formula established by the legislature, school districts are awarded funds for every day of attendance by students. Other information published by state departments includes:

- Number of students graduating from high schools
- Number of students in vocational programs
- State assessment scores
- Dropout rates in various grades
- Curricular guides in subject areas
- Booklets on special topics such as career education
- Budget proposals for the legislature
- Guidelines for certification
- Listings and addresses of all schools in the state
- Professional journals
- Guidelines for school construction

Planning and Implementing the Instructional Program

State departments are the "eyes and ears" of the citizens of the state on educational matters. Professionals, working in departments of education, respond to immediate and long-range needs in education. The mandates of state legislatures, federal and state statutes, court decisions, and federal regulations are transformed by state education department personnel into programs of studies, curricular revisions, statements of minimum standards, and monitoring procedures for compliance with regulations.

Recent instructional programs that have been mandated by state legislatures include sex education, law education, consumer education, drug education, and environmental education. The legislatures usually stop short of dictating course content or structure. Local school district leaders look to the staffs of state departments of education for help in interpreting legislation and in selecting suitable materials to carry out mandated school programs. Often state departments hold conferences to discuss how new programs can be implemented in elementary and/or secondary schools. Planning committees are organized to write study guides and select suitable materials to recommend to local school districts. State departments must publish reports indicating compliance with state legislation. Many times, dates and methods for compliance are spelled out in the legislation.

Most states have requirements governing the selection and use of textbooks. To aid in the selection of textbooks the state department of education appoints textbook selection committees to recommend textbook adoptions. Some states leave the selection of texts to local school districts but require that each book selected be on a master adoption list of ten to twenty texts.

Perhaps the most important aspect of the research functions of state departments of education is the communication of research. It is important that board members be aware of the latest educational studies being conducted by individuals and agencies around the nation. Methods of summarizing results of important research studies should be found in each state and a delivery system established for disseminating those results to board members, educators, parents, and the public. This information should also be used by members of the state board of education and legislature as they consider educational problems and proposed mandates or legislation.

Because many small school districts lack the capability for research functions because of lack of staff and budget, state departments can play an important role in helping those districts carry on research and evaluation activities.

Regulatory Functions

State departments of education perform many regulatory functions. Regulations may come from federal funding programs that are administered through the state, through legislation, and through mandates of the state board of education. Prescriptive federal programs have forced many states to adhere to certain standards. Those standards include equal opportunities for minorities, women, and the handicapped.

Funding programs for state instructional programs, school buildings, and special programs such as career education and sex education have brought with them a plethora of special provisions, standards, and regulations. It is common practice for the legislature to delegate the establishment of standards or regulations to the state board of education. More likely, the delegation is to the chief state school officer who, in turn, uses his or her professional staff to monitor the programs or activities covered by the standards or regulations.

Among the regulatory roles of state departments are the establishment of minimum enrollments for instructional programs and school facilities, teacher and administrative certification, enforcement of compulsory attendance laws, school debt limitations, textbook approval, and insuring the health and welfare of students.

An example of an increasingly important function of state departments today is the administering of mandated competency testing programs for public schools. Two-thirds of our fifty states have, since

1969, mandated competency testing programs for public schools. In the states that have such programs, all but six test at both the elementary and secondary levels. Six states test at the secondary level only and, by 1980, five states had competency requirements for the award of high school diplomas while other states are scheduled to implement such requirements.

Competency testing programs in education have not been limited to students. A number of states have moved to some form of standardized testing of persons desiring teaching and administrative certificates.

Certification of Personnel

As mentioned above, testing programs for determining eligibility for teacher certification and pay level are becoming more and more common. Such testing programs have been upheld in the courts.

State departments of education not only certify personnel, but approve teacher education programs. Teacher education programs are periodically examined by state department personnel for quality, and a report is filed with the chief state school officer and state board of education.

Facilities Standards

Although capital outlay funds for school buildings in local school districts come from local tax sources and legislature appropriation, control over school plants is exercised by state regulations administered by a state agency. That state agency is usually the state department of education. In some states other state agencies may share the control over school facilities. In New York State, for example, the State Department of Public Works shares that function with the State Department of Education. The federal government also contributes to regulations for public buildings through such acts as OSHA, the Occupational Safety and Health Administration Act.

State control over school buildings includes the approval of sites, establishment of standards for buildings, and approval of plans and specifications for new facilities.

Technical Services

State departments of education provide a variety of technical services to local districts. Those services include computer services, record keeping, long-range planning, school plant surveys, site studies for new buildings, textbook selection, analysis of test results, preparation of data for school board elections, financial studies, and legal services. A final area of technical service covers the operation of special agencies and programs such as schools for the deaf or blind.

Although some local districts have separate retirement programs, all states have state retirement systems for teachers, administrators, and support personnel. The massive records required in retirement programs are centralized at the state level. Only the state can provide the level of technical services necessary to give up-to-date information to the thousands of recipients of retirement programs. As many state retirement systems are tied to the social security program, the role of the state becomes even more important in providing assistance to state personnel.

The smaller the school district, the more reliance there is upon the technical services a state can provide. Cost factors alone dictate that many technical services should be provided by a single state agency.

Leadership

Although all functions of state departments of education can be classified as leadership functions, a number of areas of leadership deserve special mention.

The state department serves as a leadership agency in conducting workshops on innovations, and bringing in persons of national reputation for conferences and seminars. State departments of education also host a number of advisory and volunteer organizations. Examples of these groups include the ESEA Title IV Advisory Council, the Advisory Council on Career Education, and the Educational Television and Radio Advisory Council.

State departments of education also support, through publicity and technical services, professional organizations such as the state Association for Supervision and Curriculum Development, state Association for Childhood Education, the American Cancer Society, and the state Bandmaster's Association.

Financial Support

State education departments provide financial support to local school districts and intermediate units through special grants. Although funds for such grants may come from the state legislature, the federal government, or through foundations, the control of these funds is in the hands of persons in the state department of education.

State education departments, acting on mandates from the legislature or state board of education, sometimes authorize special tax levies that exceed normal tax rates to be used for supplemental purposes such as transportation or capital outlay projects.

Financial controls imposed upon school districts such as setting debt limits for borrowing, establishing local assessment practices for setting millage rates, and determining voting percentages for approval of budgets are often administered by state departments of education.

Financial controls are spelled out in legislation and an administrative board, usually the state board of education, is required to allocate state funds. That agency can exercise little, if any, discretion on how those funds are spent. The state education department is the agency that provides guidance to districts in how and when funds should be used.

Cooperative Functions with the Federal Government

The state acts as a federal proxy in allocating much of the federal educational dollars to local school districts. As a result, the number of state department personnel paid for by federal funds has multiplied in the past twenty years. In some departments of education over one-half of their staff is assigned to federal programs. Those staff members are located in the area of administration of vocational education, programs for the disadvantaged, and programs of the handicapped. Other federal dollars have gone to state education departments for planning and research. Federal funds have also been used to strengthen state departments of education.

CHIEF STATE SCHOOL OFFICER

Each of the fifty states has a chief school officer. The title used by the chief school officer varies, but the most common is Commissioner of Education or State Superintendent of Instruction.

Today those early functions of the chief state school officer remain and these state school officers exert considerable influence over education. The chief state school officer is elected by popular vote in nineteen states, appointed by state boards of education in twenty-six states, and appointed by the governor in five states. Most of the chief state school officers appointed by the state boards are employees of the board, not officers of the state. In some states the chief school officer is a cabinet official. In states where the chief school officer serves as a member of the state board of education, he or she serves as executive officer and secretary of the state board of education.

The chief school officer is charged with supervision of the public schools and, as such, is often involved in litigation. Decisions of the chief school officer frequently are appealed to the courts. Generally, since the chief school officer has legal counsel, most of his or her decisions are upheld by the courts.

INTERMEDIATE UNITS OR AGENCIES

Over half of the states have established intermediate agencies to assist in administering educational programs. Although the function of intermediate agencies often is not clear, they represent a unit of administration between local school boards and the state board of education, state department of education, or chief school officer.

ROLE OF THE GOVERNOR AND LEGISLATURE

Control over education is exerted by the legislature and executive branches of state government. The governor is a political figure who heads his party. His viewpoints on education are usually set forth in his messages to the legislature. The governor also prepares an educational budget for submission to the legislature. As noted earlier in this chapter, where an educational budget proposal comes from the cabinet acting as the state board of education, there is often a conflict of interest with the governor sitting on that board. The governor's budget recommendation may or may not match that of the state board of education. In Florida, during the 1981 legislative session, the chief state school officer, the governor, and the state board of education (the governor and chief school officer are members of the state board), all submitted recommendations for the educational budget of the state. All of the recommendations were higher than the one ultimately adopted by the state legislature.

The governor can also exert power over education by making appointments to the state board of education, filling vacancies on local school boards, and in states where he has the power, the governor can appoint the chief school officer.

The governor can also veto educational acts of the legislature. If the governor chooses to be aggressive on educational matters, his influence can be felt.

The legislature is charged by the constitution in most states with the power to establish and maintain a system of free public schools. The plenary power of the legislature has been consistently supported by the courts. District school boards are part of the machinery of state government, and their powers may be enlarged, diminished, modified, or revoked at the pleasure of the legislature. The powers of the legislature are not unlimited, however. A legislature cannot exercise its power in a way that violates federal and state constitutional provisions and court decisions. Nor can the legislature delegate its plenary power to other governmental agencies.

The legislature, through passing statutes, gets into all phases of school operation. The following House Bills introduced in the 1981 Florida legislature clearly illustrate the extent of state legislative involvement in educational matters:

HB 494 SAFE SCHOOLS (Rosen, Young, Lehtinen). Creates Safe Schools Act to provide funds for district school board to develop programs to deal with school disruption and vandalism, state funds to be included in general appropriations bill and distributed to districts on basis of unweighted FTE membership in K–12. (Same as SB 522, in Senate Appropriations Committee) Referred to House K–12 Education and Appropriations Committees. Considered by K–12 Education Committee, Apr. 22: (1) bill reported favorable, sent to Appropriations Committee.

HB 497 STUDENT EFFORTS/PENALTY (L.J. Hall). Requires all K–12 students to make a minimal effort to pass at least one grade per year, with parents required to reimburse the school board for school expense if teacher demonstrates student did not make the necessary effort. Referred to House K–12 Education Committee.

HB 533 COLLECTIVE BARGAINING/REQUIRED SUSPENSION (Danson). Requires Public Employee Relations Commission to revoke the certification of any employee unit for a two-year period if in violation of prohibition against strikes, requiring both parties in collective bargaining to follow state law on resolving an impasse. (Similar to SB 276, in Senate Personnel, Retirement and Collective Bargaining Committee) Referred to House Retirement, Personnel and Collective Bargaining Committee.

HB 544 TEACHER CERTIFICATION/TRADE AND INDUSTRIAL ARTS (Liberti). Requires State Board of Education to develop special criteria for certification of industrial arts teachers. (Similar to SB 414, in Senate Education Committee) Referred to House K–12 Education Committee.

HB 550 SCHOOL RECORDS/PUBLIC INSPECTION (S. McPherson, Brodie, Kimmel, Nuckolls). Provides that school records dealing with student behavior and law enforcement records of students can be opened to public inspection by others by court order. (Same as SB 782, in Senate Education Committee) Referred to House Juvenile Justice Committee.

HB 553   TAX ROLLS/PROCEDURES, LRE (Kimmel). Provides for courts to set interim tax roll and use of roll to calculate local required effort, changes date for appraiser to complete rolls from July 1 to June 1 and makes appropriate changes in certification dates, changing words in required newspaper ad when increasing taxes, sets up procedures for school board hearings on school budget, eliminates requirement for DOE approval of budget, setting maximum discretionary millage at 1.6 mills. Referred to House Finance and Taxation and Appropriations Committees.

HB 554   SCHOOL CONSTRUCTION/EXCEPTIONS (Upchurch). Authorizes the Commissioner of Education to approve exceptions to statutory priorities for projects funded by PECO. (Similar to SB 315, in Senate Education and Appropriations Committees) Referred to House K–12 Education Committee. Considered by Committee, Apr. 29: (1) bill reported favorable, placed on House Calendar.

HB 557   GIFTED EDUCATION GRANTS (Rosen, Young, Crotty). Creates the Challenge Grant Program for the Gifted, with state funds to be allocated for exemplary gifted education programs in a school, district, or group of districts, based on rules to be developed by State Board of Education, with no specific appropriation in the bill. Referred to House K–12 Education and Appropriations Committees. Considered by K–12 Education Committee, Apr. 22: (1) bill reported favorable, sent to Appropriations Committee.

The legislature determines how education is managed in the state. It determines the method of selecting a state board, chief school officer, what types of intermediate and local units exist and defines the power and duties of each. All these functions are subject to the restrictions set forth in the state constitution. For instance, where state board members and/or the chief school officer are constitutional officers, the legislature is restricted by the provisions in the constitution establishing those positions.

The state legislature also determines the nature of the state financial plan for equalization of educational opportunity, the level of financial support for education, and the taxing power of local school districts.

The legislature also determines basic policy questions about education including management of schools, the establishment of advisory committees, and the number and types of courses taught in the schools. Promotion standards and testing programs for students, teacher certification standards, and retirement policies are also determined by the legislature.

As greater proportions of school fundings are assumed by the state, legislatures tend to become more and more involved in the affairs of education. In the opinion of many educators legislatures often handicap the educational program of the state by enacting too many laws affecting education. As noted earlier in the chapter, decision-making power follows the dollar. Where 80 percent of school funds are provided by the states, as is the case with some states, educational decisions more often will be made in the state capitol rather than in the local school district.

Regulation of Nonpublic Schools

Nonpublic schools are not exempt from the control of the state legislature. State laws regulating organizations and those individuals conducting business or charitable undertakings apply to nonpublic schools. Other designated agencies in the state have direct or indirect regulatory power over nonpublic schools. Corporate law in the state regulates incorporated nonpublic schools. Nonpublic schools are also required to meet accreditation standards before they can operate.

In addition to the above regulations, nonpublic schools also fall under the rules applying to public schools. Teachers must be certified and compulsory education laws must be followed for students. Health and safety standards must also be met including physical examinations of students and safe buildings provided for students.

STATE COURT DECISIONS AFFECTING STATE AUTHORITY IN EDUCATION

Numerous state court decisions have affected state authority in education. State courts have held repeatedly that public education is a function of the state and the law-making power of the state. For example, a 1937 Colorado court ruled:

> We hold the establishment and financial maintenance of the public schools is the carrying out of a state and not a local or municipal purpose—Being for a state purpose, the imposition of taxes or the appropriation of

monies in the treasury, the proceeds from taxes imposed, is not unconstitutional—By vesting the power in the districts to buy and collect taxes for the support of the school or schools in such districts, the state was but adopting a means for carrying out its purpose. (*Wilmer v. Annear, 65 P. 2nd 1437, Colorado, 1937*)

A later case in Oregon maintained that position:

Education is a function or duty not regarded as a local matter. It is a governmental obligation of the state. Few of our administrative agencies are creatures of organic law. But as to schools, the Constitution mandates the legislature to provide by law "for the establishment of a uniform and general system of common schools . . . It is a sovereign power and cannot be bartered away." (*Monaghan v. School District No. 1, 211 Ore. 360, 315 P 2nd 797, 1957*)

State courts have consistently held that the legislature has the power to exercise the state's control over schools, except when that power is restricted by the state or federal constitution.

State courts have upheld the power of legislative bodies to levy taxes for school purposes. The classic case that established precedent relative to public taxing power for states was the Kalamazoo, Michigan, case where the court upheld the use of Kalamazoo School District funds for secondary schools, even though it was not required by the state constitution (*Stuart v. School District No. 1 of the Village of Kalamazoo, 30 Mich 69, 1874*).

Later cases in the 1960s and 1970s challenged state methods of allocating and distributing tax funds for public schools. The states historically have had the power to determine the method of distributing school funds. This has been upheld in both state and federal courts. The historic California case, *Serrano v. Priest*, was precedent-shattering in that the court held that the method of raising the funds in California violated the U.S. Constitution and the California Constitution because it denied each school child equal expenditures for education (*Serrano v. Priest, 5 Cal. 3rd 584, 487 P 1241, 1971*). Since the method of financing public education did not result in equal expenditure for each child because of the disparity in the ability of the state's school districts to support education (some districts were much wealthier than others), the equal protection clause of the federal and state constitutions was violated.

Later court decisions by both the Supreme Court of the United States and state Supreme Courts forced states to reform their educational finance systems significantly. State courts have ruled on other matters than school finance. State compulsory attendance laws have been confirmed. Discipline procedures for students have been clarified.

Courts have ruled that state tenure laws for teachers did not constitute a contract between teachers and the state. The right of states to
prescribe teacher qualifications has been upheld. Recently, state and
federal courts have rendered decisions on the right of states to with-
hold high school diplomas from students not passing minimum competency tests.

State courts have rendered decisions that have affected just about
every aspect of state authority in education. School board members
are more and more concerned that educational policies are becoming
the product of statutory, constitutional, and case law interpretations.

Court decisions rendered in the courts of one state are not binding
in another state although they may serve to set a precedent. There
have even been conflicts between court decisions made in one state
and those in another state. However, on most issues relating to control
of schools there has been a remarkable consistency in court decisions
from one state to another.

---

*You should now be very knowledgeable about the role and influ-
ence of the state in educational matters.*

*Even though your local board has considerable power to determine
educational policies, remember that your board is an extension of the
state and is subject to the will of the legislature. Every board member
acts as an agent of the state and as a representative of the local citizens
of the district.*

LIABILITY OF SCHOOL BOARDS AND THEIR EMPLOYEES

Under the doctrine of sovereign immunity, a school board, acting as
a corporate body, was immune to liability. As more and more school
boards came under attack, the doctrine of sovereign immunity was
removed either by state supreme courts or by state legislatures. Where
liability has been imposed on school board members, states have provided liability insurance and legal defense to school board members.
It would be difficult to find anyone to serve on school boards without
such protection.

The school board, as a state agency, delegates certain duties to its
employees, such as teaching, supervision, and maintenance. It is a

governmental function to educate our youth, and the school board assumes the responsibility of fulfilling this objective. However, in this capacity the board does not create a relationship of master and servant. Public officers are not liable for the negligence of subordinates, unless they cooperate in an act complained of, or direct or encourage it.

Since individual liability of agents and employees of the school board depends upon proof of their negligence, examination of a few principles of the law of negligence is pertinent.

Members of school boards and school administrators must be cognizant of school law and other laws pertaining to tort and criminal liability.

Liability is defined in *Black's Law Dictionary* as "the state of being bound or obligated in law or justice to do, pay, or make good something." The school administrator faces many obligations. He must comply with the law and be aware of the limitations of his powers under the law.

Principals and assistant principals under the statutory authority given the school board have express authority to discipline, suspend, and expel pupils. The only curb upon the exercise of this authority lies in proof that the cause is unreasonable or the action malicious and arbitrary. The courts, unless there is evidence of the above nature, will not interfere with an order suspending or expelling a pupil if due process, e.g., hearings and legal representation, is followed. Until the West Virginia decision on the flag-salute requirement, expulsion for refusal to salute the flag was generally held as reasonable (*West Virginia State Board of Education v. Barnette, 319 U.S. 624, 1943*).

In addition to the right to refuse to salute the flag, other major cases supporting student rights have involved religious holidays and school prayer. The courts have also supported school boards and administrators in many cases involving challenges by students. Examples are found in the right of school districts to require physical examinations and vaccinations and the right of administrators to administer corporal punishment.

As a general rule, a school teacher, to a limited extent at least, may exercise such powers of control, restraint, and correction over students as may be reasonably necessary to enable him (or her) properly to perform his (her) duties (Corpus Juris. Vo. 56, Secs. 1088. 1100). Statutory and common law rules restrict the corporal punishment that a teacher may inflict. Teachers and administrators (principals and assistants) may be liable under laws forbidding cruelty to children (laws found in all states) if corporal punishment is excessive or administered with a dangerous instrument. Many local boards take the responsibility of administering corporal punishment out of the hands of teachers entirely, forbidding them to use corporal punishment and requiring that such punishment be inflicted only by administrators. This serves to protect the teacher and the school administrator (because of the actions of one of his teachers), but at the same time adds more responsibility to the administrator who is already subject to liability in so many areas.

The question of liability arises most frequently in connection with pupil injuries. Two-thirds of the states have imposed direct liability upon school boards for the payment of damages to pupils injured through the negligence of the board or its employees. In 1964 only two states had imposed liability on school boards.

In private employment, the employer is usually legally responsible for negligence of his employees under the theory of "respondent superior" (employer is responsible legally for the harm caused by the negligence of his employees).

Negligence is any conduct that falls below the standard established by law for the protection of others against unreasonable risk of harm. In general, such conduct may be of two types: (1) an act that a reasonable man would have realized involved an unreasonable risk of injury to others, and (2) failure to do an act that is necessary for the protection or assistance of another and that one is under a duty to do.

The law prohibits careless action. Failure to use care, skill, preparation, or warning may be negligence. It is negligence to use an instrumentality, whether a human being or thing, that a person knows or should know is incompetent, inappropriate, or defective so that its use involves an unreasonable risk of harm to others. It is negligence for a principal to permit a third person, for instance, a teacher or pupil, to use a thing or engage in any activity that is under his control if he knows or should know that the person using it intends or is likely to use the thing, or to conduct himself in such a manner as to create an unreasonable risk of harm to others. A principal may be negligent for permitting a continuing danger to exist, i.e., defective bleachers in the gym.

The first test for determining liability is foreseeability. If a reasonably prudent person could have foreseen the harmful consequences of his actor, the actor in disregarding the foreseeable consequences is liable for negligent conduct. The principal is considered to be a reasonably prudent man and must be able to foresee harmful consequences on the part of his employees and himself.

Injuries may occur to pupils and teachers because of defects in construction or poor maintenance of buildings. Many states have "safe place statutes" which require school grounds to be kept in a safe condition, but relieve school boards and administrators from liability for injuries caused by defects in the construction of the grounds.

Personal Liability of Superintendent

The superintendent is the chief administrative officer of the school system. Subject to policy decisions of the school board, the superintendent engages in many activities and performs a wide range of functions.

In many of his multiple activities he exposes himself to possible legal liability but, unless he is personally at fault either in a negligent or criminal sense or binds himself by contract in a personal capacity, this threat of liability should not be disturbing to a competent, careful, and honest superintendent. Superintendents are not held liable for nonfeasance unless under a positive duty to act individually, but if he does act and does so improperly, he may be liable for misfeasance even if doing so as an official duty. Thus, the superintendent is subject to suit but only for his wrongful torts or acts.

Superintendents may be liable for the wrongful acts of principals, teachers, or other school personnel. Employees are considered to be the servants or employees of the school board (master-servant relationship) which is normally immune from suit. However, a superintendent may be liable only if he personally joins a subordinate in committing a wrongful act, hires an employee when he knows him to be incompetent, or negligently, or with malice, directs that the subordinate perform a wrongful act.

Many states have adopted a "save-harmless" statute which provides that the school board protect all teachers and members of the supervisory and administrative staff from financial loss arising out of any claim or suit resulting from alleged negligence while discharging their duties both within and without the school building. This statute seems to be a solution in relieving school superintendents and other school personnel of the costs of lawsuits and allows them to carry on their duties effectively and not overcautiously.

Personal Liability of School Principal

Courts are universally agreed that any cloak of immunity enjoyed by school districts and school board members does not cover principals or teachers. One reason for differentiating between the liability of school board members and principals and teachers is the difference in their legal status. Board members are held to be public officers while teachers and administrators are classified as employees. Board members are officers because their office is created by statute, terms of office are definite, duties require discretion, and the officer holds office by virtue of commission, not contract. The superintendent in some states is considered an officer and in some an employee.

Few actions in tort have been brought against principals. Principals have less direct contact with pupils. In most cases suit is brought against the teacher. Public school principals, like other school employees, will be held liable for their negligence if there is a direct connection between the alleged negligent acts and the injury that is alleged. It seems clear that the negligence of a teacher cannot be imputed to a principal or superintendent unless either directs the teacher to do a harmful act or could foresee possible harm. The teacher is an employee of the school board and not of the principal or superintendent; therefore, the principal is not liable under the master-servant relationship. The principal, in addition to avoiding personal liability himself, is responsible for informing all those under him of their legal responsibilities and, with them, developing rules and regulations that, if followed, will result in the elimination of negligent behavior.

Principals are responsible for providing for student supervision. Failure to do so may result in a charge of negligence if injury should occur. The principal should not take teachers out of the classroom for extra duties and should also insist that classes be supervised at all times. The principal should also require that safety precautions be taken in gyms, shops, and in science laboratories. The area of physical education must constantly be examined to prevent injuries. The principal should encourage physical education teachers to act prudently. The principal should insure that driver education classes also exercise great care. Courtyard and stairway regulations should be clear to all teachers and students. Principals have been held liable, even though not present at the time of an accident, because they failed to promulgate adequate regulations governing student conduct on stairways. Recess, parking lot, and lunchroom supervision should not be overlooked by the principal. The right of the principal to restrict pupils to the school grounds during lunch periods and recess has been upheld by the courts.

Transportation is another concern of the principal. Many districts provide insurance for accidents even though not bound by law to do so. Principals do not have the responsibility for determining bus routes, bus stops, etc., but are responsible for supervising children waiting for buses or getting off buses.

Athletics, field trips, and extracurricular activities should also be adequately supervised and planned to prevent liability. This includes teacher supervision, parent permission, and provisions for adequate transportation.

Principals should also exercise care in cases of injury. Failure to permit a student to see a nurse may be grounds for negligence. Unwise actions that aggravate injuries may constitute negligence. It is no wonder that students may not even obtain an aspirin in a school office.

All states have statutes requiring regular fire drills. Failure to follow fire drill rules could be construed as negligence in a suit for damages.

The administrator is responsible for the safety and welfare of students. He or she must exercise good judgment and see that the staff does the same. If he sees that a competent staff is employed, if he does not direct them to do improper acts, if he warns them as to duties in specific instances, and if he takes the time to plan and promulgate safe procedures, his personal liability is at a minimum.

Since the board is ultimately responsible for its actions and those of its employees, you should be aware of the liability of school boards and their employees. Know the legal responsibilities of each group of employees in the school district.

RIGHTS OF STUDENTS

Increased demands to hold government and professionals accountable have been expressed by parents through a growing tendency to seek redress from the courts. Because most students are minors, suits involving students' rights have been instituted by parents, guardians, or civil liberty groups. Discrimination, student records, and sexual classifications have been dealt with recently in courts and legislation. Student rights have advanced rapidly in those areas.

Today most states have legislation implementing codes of student conduct. Such codes must be printed and discussed with students and parents. This process tends to eliminate charges of arbitrary action on the part of teachers and administrators. Some codes, however, have been challenged in the courts because they contained rules that were considered discriminatory.

In some areas relating to students' rights there seems to be some regression. Search of student lockers, for instance, has stood the test against charges of unreasonable search and seizure. School lockers were held by the courts to be school and not personal property. Of course, there still has to be reasonable suspicion that contraband material (usually drugs) is stored in the lockers. Students also need to be present when lockers are searched.

Right to be Educated

Educational malpractice has been the subject of court suits in recent years. The most celebrated case was *Peter W. v. San Francisco School*

District (Peter W. v. San Francisco Unified School District, 131 Cal. Rptr. 854, 1976). That case set the pattern for similar malpractice cases that followed. Peter W. was graduated from high school but could barely read and write. His parents sued for damages based on the fact that Peter would be unable to earn a living. The parents lost in both the lower and appeal courts. At both levels, the judges ruled that the achievement or failure of literacy in the schools is influenced by a host of factors apart from the teaching process. As a result, there was no way to assess the schools' negligence. In a later case a New York judge stated, "the failure to learn does not bespeak a failure to teach" *(Donahue v. Copiague Union Free School District, 47 N.Y. 2nd. 440).*

In both cases the judges ruled that the courts were not the places to test educational programs and methods. Through 1981, state courts in California, New York, Iowa, Florida, and Maryland had turned away cases dealing with the legal duty of schools to educate. The issue of a legal right of schools to educate is far from settled, however. A number of states have not been involved in such cases nor have the federal courts. Those states are not bound by the earlier cases.

Ability Grouping

Ability grouping is widely practiced in American schools. Many school districts, especially those with enrollments of over one hundred thousand students, use grouping practices systemwide.

Ability grouping may be based on teacher judgment, a single test, or on a composite of several tests and/or judgments. Ability grouping may occur for learning of individual subjects, within classes for basic skills, for school activities, across age groups for physical activities, or within school programs as in high school vocational or college preparatory programs.

Recent court cases involving ability grouping have upheld student claims that grouping practices discriminate against those from low socioeconomic families. Data from those court cases show high socioeconomic groups and mainstream ethnic groups overrepresented in high ability tracks or groups while low socioeconomic groups and most ethic minorities are overrepresented in low ability groups or tracks.

The board member must be prepared for legal challenges where his or her district uses tracking or ability grouping. Flexible grouping for skills is acceptable, but static grouping where students travel daily in homogeneous groups should be avoided.

Summary of Student Rights

Personal and symbolic expression such as the wearing of armbands, display buttons, or other badges of symbolic expression where the manner of expression does not materially intrude on the rights of others or the school are rights of students (*Tinker v. Des Moines, 1968*).

Religious expression is a right of students. Students can observe their own religion or no religion. They can't be forced to recite a prayer or read Bible verses. Students may decline to salute the flag or recite the Pledge of Allegiance. The Ten Commandments may not be posted in a school (*Stone v. Graham, 101 S Ct., 1980*).

Assembly and petitioning allow students the right to assemble within the school or school grounds and to demonstrate and picket peacefully. Signatures can be collected for dismissal of the school principal.

Freedom of speech and literature distribution are rights of students. Students can plan public meetings and invite speakers. They may also distribute literature on the school grounds. School officials can regulate outside visitors who have violated laws and can set rules for students distributing literature.

Access to student records must be provided students and parents under the Buckley Amendment. The schools may not allow a third party access to a student's records unless the student's or parent's permission is obtained.

Police in schools are governed by rules such as invitation by school officials, warrants, or entry if a crime has been committed. School lockers and students can be searched without warrants if there is reasonable belief that drugs are in the locker or on the person of a student.

Suspensions and expulsions are governed by rules of due process (*Goss v. Lopez, 1975*) and recently by rights of handicapped students under Public Law 94-142 (*Sl v. Turlington, 1981*). Students who are facing expulsion have a right to representation by an attorney and have to be given a formal hearing before the school board. Handicapped students must be given continued public educational services when expelled from school. Also handicapped students cannot be expelled until a qualified group of professionals determines whether a student's misconduct bears a relationship to his handicapping condition.

Pregnancy and marriage cannot prevent a student from an education.

Grades and academic penalties should not be affected as a result of student punishment. Diplomas cannot be withheld for breaking rules of discipline.

Corporal punishment was upheld by the U. S. Supreme Court in 1977 (*Ingraham v. Wright*). Students are protected by safeguards against unreasonable punishment.

The right to participate in student government is guaranteed all students who meet the qualifications of the school's constitution. Faculty or administration cannot veto winners of elections.

Title IX (86.34), an act of Congress, states that an institution or agency may not provide any course or carry out any educational program or activity separately on the basis of sex. Contact sports and sex education courses were excluded under Title IX.

RIGHTS OF TEACHERS

School boards are authorized to dismiss teachers on permanent tenure by provisions in tenure laws many of which include dismissal for personal reasons, such as immorality. Probationary teachers in tenure situations may be dismissed if they do not achieve the standards set by school boards and administrators, standards of personal conduct as well as professional. So also teachers under contract for a specified term may be dismissed before the termination of their contract without liability for breach of contract on the part of the school board if certain charges can be upheld by sufficient evidence.

By any one of these methods a teacher may be excluded from the profession for which he or she has trained, upon charges of immorality, conduct unbecoming a teacher, dishonesty, intemperance, mental derangement, inefficiency, or incompetency.

Summary of Teacher Rights

Teacher rights have been the subject of numerous court cases involving academic freedom, sexual behavior, religious discrimination, mandatory retirement, political activity, and tort liability.

In a majority of the cases school boards were upheld in their actions against teachers. Some examples of court rulings involving teacher rights include:

- Boards can fire teachers for advocating open marriage or drug use to teen-agers.
- Boards can fire teachers for unconventional sexual behavior including homosexuality.
- Boards can enforce retirement policies for teachers such as mandatory retirement at age 65.
- Boards cannot fire teachers for religious beliefs.
- Boards can dismiss teachers having illegitimate children.

Teacher certificates may be revoked by state boards of education or other designated state agencies. In one state (Florida, 1980–81) forty certificates were revoked by the state board. Of the forty revocations, eighteen were for sexual misconduct, primarily with students; eleven related to alcohol or drug use or possession; the rest of the cases were for such causes as incompetency, shoplifting, rape, attempted murder, and petty larceny.

The modern school board member and school administrator must be aware of all laws regarding the teachers' rights. Where questions may arise about actions to take against teachers, the administrator should ask for legal advice from the school board attorney. The attorney representing the school district is the person most knowledgeable about recent court decisions, legislation, school board policies, and state regulations. Arbitrary action on the part of an administrator may lead to a costly suit for the administrator and school district.

Teacher Evaluation

Teacher evaluation is an essential task of the school administrator. In the 1980s teacher evaluation is guided by accountability laws and negotiated agreements with teacher unions. With declining enrollment, some school districts are using performance criteria to determine the order of teacher layoffs.

SCHOOL LIBRARY AND TEXTBOOK CENSORSHIP

The American Library Association reported over one thousand incidents in 1982 involving requested censorship of books and materials in schools and public libraries. Groups have tried to remove books from library shelves. School boards have banned required reading of certain books. Book-banning has resulted in a review by the U. S. Supreme Court of a case involving freedom of speech (*Pico v. Island Trees Union Free School District*). That landmark case, decided in June, 1982, restricted the right of school boards to remove books they thought were offensive. The U. S. Supreme Court decision stated that the First Amendment's guarantee of freedom of speech would allow students "access to ideas" with which school officials disagreed.

CONTROL OF THE CURRICULUM

As noted earlier, the Zycan case struck a blow for school board authority in determining book selection and the curriculum.

Recent state cases have involved the battle over teaching "creationism" in schools. The Supreme Court of Arkansas ruled against the inclusion of creationism in the school curriculum in 1981. Although the Arkansas case only affected that state's schools, the ruling would set a precedent for cases in other states in the future. In 1982 the New York School Board rejected three adoptions of biology textbooks that accepted creationism even though two of them presented both the view of creationism and of evolution.

Issues such as teacher authority to determine classroom methodology, educational malpractice (*Peter W. v. San Francisco Unified School District, 1976*), and the right of a school board to determine the curriculum will continue to surface in the 1980s. Board members must be alert to state and federal court decisions involving these issues and be ready to change conflicting policies if necessary.

The modern board member must be aware of legal issues facing school boards. Rights of students and teachers must be understood. Areas of previously uncontested board authority, such as control of materials and curriculum, are now subjects of numerous court suits. The board must remain alert to almost daily changes in law regarding fundamental issues in education.

IMPLICATIONS OF SCHOOL LAW FOR SCHOOL BOARDS

School boards operate under a system of state law and federal law. Where administrators and teachers in past years assumed they *were* the law, they now work *under* the law. Faced with increased regulations and encountering a better-educated class of parents than ever before, school boards are having to rely more and more upon their attorney.

School boards and individual board members are no longer immune to damaging lawsuits.

The school attorney must know more than just the law affecting school governance to be an effective advisor on matters of school law. He must know about school administration and be acquainted with the aims and goals of the school board and superintendent. By knowing where the board and superintendent stand, the board attorney can help select optimum courses of action.

The board attorney must understand the legislative, judicial, and executive functions of both state and national government. Legislation, court decisions, and mandates must be interpreted for lay citizens serving on the board. Litigation can be costly for the school district and can cost administrators their jobs. A successful board attorney will help school boards avoid such costly court suits. Because we exist in an era of litigation, it is even more important that the board select a competent attorney and listen to his or her advice and counsel.

By now you must realize the importance of your board attorney. Hire the best attorney possible and trust his or her judgment on legal matters.

You may also need to know what certain legal terms mean. Read over the glossary of Legal Terms found at the end of this section. Put a tab in the book at this page so that you can easily refer to the glossary when reading or listening to reports of the board attorney.

LEGAL TERMS

ad valorem	"According to the value"; a tax or duty assessed in proportion to the value of the property.
appellant	Party, be she/he plaintiff or defendant at the lower court level, who upon losing at the lower level brings an appeal.
appellee	Party, be she/she plaintiff or defendant at the lower court level, who is put in the position of defending the decision upon its appeal. It should be noted that the same party may become "appellant" and "appellee" at successive stages of the litigation.
certiorari	"To be made certain of"; the name of a writ of review for a case falling in the discretionary area of the Supreme Court's appellate jurisdiction, requiring an affirmative vote of four justices.
class action	An action brought on behalf of other persons similarly situated.
concurrence	An opinion separate from that of the majority filed by one or more justices who agree(s) with the general result of the majority decision, but who choose(s) to emphasize or differentiate the reasoning or grounds for the decision.
de facto	"In fact"; actually occurring.
de jure	"By law"; occurring as a result of official action.

dismissal	Decision without opinion by the United States Supreme Court in the mandatory area of its appellate jurisdiction which summarily disposes of the case because of the procedural status of the parties or the issues, e.g., mootness, standing, or lack of substantial federal question.
dissent	An opinion that disagrees with that of the majority and is handed down by one or more members of the court.
due process	The regular course of administration of justice through the rules and forms that have been established for the protection of private rights in courts of law.
enjoin	To require a person by an injunction to perform or to abstain from performing some act.
ex post facto	"After the fact"; a law passed after the occurrence of an act which retrospectively changes the legal consequences of the act.
ex rel	"Upon information of"; legal proceeding instituted by the attorney general or other appropriate official in the name of and on behalf of the state, but on the information and the instigation of an individual who has a private interest in the matter.
in loco parentis	"In place of parents"; charged with a parent's rights, duties, and responsibility. In the case of a teacher, this is a condition applying only when the child is under the reasonable control and supervision of the school.
in re	"In the matter of"; designating a judicial proceeding, e.g., juvenile cases, in which the customary adversarial posture of the parties is deemphasized or nonexistent.
incorporation	Evolving doctrine by which the United States Supreme Court has applied a substantial part of the Bill of Rights, e.g., First Amendment, to the states and thereby public school officials via the Fourteenth Amendment.
infra	"Below"; cross-reference to a fuller citation appearing subsequently in the document.
inter alia	"Among other things."
one-judge opinion in chambers	Special ruling issued by a Supreme Court Justice under unusual circumstances and thus not carrying full precedential effect.
moot	An issue that is not considered by the court because it no longer contains a live dispute of the sort proper for a judicial decision. A moot case seeks to determine an abstract question that does not arise upon facts or rights existing at the time.

parens patriae	"Parent of the country"; referring to the states as having sovereign power of guardianship over persons under a disability, such as minors and insane persons.
per curiam	"By the Court"; an opinion concurred in by several/or all the members of the court but without disclosing the name of any particular justice as being its author.
police power of state	The power vested in the legislature to make and establish laws, statutes, and ordinances which would be for the good of the state and its people. This power extends to all areas of health, morals, safety, order, and comfort of the people.
prima facie	"On first appearance" or "on its face"; evidence that is presumed to be true unless rebutted by proof to the contrary.
remand	"To send back"; action by an appellate court to send the case back to a lower court for further proceedings.
standing	Status as a proper party before the court as determined by the court; requires an actual injury or immediate interest in the action at hand.
statute	A law enacted by the legislative branch of the federal or state government.
sub nom	"Under the name of"; designation for the change in the name of either party (or both parties) in the course of the litigation, e.g., upon the death of one of the parties during the appellate process.
supra	"Above"; cross-reference to a fuller citation appearing earlier in the document.
summary affirmance	Decision without an opinion by the United States Supreme Court in the mandatory area of its appellate jurisdiction which gives binding effect to the lower court's decision* but which does not have as much precedential value as a full opinion by the court on the merits. Thus, the court feels less constrained to overrule summary affirmances than full opinions while it expects lower courts to follow both equally. The jurisdictional statement filed in the parties' briefs to the court, rather than the lower court opinion, must be the focus of any inquiry regarding the scope and meaning of the summary affirmance.
U. S. Reports	Official reports of the United States Supreme Court decisions, as contrasted to parallel citations of unofficial reports of the decisions which are available through Shephard's and other such reference volumes.

void for vagueness   Constitutional infirmity when a law is so unclear that it does not provide the specificity required by due process, thus making it void.

CHAPTER 4

Personnel Matters

School board members today are spending an ever-increasing amount of time dealing with personnel matters. Developing policies for evaluation of teachers and administrators, hiring and evaluating superintendents, and negotiating with teacher unions and management groups occupy prominent positions on board agenda. Retrenchment and inflation have taken their toll on school budgets and different groups are demanding bigger slices of a shrinking pie. Since personnel costs account for over 90 percent of most school budgets, the greatest attention of the public is focused on that area of the budget. The board member must balance demands for cutting the budget and reducing personnel with demands for more and better services provided by the schools.

In Chapter 4 we will examine the area of personnel reviewing, first of the role of the superintendent. Other areas of review will include collective bargaining, negotiations, and evaluation of personnel.

ROLE OF THE SUPERINTENDENT

In the United States today some fourteen thousand men and women serve as chief school officers in our public school systems. The title, Superintendent of Schools, is most often used to describe these leading educators, although they are sometimes called chief executives or even supervising principals. Most superintendents are appointed by school boards (most of whom are elected), but some superintendents are still elected by the public for fixed terms of office. Collectively, these district administrators represent the highest level of management in public school systems.

District administrators are important people because of the vast scope of their discretionary decision-making powers. From an operational standpoint, they determine, either directly or indirectly, who shall teach, what is taught, how it is taught, what materials will be used in teaching, the type of facilities available for instruction, and the rules and regulations for conduct in schools. While in theory most superintendents make recommendations to school boards to establish policy in these areas, in reality (practice) the superintendent is the final arbitrator in these matters. The superintendency is a powerful position in public schools, and the selection of such a leader is the most important task of any school board.

Origins of the Superintendency

Four major stages have been identified with the development of the superintendency. The first stage was basically a clerical one. Superintendents were hired to relieve board members of minor tasks. The superintendent was hired as an employee of the board. Many of the early superintendents were trained in business, not education.

Later, as the educational program became more complex, the need for trained educators resulted in the employment of educational scholars. This stage was followed by the hiring of a superintendent for business. Boards often had a dual administrative organization with an executive for business and one for the educational program. The dual system soon gave way to a development of the superintendency where the school executive was the business manager. The early part of this century was an era in which business and the industrial model heavily influenced schools. The concept of the superintendent as a business manager fit the times. The superintendent became responsible for preparing budgets, passing tax levies and board issues, and managing programs.

The next stage of the development of the superintendency, still evolving, makes the superintendent a chief executive who is responsible for both the educational program and the business affairs of the district. Superintendents do have supportive staffs to help in these functions. The larger the school district, the more the superintendent can become the chief executive and adviser to the district. Superintendents' cabinets in larger districts often include assistant superintendents for business, program development, and personnel. In smaller school districts those functions are often assumed by one deputy superintendent or by the superintendent alone. Furthermore, in some rural districts the superintendent may also serve as a school principal or even as a part-time teacher.

During the 1970s and early 1980s the superintendency may have evolved through even another stage of development, that of a master politician. As a politician, the superintendent must strive to help citizens and professionals to keep the goals of public education in view. By far the most important part of any modern superintendent's job is to provide adequate financing for the schools by passing periodic tax referenda. The superintendent must also build up a constituency of support while at the same time pursuing purposeful change in the improvement of school programs. Like the congressional model, this role calls for continuous compromise. Vision, and the ability to constrain action toward desired ends, thus becomes a preferred commodity in the office of the superintendent.

Legal Requirements for the Position of School Superintendent

In states where the school district is a part of the county structure, e.g., Florida and Utah, the legal role of the school superintendent is well defined. In many states the laws do not deal in detail with the position of school superintendent. Often the law simply authorizes the hiring of a school superintendent. The local board defines qualifications and conditions for employment. Among the states, only Florida, Michigan, and the District of Columbia have no certification requirements for school superintendents.

In most states where superintendents are elected or where the position is a constitutional office, the laws governing the superintendency are more specific. This is also the case where the position is defined in a municipal charter.

The qualifications for superintendents vary from no education required to the holding of a Ph.D. degree. The tradition of local control of schools has resulted in few uniform professional standards for superintendents being adopted by boards of education. In the states where certificates are required, the most common requirement for a superintendent's certificate is a master's degree in education.

Very few of the administrative training programs in institutions of higher learning have formal superintendency preparation programs leading to a graduate degree. Most programs prepared administrators for elementary or secondary principalships or supervisory positions.

Legally, the superintendent of schools is viewed in two ways. He or she may be considered as an employee of the school board or as an officer of the board. A person holding the position of officer usually is elected, has a salary fixed by law, and has duties of a continuing nature in a position created by constitutional or statutory authority. Various state court decisions have examined the issue of legal status of the superintendent with some courts holding that the superintendent is an employee and others that the superintendent is a legal officer of the board.

School codes in about one half of the states contain language relating to the relationship of the superintendent to the board.

Duties of Superintendent

Few powers are legally granted to a superintendent since the public prefers keeping the major responsibility for defining the superintendent's functions in the hands of the school board. Although there is considerable debate as to how much statutory definition there should be, certain duties of school superintendents can be identified. Generally, the important duties include:

1. Serving as chief executive officer of the board and school system.
2. Helping the board in formulating policies.
3. Providing leadership in planning and carrying out the instructional program.
4. Selecting and recommending personnel for appointment and guiding staff development.
5. Preparing and administering the budget.
6. Determining building needs and administering building programs.
7. Serving as the school leader in the community and as chief spokesman for the educational program.

Problems of Superintendency

Lately the superintendency has not been the attractive position it once was in American education. Among the problems faced by modern superintendents are the following:

1. Declining resources combined with the escalating power of teacher organizations and their demands in the collective bargaining arena have put new pressures on the superintendent. The superintendent must decide what role he will play in the dialogue between school board and teachers' organization.
2. With the decline in school enrollment, less professional and nonprofessional personnel are required. The superintendent must in-

spire, coordinate, evaluate, and support all personnel, and operate a more complex administration with less supporting staff.

3. Citizens elected to school boards today are better educated, more articulate, and sometimes more critical than ever.

Role and Tasks of Superintendent

The superintendency, as observed, is an emerging role in the 1980s. The complexity of school operations has altered the role from a purely academic one to one which might be characterized as managerial and political in this century. As such, the superintendent has two genetic roles: to serve as executive officer for the school district (advising the board and promoting technical changes) and as *the* individual accountable for all school operations. In the first role, the superintendent serves the board directly and the public indirectly. In the second role, he or she serves a variety of clientele including the board, administrators, teachers, parents, students, taxpayers, and citizens-at-large.

The superintendent works within the framework of state law and local board mandates. Depending upon the size of the district, he or she has a number of assistants including area superintendents in decentralized districts, deputy superintendents (direct assistants), associate and assistant superintendents, and directors in areas of specialization such as facilities planning or transportation. How the superintendent operates through this bureaucracy of second- and third-echelon officers is, in most districts, a discretionary matter dictated by what might be called "administrative style." Additionally, what duties and decisions are reserved exclusively for the superintendent are also a professional decision of the status leader. In many districts the degree of energy required of superintendents to serve the school board and maintain the lines of communication with various public groups has diminished the time allocated to educational management. The day-to-day tasks of running the school district are often delegated to subordinates.

In the larger sense, all superintendents must be generalists because their responsibility for school operations cannot be delegated. The superintendent must have a working knowledge of facilities management, personnel matters, school finance, curriculum and instruction, auxiliary services, and evaluation. In a general sense, the competence of a chief executive officer might be thought of as being on two levels. At the first level is the ability to maintain the administrative flow—to deal with the technical aspects of the job. At a second level is the ability to open and maintain communication lines among all the interested parties. This often calls for an unusual understanding of people as well as a knowledge of institutional behaviors.

LINE-AND-STAFF ORGANIZATION

In planning a suitable organization for any district the superintendent must be concerned with both formal and informal staff relationships. Formal structure will identify lines of authority needed to distribute tasks that must be accomplished. Informal relationships will clarify the actual working relationships and "style" in which authority will be exercised.

Common to most school districts is a line-and-staff organization that maps the administrative lines of authority. By such a chain of command, authority passes from one position down to the next in an orderly fashion. Line authority communicates openly the ground rules for formal leadership in schools. Figure 4.1 contrasts line authority in a small and a large school district.

Complimenting the line structure of an organization are the staff relationships. Staff personnel are specialists who advise and consult with other members of the organization, formally and informally, but have no authority. Staff members can be "delegated" authority for special assignments, but they always serve in a temporary (ad hoc) role in such cases. Assistant superintendents for instruction and supervisors of instruction are often in such a staff relationship to administrators in the school district.

Titles will often give a clue as to whether an individual is a line or staff officer in the district. Titles such as director and coordinator (as opposed to department head, principal) indicate a "helping" role.

Line relationships describe the vertical organization in the school district, but there is also a horizontal structure in districts of any size. In the horizontal organization various assistants are deployed to look after specific tasks, usually by the level of schooling (such as elementary or secondary). An example of a horizontal line position might be director of secondary education in a fairly large district. Horizontal positions on a line-and-staff chart may indicate the complexity of the district and the type of special programs present in the curriculum.

The utility of a line-and-staff organization in most districts is two-fold. First, the "organization chart" is a shorthand drawing of the way things are supposed to be. It allows a quick study of responsibility among district officers. Second, such a line-and-staff chart allows the superintendent and his team to create a set of workable relationships in the district. It formalizes, where appropriate, the informal relationships that have developed naturally and maintains balance among all of the roles and tasks within the district.

Selecting the Team

The selection of subordinates reflects the judgment of the superintendent and constitutes one of the most important jobs of the office. Poor

Figure 4.1 Line Authority in Small and Large Districts

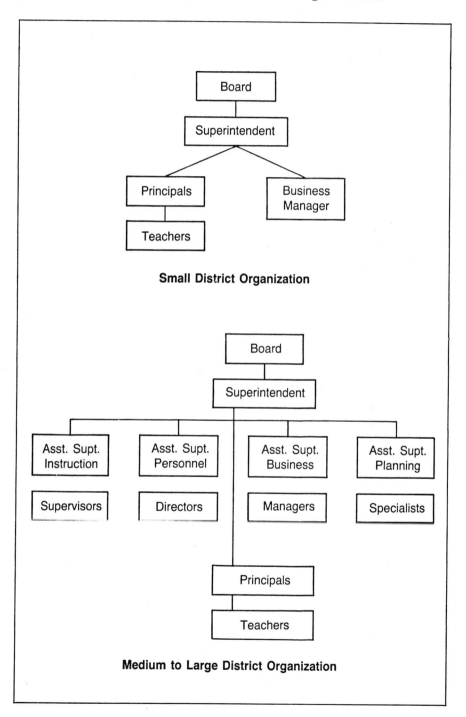

Small District Organization

Medium to Large District Organization

choices will plague an administration and divert the energies of more competent colleagues into "back filling" and "covering" operations on a day-to-day basis. At least five criteria are time-tested traits worthy of consideration:

knowledge and confidence
strong communications skills
loyalty and tact
experience in technical aspects of the job
self-direction and motivation

THE SUPERINTENDENT'S CONSTITUENTS

In addition to his or her staff, the superintendent attends to other important groups. Of these groups, the three most important constituents, from a political perspective, are the school board, the community, and the teachers.

In most of America's school districts board members are elected on a rotational pattern so that there are always veteran board members and new board members. School boards are almost always comprised of an odd number of members, and they represent certain political factions (an area of the city, an ethnic group, a political party). The superintendent's job is to meld these members into a working majority for the betterment of school programs. This is generally achieved by finding areas of consensus, usually philosophical in nature, and focusing improvement activity in that area.

In many districts the superintendent is hindered in this role by the fact that he or she is appointed by the board for a term of office. Serving at the pleasure of the board reduces the ability of the superintendent to be forceful and encourages a quiet style of diplomacy. The fact that the superintendency is a highly mobile role in public schools suggests that not all superintendents possess the diplomatic skills needed for working with school boards.

A second constituency for the superintendency is the community which includes parents, concerned citizens, and the press. During the 1960s some communities put pressure on district superintendents for more local control. While this movement appears to have lost steam in the 1980s, it is clear that a superintendent must "keep in touch" and "clear" controversial items with this group. This is particularly true if the office of the superintendent is elective because parents will always form a critical core of voters in local school elections.

In the 1980s concerned citizens make up a significant pressure group in American education. With the continuing rise in property taxes to support local education efforts, an ever-growing number of private citizens seek to influence the direction of education by pressuring the superintendent directly. Skill at intersecting these efforts, and being adroit at avoiding these pressures, is fast becoming a prerequisite for survival.

Finally, working with and through organized teacher groups is a third area given attention by today's superintendent. In contrast to even 1970, today most teachers are unionized and their presence is reflected in negotiated contracts, grievances, and the continuing pressure for involvement in decision making. Such input, and pressure, can be expected to grow even more in this decade and the next as shrinking resources more clearly define educational roles and performance.

Whether a superintendent is appointed by the board, elected, or appointed independently of the board, he or she holds the most powerful and important position in the school system. The board and superintendent are one—a team that leads in a school district.

It is important that board members learn about the origins of the superintendency, know the duties of the superintendent, and understand how the administrative structure facilitates the management of the district.

In districts where superintendents are elected or appointed independently of the board, competition rather than cooperation between the board and superintendent might arise. Policies have to be worked out cooperatively between board and superintendent.

The superintendent can't set policies independently of the board and the board can't engage in administration. Where their roles are confused, both end up the losers.

MAINTAINING EFFECTIVE PERSONNEL POLICIES

The employment of school personnel is justified only as it contributes to the instructional program. Because school programs change from time to time, personnel needs also change. Boards approve all personnel hired in the district; therefore, they must have effective personnel policies in place.

One of the dangers of having weak personnel policies is that positions become perpetual in districts and continue to exist long after there are instructional needs for these positions. A conscious effort must be made to adapt personnel practices to a changing instructional program. One way of monitoring is not to automatically fill a vacant position until that position is reexamined to see whether it should be redefined or eliminated.

The board hires and evaluates the superintendent in most districts and must approve his recommendations in all districts. The superintendent is charged with developing effective personnel policies and working with the board to put those policies in place. To assure that personnel policies compliment the instructional program, it is essential that those policies relate directly to the educational goals of the district. That relationship can be accomplished through a comprehensive, long-range plan for school improvement in the district (See Chapter 9 of this guide for information on comprehensive planning). In a comprehensive plan, there would be provisions for evaluating personnel and personnel positions along with a design for instructional personnel to be responsive to the goals of the district's overall instructional program.

Specifications of personnel needed for schools should include at least the following: the number of positions needed; a job description for each position indicating how it is related to stated educational goals of the district; qualifications required to perform the job; and the method of evaluation to be used. Put simply, how many people are needed, what should each of them be doing, and knowing how well each of them is doing it.

Selecting a Superintendent

Sometime in your career as a board member you will more than likely face the task of hiring a new superintendent. The selection of a superintendent is the most crucial decision a board must face and a complex task. There may be a time when the right person is available in the district, but more likely a systematic search will be undertaken. Even if a board is sure it wants an insider, more than likely it will still initiate a search, if for nothing else than to match the inside candidate from the best candidates outside the district.

The superintendent of the 1980s is expected to provide leadership in the instructional program, deal with declining enrollments and test scores, carry out new mandates on funding and rights of the handicapped and minority persons, interpret court decisions, and be a part of the management team in collective bargaining. In short, the job of superintendent of schools has evolved into a complex, challenging, and often exhausting position.

The first step in selecting a chief administrator is to have a plan. Such a plan will include a systematic procedure for choosing a superintendent. A rational, systematic process can be developed that will prevent quick decisions from being made—decisions that the board may later regret.

Hiring a superintendent can give a board a chance to review its priorities and take a new direction. New priorities will force the board to look for a "new kind of leader." Many boards reorder priorities and develop new policy thrusts when faced with having to have a new superintendent. That often spells bad news to inside candidates who were identified with the philosophy of the previous administration.

The following steps for selecting a superintendent are suggested by the National School Boards Association and the American Association of School Administrators:

1. Examine goals and priorities of the district. Listen to persons within the system and those in the community about what they think the district's future needs should be and what kind of superintendent is needed.
2. Secure outside or inside consultants to carry out the search process. Check with the board attorney to make sure all federal and state guidelines are followed concerning the promotion of women and minorities.
3. Develop criteria for selection of the superintendent. Utilize your consultants to help identify the characteristics you want in a superintendent and agree on a job description and salary parameters. Set up a budget to carry out the selection process.
4. Set up a plan that will include systematic procedures and timelines to be met in selecting the superintendent.
5. Utilize a screening committee to review resources. Use parents, retired educators, teachers, administrators, and students on the committee to do the initial screening. Make sure that committee members clearly understand that they are to conduct only an *initial* screening to eliminate unqualified candidates and to compile information on all eligible candidates. The final screening with names of candidates to be interviewed should be done by the board as a whole.
6. Keep the media and public informed at all stages of the selection process. Be open and frank with the community about what the board is doing.

7. Don't hesitate to reinstitute the search process if good applicants aren't on the final selection list. Good candidates sometimes withdraw, leaving the board with a choice of taking "second best." Hurried decisions by the board whether in selecting a superintendent or on any other matter are usually decisions that the board will later regret.

Superintendent's Contract

An important task is to develop a suitable contract between the board and its chief administrator. Since superintendents usually do not have tenure, they serve at the mercy of the board. A carefully developed contract can provide security to a superintendent and allow the board to spell out exactly the terms and conditions of employment.

The superintendent's contract is in reality a basic policy established by the board for the performance of the superintendent. The contract lets everyone know what the expectations of the superintendent and board are in carrying out the goals of the school district.

Superintendents' contracts have to comply with existing statutory and other legal requirements and guarantee "due process" to the superintendent if he or she is removed from office. The National School Boards Association and the American Association of School Administrators both can provide model superintendent's employment contracts to guide the board and its attorney in drawing up a proper contract.

Elements of a superintendent's employment contract include a preamble, term of office, salary terms and benefits, provisions for termination, superintendent's professional certification (where certification requirements exist), and professional responsibilities. Other elements might include vacation benefits, provisions for an automobile, life insurance and medical protection, and exact procedures for evaluation of the superintendent by the board.

Evaluating the Superintendent

A relative timetable and format should be developed by the board and superintendent for evaluation of the superintendent's job performance. The evaluation format should include an examination of whether goals and objectives set by the board and superintendent have been met. Other means of evaluation should include board-superintendent relations, the instructional program, budget practices, personnel and community relations, and professional development.

A number of rating systems can be used to look at the superintendent's leadership, including both checklists and narrative comments.

For protection of the board and superintendent, evaluation should be in writing. If performance criteria are carefully spelled out and used as a basis for evaluation, then evaluation data are useful.

Following a written evaluation, the superintendent and board should sit down together to discuss the results. In reality, where district goals and objectives are mutually developed by the superintendent and board, the evaluation process represents an examination of the performance of both parties. Frank discussions between the board and superintendent should result in growth for both and a better school system.

A definite timetable for the evaluation process to begin and end should be established by the board and superintendent. If there are strong indicators that a superintendent is not performing well, a board should not wait until the end of the year to begin an evaluation process. On the other hand, a superintendent who must constantly undergo an evaluation to satisfy the whims of one or two board members soon becomes totally ineffective. Only the board loses in that situation.

Your most important task as a board member will probably be the selection of a school superintendent. It is essential that you know the correct procedures for selecting and evaluating the superintendent. Don't ever be a part of a hurried-up process in selecting a superintendent or fail to insist on a carefully worded contract between the board and superintendent. Finally, make sure a suitable format and timetable for evaluating the superintendent's job performance is in place at the beginning of each school year.

IMPROVING PERFORMANCE OF SCHOOL DISTRICT PERSONNEL

Since board members usually are successful business and professional persons, they are concerned about setting strong standards for job performance for all employees of the district.

Policies, rules, and regulations for employment of all personnel should be carefully developed by the board and superintendent but it is the sole responsibility of the superintendent to select the most qualified persons for available positions in the district. A board or board member should not get involved in hiring school personnel. A superintendent who allows a board member to interfere with the selection process is inviting trouble for both individuals. If policies are carefully developed for selecting district personnel, then those who do not follow those policies should be held accountable.

Two major groups of school district personnel who deserve special attention are administrative and supervisory personnel and teachers. Non-certified personnel are key employees in any school district but they don't require the specialized skills needed by the other two groups. The superintendent or his designee (usually an assistant superintendent in charge of business or personnel) should be accountable for exercising strong quality control on the selection and performance of non-certified personnel. Civil service requirements, where they exist, may or may not be beneficial to the district administration charged with working with non-certified personnel. If strict requirements for employment are found in civil service regulations, better employees will be hired. Where civil service rules are weak and result in poor-performing employees, then the school system will suffer.

Administrative and Supervisory Personnel

The administrative and supervisory leadership team provides support for the superintendent to carry out the many specialized tasks found in a modern school system. Administrators and supervisors today are part of the management team that is responsible for developing and implementing programs and policies.

Today's middle-management personnel are growing more and more restless. Charged with carrying out policies dictated by others (often from outside the district), and caught between teacher unions and top-level management in negotiations, administrators and supervisors are seeking to establish their own identity as a group. More and more, mid-level personnel are turning to negotiations and management organizations to resolve their identity crisis.

School boards faced with middle-management groups who are beginning to act like teacher unions are bound to feel hemmed in. A board and superintendent isolated from a teacher group and non-certified personnel in a management-labor world can ill afford to have yet another organized group making demands upon the system.

The key to the dilemma facing boards and superintendents today is to include administrators and supervisors in major decisions through a concept known as "participative management." Participative management is accomplished through an "administrative team." An administrative team utilizes cooperation and collaboration to accomplish educational goals and objectives.

If you are in a district where the superintendent refuses to relinquish any decision making to his staff and tries to go it alone, then there will be no team concept. Participative management requires just that—participation by everyone on the management team.

A board can sit around and hope that administrators and supervisors work together or it can take the initiative and develop a comprehensive policy that will insure that a district management team structure is in place.

A board policy that provides for an administrative-team approach must be developed with the superintendent's full cooperation and support. The policy should clearly state that the superintendent is still accountable for all decisions and that the administrative team serves in an advisory capacity. The superintendent is the leader of the team and all communication to the board continues to go through the superintendent.

The administrative team should be comprised of representatives of district level personnel and support personnel and school principals. The superintendent may suggest certain tasks and responsibilities for the team. One important task would be to provide necessary research for board members as they deal with complex questions and issues.

Board policy will set the tone for the operation of the administrative team, and leadership in seeing that the team concept works rests squarely on the shoulders of the superintendent. Regularly scheduled meetings, procedure guidelines, and constructive agenda will facilitate the workings of the administrative team. Board members should not attend meetings of the administrative team or become involved in any way in administrative decisions made by the team.

One promising spin-off of the administrative team concept is the feeling of mid-level managers that they are being heard by the superintendent and board and are truly a part of the administration of the district. Such feelings will result in less movement on the part of middle managers to organize and participate in union-like negotiating groups.

Preparation Programs for Administrators and Supervisors

School boards should insist on strong credentials and proper certification as well as successful job performance for all persons employed in administrative and supervisory positions. Where certification standards don't exist or are weak, boards should develop policies that require a high level of competence for each administrative or supervisory position to be filled.

Estimating Administrative Needs

Predicting future administrative needs in a school district is risky these days with declining enrollment in most areas of the country. In order to predict future administrative needs one must analyze employment and population needs, tie administrative needs to number of teachers or students, or estimate number of administration personnel based on program needs. In assessing administrative requirements for the district, the superintendent must estimate the kinds of administrators needed over time, their future productivity, and levels of responsibility.

In many districts facing declining enrollment, there has been a tendency to maintain certain administrative and supervisory programs long after the need for such positions existed. With fewer students generating fewer dollars to support administrative and supervisory jobs, the boards in those districts are in reality subsidizing those positions at the expense of actual dollars going to classroom instruction. The need for evaluating each vacant position before advertising to fill it has never been more critical.

Another particular problem of declining resources is the aging of existing administrative staffs. Seniority usually dictates who remains in top-level and mid-management positions when reductions have to be made. No business can maintain or improve its management unless there is a continuing input of developable talent. An analogy to the present situation is what happened to certain companies in America after World War II. In those companies older managers were encouraged to stay in jobs during the war while younger persons were involved in the armed service. After the war, many companies found most of their managers retiring with no experienced company persons to take their place.

Boards today are faced with running a more complex organization than ever before. Talented leaders must be maintained and new leaders carefully developed. Doing business as usual won't be good enough in the 1980s. Board policies must encourage a constant evaluation of management positions, develop a plan to select only the best and not necessarily the oldest administrator or supervisor when choices are forced by retrenchment, and maintain a developmental management program to train and nurture future leaders.

Fortunately, few districts have tenured administrators or supervisors in any position other than a teaching position. Tenure for administrators is usually found in large city districts and those tenured are school principals. In districts where there are tenured administrators an option would be simply to abolish all positions and re-create fewer new positions, thus allowing the superintendent to choose the best talent from the pool of educators available. When districts have exercised that option though, the result has been a residual bitterness and low morale on the part of all personnel.

Work for the establishment of a comprehensive board policy for improving performance of educational managers that will include a management-team structure, a developmental program for new educational managers, and procedures for selective reductions in force.

Evaluation of Administrative and Supervisory Personnel

All districts have some sort of formal evaluation procedures in place to evaluate administrative and supervisory personnel. Management by Objectives (MBOs), checklists, observations, and conferences are some of the common means of evaluation used in school districts.

Performance evaluation by a management team is the concept used in more and more districts today to evaluate educational managers. In earlier days performance evaluation usually meant the boss developed a series of objectives for the subordinate to improve performance and the subordinate either accomplished those objectives or was fired. In today's school districts there is still a recognition that the subordinate must accomplish certain objectives, but those objectives are developed in partnership with the supervisor or evaluator. In fact, there is less emphasis upon "superior" or "subordinate" and more emphasis on a management-team approach. The team approach does not negate an administrative hierarchy, it simply means that everyone is responsible for improvement of performance. The relationships developed through open, work-focused, face-to-face communication in a team operation will result in improvement efforts at all management levels.

Participate in the development of policies to build an advanced performance evaluation program in your district. Begin with an administrative management-team concept, develop meaningful evaluation procedures, and ask that the superintendent and his subordinates work in partnership with administrative and supervisory personnel in carrying out the evaluation process.

TEACHER EVALUATION

A review of studies of teacher evaluation has to leave one with the conclusion that teacher evaluation is indeed a complex problem. Faced with union demands, retrenchment, and educational accountability, boards today are finding little is being done to develop effective procedures for evaluating teachers. In fact, because of distrust and disagreement about the kinds of evaluation instruments and use of evaluative information, much of what suffices for evaluation today is so watered down that it yields little useful information.

As noted earlier, when examining the need for administrators and supervisors, the employment of instructional personnel is justified only as it contributes to the instructional program. Districts faced with continued decline in the number of students must cut staff. With seniority often being the only criterion for retaining staff, boards may soon find themselves employing fewer and older teachers at higher salaries. Not only is that situation not cost-effective, it leads to stagnation. A further problem is that teachers with seniority may not be the teachers needed to carry out a balanced educational program. What do you do, for instance, with four senior social studies teachers when you need science or mathematics teachers?

Here are some sound evaluation principles that can be used for teacher evaluation:

1. Multiple approaches should be used. When this is done, the limitations of one method of evaluation are balanced by the strengths of another.
2. Instruments should be used that really look at the teaching-learning situation. Simple checklists that include such things as room arrangements do little to provide information to teachers or supervisors. There are instruments available that do relate teacher performance to student learning and they should be used.
3. Systematic student ratings, administrative evaluation, self-evaluation, colleagues' opinions, and evidences of student learning should all be used in evaluation of teachers.
4. Assistance should be provided teachers who do not perform according to expectations. That assistance should be systematic and be offered over a reasonable period of time.

Only when a meaningful evaluation process is in place can educational decisions be made conerning improvement in teaching competence; employment, placement, tenure, and transfer; and effective use of the abilities and skills of the teaching staff.

New Ways of Assessing Teacher Performance

Several states have implemented new statewide programs to assess performance of newly certified teachers. Georgia and Florida have been two of the leaders in requiring prospective teachers not only to pass a written criterion-referenced test on the content of the certification field, but to demonstrate successful teaching performance during the first year of teaching. Observational instruments and procedures have been developed to measure performance of teachers on the job. This performance-based certification model, which includes provisions for assisting teachers who don't measure up, promises to improve performance of beginning teachers. Unfortunately, it does not address the problems of what to do with incompetent teachers who have somehow successfully received tenure and have built up years of seniority. Declining enrollment has offered school administrators the opportunity to eliminate teaching positions but not to dismiss poor teachers.

School boards that are future-thinking will begin to take a critical look at traditional methods of evaluation. As a board member, you should push for updating means and methods of teacher evaluation in your district. Since the instruments and methods of evaluation have become negotiable items at the bargaining table, don't hesitate to "bite the bullet" and fight the battle for an accountable evaluation system. You were elected to look after the interests of students and that should always come first in your thinking and actions.

Tenure/Dismissal for Professional Incompetence

Many believe the 1980s will be the decade when teacher tenure will be eliminated in this country. Many argue that the conditions that originally precipitated tenure laws no longer exist. With the protection of recent court decisions regarding individual rights, e.g., due process, provisions of collective bargaining laws, and federal and state statutes, teachers today have much protection against arbitrary and malicious dismissal. Also, school administrators today are better trained and more cognizant of teachers' rights. The protection of tenure laws is simply not needed for competent teachers. What has resulted is that incompetent teachers are being protected by tenure laws while the competent majority suffer in reputation from being identified with the few incompetent teachers in a school system.

Incompetent teachers can be dismissed even if they are tenured. The process is usually a detailed and drawn-out one but is worth the price. Most tenure/dismissal statutes simply list incompetence as one of several reasons for dismissal. In order for a board to dismiss an incompetent teacher, specific teaching behaviors must be documented clearly over time. Most courts have upheld the dismissal of teachers where teaching methods, effects on pupils, personal attitudes, e.g., refusal to teach or accept supervision, or knowledge of subject matter have been found to be severely lacking.

Teachers facing dismissal must be offered assistance and have the right to second and sometimes third opinions from evaluators. Boards must have policies that spell out step-by-step procedures to be used in the determination process.

In summary, there are six purposes of evaluation:

To improve teaching
To supply information for modification of assignments
To protect individuals and school systems from incompetence
To reward superior performance
To validate the selection process
To provide a basis for a teacher's career planning, growth, and development

---

Perhaps one of the most trying and time-consuming activities you may engage in will be participating in a dismissal hearing. If your superintendent and his staff have done their homework, you must simply weigh the evidence and render a decision. The board attorney must provide guidance to the superintendent and board. One thing to remember is that dismissed teachers have the right (and most exercise that right) to an appeal in the courts. Also, separate state hearings requiring testimony of school officials may be necessary where recommendations are made for the lifting of a teaching license.

AFFIRMATIVE ACTION

During the decade of the 1970s a great deal of federal legislation, mandates, and federal court rulings were aimed at reducing employment discrimination in education. The two groups most affected by those actions were women and minorities. Title VII of the Civil Rights Acts of 1964 became applicable to school boards in 1972. Title VII prohibited discrimination in employment practices on the basis of color, religion, national origin, or sex. In 1972 federal courts ruled that it was illegal for boards to require pregnant teachers to resign. Title IX of the Educational Amendments of 1972 extended further the rights of women, especially in particular sports programs.

Exert leadership on the Board to get the administration to review all policies relating to women and minorities, adults and students, in the school system.

If policies need modifying or strengthening, make sure that they are rewritten by a representative committee of students, teachers, and administrators.

Set up a communication system in the district to insure that everyone knows that jobs and programs are available to all persons regardless of sex or race.

Affirmative action does not mean that persons are hired solely on the basis of their being one of a minority group or being women. School board policies must be clear that only the best qualified persons will be hired.

NEGOTIATIONS — DEALING WITH WORK STOPPAGES

Negotiations

Since employees of federal, state, and local governmental agencies are exempt from the National Labor Relations Act, collective bargaining for teachers is almost exclusively a matter governed by state statute. All states now have legal precedent that either authorizes or mandates collective negotiations. Collective negotiations between teacher organizations and Boards of Education have become a way of life in America's school districts.

Even though teachers have the right to organize and bargain with a school board, the board has the full authority to make the final decision on any topic raised at the bargaining table. Teachers can either strike (strikes are illegal in many states) or work to defeat the board members at the next election. The Supreme Court has ruled that boards have the right to fire striking teachers in states where teacher strikes are illegal (*Hortonville Joint School District No. 1 v. Hortonville Educational Association*, 1976).

Collective bargaining is strictly an adversary process with both parties striving for advantage. Boards and teacher unions usually have outside assistance, usually an attorney, to represent them in the bargaining process. Negotiating teams on the board's side may consist of any combination of board members, chief school administrators including the superintendent, representatives of the administrative team, the board attorney, and other legal counsel. The union or professional teacher association may have a team of teachers, union or professional association officers, state and national union or association representatives, and legal counsel at the table.

Many districts have organized a new position in the school district, Director of Employee Relations. That person helps the board team prepare for negotiations, becomes the chief spokesman at the bargaining table, administers the negotiated contract, and administers the management-employee relations program. Boards can obtain a model job description for the position of Director of Employee Relations from the American Association of School Administrators (AASA).

While Boards of Education are ultimately responsible for representing the school system, most boards delegate the negotiation responsibility to the superintendent, thereby keeping the board posture as one of a ratifying body. Various estimates hold that the complete negotiation process, without unusual circumstances, may consume three to four hundred clock hours. Thus, the superintendent and other administrators must develop some techniques for effective negotiating. Listed below are some suggestions compiled by the Ohio School Boards Association:

1. *Keep calm—don't lose control of yourself.* Negotiation sessions can be exasperating. The temptation may come to get angry and fight back when intemperate accusations are made or when "the straw that broke the camel's back" is hurled on the table.
2. *Avoid "off the record" comments.* Actually nothing is "off the record." Innocently made remarks have a way of coming back to haunt their author. Be careful to say only what you are willing to have quoted.
3. *Don't be overcandid.* Inexperienced negotiators may, with the best of intentions, desire to "lay the cards on the table face up." This may be done in the mistaken notion that everybody fully understands the other and utter frankness is desired. Complete candor doesn't always serve the best interests of productive negotiation. This is not a plea for duplicity; rather, it is a recommendation for prudent and discriminating utterances.
4. *Be long on listening.* Usually a good listener makes a good negotiator. It is wise to let your "adversaries" do the talking—at least in the beginning.
5. *Don't be afraid of a "little heat."* Discussions sometimes generate

quite a bit of "heat." Don't be afraid of it. It never hurts to let the "opposition" sound off even when you may be tempted to hit back.

6. *Watch the voice level.* A wise practice is to keep the pitch of the voice down even though the temptation may be strong to let it rise under the excitement of emotional stress.

7. *Keep flexible.* One of the skills of good negotiators is the ability to shift position a bit if a positive gain can thus be accomplished. An obstinate adherence to one position or point of view, regardless of the ultimate consequences of that rigidity, may be more of a deterrent than an advantage.

8. *Refrain from a flat "no."* Especially in the earlier stages of negotiation it is best to avoid giving a flat "no" answer to a proposition. It doesn't help to work yourself into a box by being totally negative "too early in the game."

9. *Give to get.* Negotiation is the art of giving and getting. Concede a point to gain a concession. This is the name of the game.

10. *Work on the easier items first.* Settle those things first about which there is the least controversy. Leave the tougher items until later in order to avoid an early deadlock.

11. *Respect your adversary.* Respect those who are seated on the opposite side of the table. Assume that their motives are as sincere as your own, at least until proven otherwise.

12. *Be patient.* If necessary, be willing to sit out tiresome tirades. Time has a way of being on the side of the patient negotiator.

13. *Avoid waving "red flags."* There are some statements that irritate teachers and merely heighten their antipathies. Find out what these are and avoid their use. Needless waving of "red flags" only infuriates.

14. *Let the other side "win some victories."* Each team has to win some victories. A "shut out" may be a hollow gain in negotiation.

15. *Negotiation is a "way of life."* Obvious resentment of the fact that negotiation is here to stay weakens the effectiveness of the negotiator. The better part of wisdom is to adjust to it and to become better prepared to use it as a tool of interstaff relations.

Finally, the language of negotiation is new and must be mastered by the beginning board member. Among the more common terms which should be familiar to the board member are the following:

agenda	The agreed-upon list of requests or demands that become items for negotiation
agreement	The contract that binds the parties to certain actions for specified periods of time
conciliation	Use of a third party to help reach an agreement without coercion
grievance	An intensified complaint that cannot be settled at an operational level and is referred to a specific grievance process
negotiation	A simplified form of collective bargaining where teachers and the board settle common matters

sanctions   Severance of a relationship with an agency or with-
                        holding services as one step toward applying pressure

union affiliation   Identification with an organized labor organization
                        for the purpose of entering into negotiations

Dealing with Work Stoppages

Strikes don't just happen. Strikes result after prolonged negotiations
have broken down. Board members and administrators who get
caught without a carefully developed strike plan have only themselves
to blame. Neither teachers nor administrators want strikes but they
happen. A strike plan then is essential for every district no matter how
good management-labor relations have been in the past.

The scope of a strike plan will vary with the size of the district but
should include the following essential elements:

1. A plan to manage the district during the strike: keeping buildings
   open, assigning district level personnel to key schools, consolidat-
   ing remaining staff in a few schools to keep school programs going,
   revising bus schedules, and communicating with school principals
   are some of the major elements necessary in managing the district
   during a strike.
2. A communication network for all administrators and management
   persons: special phone or radio linkages, and radio and television
   announcements are a part of this network.
3. Carefully worked-out job roles for all administrators during the
   strike: responsibilities for administrators may include everything
   from driving a school bus to manning a radio transmitter at the central office. All administrators will have to know the rules regarding
   the handling of pickets. (Pickets, for instance, cannot picket on
   school grounds or use school facilities such as lavatories. Nor can
   they engage students or other adults.)
4. Procedures for communicating with parents about school closings
   and openings. Board policy should be to keep schools open within
   the bounds of health and safety for students and other persons who
   continue to work.
5. A letter to each school employee should be drafted and mailed outlining applicable strike law and board policy relating to the strike.
   The letter should also be informative, listing steps the board has
   taken along with issues that have been agreed upon.

It must be emphasized that the board must work until the last moment to prevent a strike. When an impasse has been reached in bargaining, often the board and school employee organization will agree

to the involvement of a third-party mediator. When the "last and best offer" is made by the board team and rejected by the teacher group, a strike usually follows. A third-party mediator can keep negotiations going so that a "last and best offer" does not have to be made.

Once a strike has occurred, the board must continue to negotiate with teachers. Negotiations continue while the board is carrying out its strike plan to keep the schools operating. Even after strikes have begun, the board and teacher group may still utilize a third-party mediator to help resolve the strike. Arbitration cannot be binding on a school board but can help remove a total impasse.*

Once a strike is settled, it is important that schools begin operating again as smoothly as possible. Hard feelings may exist on both sides and it will take time to "heal the wounds." Board members may have a difficult time adjusting to the new power of teachers if they win, or to administrators who lost and forced the board to raise taxes. If teachers lose, they may look for issues to get back at board members.

A strike is a no-win situation for board members. "Giving away the store" or a no-compromise stance will both bring grief to the board member. The best advice is for board members to select a good negotiating team, study the issues, make the best possible offer, and maintain a calm professional demeanor even when engaged in a heated strike. One further word of advice is always to know the law and follow it to the letter.

---

*Arbitration is binding in some states, e.g., Wisconsin.

CHAPTER 5

What Are Schools All About?

The school board is responsible for the development and operation of the total school system. That includes the curriculum, instructional program, and organizational structure of schools.

The curriculum includes both the formal and informal curriculum. The formal curriculum includes courses of study found in all school districts such as mathematics, sciences, art, music. The informal curriculum consists of all the other experiences of students under the direction of the school such as guidance, student government, and competitive sports. The curriculum is dictated by state requirements as well as local requirements.

While the curriculum is "what is," the instructional program represents the processes or means of carrying out the curriculum. It includes the activities, materials, textbooks, and methods used by teachers and support personnel to deliver the curriculum to students.

The organizational structure of schools relates to the grades assigned to schools, e.g., grades K–5 for elementary schools; how students are grouped, e.g., by ability; and how teachers teach, e.g., in teams, by departments, etc.

In a typical system schools are organized according to the age/grade of students in elementary, middle or junior high, and high school. Some districts have organized schools as simply elementary (grades K–8 or K–6) and secondary (grades 9–12 or 7–12). In a few small school districts grades K–12 are housed in one school.

SCHOOL CENTERS

The operating units of a school system are the individual schools. School centers are usually coded by number. Where school districts are divided into areas, schools may also carry an area identification number.

School Attendance Areas

A school attendance area is that geographic portion of a district served by a particular school. Most school districts have several attendance areas. Only where there is a single school center is the boundary of the attendance area congruous with the boundary of the school district.

It would appear that the setting of an attendance area for a particular school is a rather simple administrative task allowing school leaders to move ahead to more important matters of teaching and learning. In the world of today, that unfortunately is not the case. The supporting public has joined in an intense debate with school boards and state and federal agencies about school attendance areas being determined by busing for social integration. Adding fuel to that debate has been the concern of parents and community leaders about school closings necessitated by declining enrollment. A rich tradition in America has been the association of a school with a community or geographic area. Schools are often meeting places for civic groups, polling places, and evacuation centers in times of emergency. To lose a school in many cases is to lose the heart of a community. Many school districts have experienced such turmoil when trying to set attendance areas that school superintendents and school board members have lost their jobs. "Neighborhood schools" has become a rallying cry for many community groups.

District Organizational Patterns for School Centers

There are many patterns that may exist in a school district. School attendance zones may not be uniform. For instance, there may be within a school district a K–12 center that draws students from the total district, elementary attendance areas, middle school or junior high attendance areas, and senior high areas. Some districts have attempted an open enrollment policy allowing students to choose a school of their choice in the district no matter where they live in the district. After the historic first Brown case in 1954 that ruled against segregation of pupils on a racial basis, some district boards tried gerrymandering of attendance areas to perpetuate racial segregation. Other boards attempted "freedom of choice" patterns where students could choose the school of their choice. Where federal officials determined that free choice was a ploy to maintain racial segregation of schools, that organizational pattern came under attack in the courts.

Where open enrollment patterns failed, the next move in school districts was the massive restructuring of attendance areas. Large city districts, in particular, developed strip or pie-shape attendance areas running from the inner city to the outer fringes of the districts, e.g., St. Louis and Denver. The 1960s and 70s saw other attendance organizations attempted such as pairing of schools, school clusters, and magnet schools. Pairing simply took one attendance area where there were mostly white children and grouped it with a predominantly black area. The areas were not necessarily congruous. All students would attend the schools in both areas part of the time, i.e., morning and afternoon or grades K-2 in one area and grades 4-5 in the other attendance area. Clustering involves three or more attendance areas and school centers. Magnet schools emphasize a particular curriculum, i.e., music, science, or athletics. The attendance areas for these schools generally include the total area of the school district. Magnet schools are different from the "freedom of choice" schools in that they maintain a racial balance.

The authority of school boards to establish attendance areas has been challenged frequently in recent years. For many years racial imbalance among students in one attendance area of a school district was held by courts and the federal Justice Department to constitute total district segregation. Late in 1981 the Justice Department announced that attendance areas within a district could be dealt with separately to achieve racial balance. The trend toward massive bussing across a total district seemed to be reversing with the decision and the philosophy of the Reagan administration. Courts, however, are a separate branch of the federal government, and there appears to be little backing down in implementing racial integration of schools in recent court decisions. The 1980 and 1981 federal court decisions in St. Louis not only mandated attendance zones be changed for racial integration within the St. Louis School district, but that county school districts surrounding the city districts be merged into the attendance zones of the City of St. Louis. That decision and others involving "cross-bussing" between districts are sure to have great implications for school leaders attempting to set attendance areas in the future.

INTERMEDIATE UNITS — REGIONAL EDUCATIONAL AGENCIES

The term "intermediate unit" has historically been used to designate a school agency that exists between the state and local school district.

Originally designed as arms of the states to regulate or supervise state programs, intermediate units have evolved so that they now provide services that local school districts are unable to afford. Initially conceived in the Midwest in the late 1800s, these units were created in thirty-five states. The intermediate units, first as regulating units and later as service units, functioned to serve rural school districts. After World War II the intermediate unit was eliminated by some states and modified by others. The most widely known of the state intermediate units are the Boards of Cooperative Educational Services (BOCES) found in the state of New York. Authorized in 1968, BOCES provided high-cost services such as vocational and special education programs to school districts. BOCES services and programs are determined by a board elected from participating school districts. All districts participate in BOCES programs with financing coming from the state and local districts.

There is considerable variety of organizations of intermediate units. In those states having intermediate units a three-echelon educational system exists composed of the state, intermediate or regional agency, and local school district. Debate today revolves about the need for an "extra" layer of government between the state and local district. Increased urbanization and consolidation of smaller districts have resulted in more sophistication and ability to provide resources on the part of local districts. The intermediate unit is clearly "on trial" in many states as declining funds force the elimination of state agencies. The function of intermediate units is another question that is debated: local boards and superintendents are reluctant to give up decision making to a regional agency. The service function of intermediate units seems to be accepted by most educators. As school enrollment continues to decline and districts continue to consolidate, the intermediate unit faces an uncertain future.

If the district you represent is small, there may be only two or three school centers in the district. In a larger district you may represent hundreds of schools. You may also represent just an elementary or secondary district rather than a unified school district. You may even represent an intermediate district. No doubt, in your board career you will have to deal with decisions involving attendance zones for schools in the district, reorganizing grade levels in schools, open schools and/ or close schools. You will be called upon to make some tough decisions that will always anger one group or another. If the school superinten-

dent and his staff do their homework, your decisions will be based upon sound information. Study the recommendations of the professional staff and the issues involved before making your decisions.

BASES FOR ORGANIZING SCHOOLS

Schools are organized around certain grade levels of students. Each school organization must have a purpose. The three basic organizational patterns of schools includes elementary, middle, and high school. The purposes of those three school patterns are:

Elementary School
  Introduction to school
    Socialization
    Beginning skills
    Communication skills
    Mathematics skills
    Study skills
  Beginning Learnings: Introduction to disciplines
    Social studies
    Science
    Other subjects
Middle School or Junior High
  Personel Development
    Guidance
    Physical education
    Health
    Etc.
  Refinement of skills
  Continued learnings
    Education for social competence
      such as Social Studies, Science
      General Subject Areas studied in more detail
    Interdisciplinary learnings
High School (Comprehensive-Vocational-College Preparatory)
  In-depth Learning
    Chemistry
    Algebra
    World history
    American literature
    Etc.

In-depth Study of Interest
  Sports
  Music
  Journalism
  Languages
  Etc.
Career Planning

The best determinant for assigning grade levels to a school is to assign grades based on normal developmental patterns of students. Those patterns and school organizations are:

Elementary – Grades K-5
  K–2 Early Childhood
  3–5 Middle–Late Childhood
Middle School – Grades 6-8
  Transescence (the traditional period between childhood and adolescence)
High School – Grades 9-12
  Adolescence

The modern board member may be called upon to organize schools for much different purposes than normal developmental patterns of students. Because of declining enrollment, lack of school buildings, bussing patterns, and court mandates, schools are being organized for every reason other than what is best for students. One-grade schools, for instance, are used in a number of school districts for purposes of racial integration or as holding schools pending further reorganization. Such one-grade schools or "centers" are particularly disruptive to students when they are established in the middle grades (grades 6–8). Resist organizing one-grade schools or any other school organization for the sole purpose of expediency. By insisting on long-range comprehensive planning for school organizations, you can avoid having to defend a school that makes no sense educationally or economically.

THE SCHOOL CURRICULUM

All school districts offer students courses in English, mathematics, science, and social studies. Most districts offer other courses such as physical education, health, music, art, industrial arts, home economics, and vocational education. These courses are considered as part of the general education or basic program of students.

In addition to the basic program, schools today provide a variety of special courses for gifted students, special education students, handicapped students, and others with special needs.

Schools also provide a variety of experiences for students during school hours including such things as lunch programs, guidance, clubs, drug education, sex education, and career education. Schools even offer after-school and evening programs such as band, intramurals, and competitive sports.

School districts now include programs for adults as well as younger students. Adult education in many districts accounts for as much school enrollment as regular school programs.

While schools are now serving an increased variety of population and demands are being made to improve test scores of students in regular courses, schools have been asked to expand their curriculum to include such programs as:

Drug Education	Career Education
Driver Education	Law Education
Sex Education	Moral Education
Parenting Education	Citizenship Education
Environmental Education	Bilingual Education
Consumer Education	Economic Education

The school curriculum has expanded, then, to include a variety of programs and experiences that society deems necessary for its youth. As other institutions such as the family, church, and neighborhood lose influence, the school has gradually assumed the roles of those other institutions. Schools today are called upon to do much more than provide students with a basic education. They are responsible for truly educating our youth by providing for personal development, affective growth, and cognitive learning.

Balance in the Curriculum

In the past, most curriculum experiences were divided into "curricular" or "extracurricular." The broadening of the definition of curriculum to include many experiences other than formal courses of study has diminished somewhat the distinction between curricular and extracurricular experiences.

Within a school program all learning experiences can be classified under one or more of the following headings: personal development of the individual; skills for continued learning; education for social competence. These classifications can serve as the basis for planning school programs and should provide direction for instruction at the classroom level. Clear attention must be given to each of the three phases of the school program.

Under such a classification system, curriculum planning can provide a rich variety of learning opportunities in each area. The personal development phase should include exploratory and enrichment experiences in a broad range of human activities. There can be activities leading to a better understanding of one's self, health, and physical activities appropriate to levels of maturity, and various school services that involve the learner's family and home.

The skills-for-continued-learning phase should include diagnosis of learning needs with cognitive learning experiences so structured that students can master critical skills and progress in an individualized manner.

The social competence phase should include courses of study in the sciences and mathematics, social studies, humanities, language and literature, and the vocational fields.

The classification system is primarily a check on the scope of the school program but it can also provide teachers with a guide for determining balance in the curriculum as they develop lesson plans or participate in the writing of curriculum guides. The classroom teacher would also use different means of organizing instruction as he or she provides learning experiences in the different phases of the curriculum. For instance, there might be more organized group instruction in the social competence phase than in the personal development phase. Group sizes would also vary with respect to the particular phase of the curriculum.

As a board member, you will often be called upon to approve new programs, courses of study, and curriculum guides and materials. All programs, courses of study, guides, and materials should be screened to see if they reflect a balance between the areas of personal development, skills for continued learning, and education for social competence. If the test for balance is not met, send the persons responsible back to the drawing board. While serving on the board, you will also hear educators use all kinds of acronyms and abbreviations. See Table 5.1 for a list of acronyms and abbreviations commonly used in school districts.

Table 5.1 Acronyms and Abbreviations

AAAS	American Association for the Advancement of Science
AAMD	American Association on Mental Deficiency
AAUP	American Association of University Professors
ABD	all but dissertation
ABM	automated batch mixing
ACT	American College Testing
ADA	average daily attendance
AERA	American Educational Research Associates
AFDC	Aid to Families with Dependent Children
AFT	American Federation of Teachers
AIM	American Indian Movement
ANOVA	analysis of variance
APGA	American Personnel and Guidance Association
ASHA	American Speech and Hearing Association
ATI	aptitude-treatment interaction
BA	Bachelor of Arts
BEH	Bureau of Education for the Handicapped
BIA	Bureau of Indian Affairs
CA	chronological age
CAI	computer-assisted instruction
CBTE	computer-based teacher education
CEC	Council for Exceptional Children
CEEB	College Entrance Examination Board
CFF	critical flicker frequency
COBOL	common business-oriented language
CP	cerebral palsy
CR	conditioned response
CVC	consonant-vowel-consonant
DAT	Differential Aptitude Test
db	decibels
DNA	deoxyribonucleic acid
DSM	Diagnostic and Statistical Manual
EEG	electroencephalogram (or -graph)
EKG	electrocardiogram (or -graph)
EMR	educable mentally retarded
ERIC	Educational Resource Information Center
ESEA	Elementary and Secondary Education Act
ESL	English as a second language
ESP	extrasensory perception
ETS	Educational Testing Service
FORTRAN	formula translation
GATB	General Aptitude Test Battery
GED	General Education Diploma
GPA	grade-point average
GRE	Graduate Record Exam
GSR	galvanic skin response
4 H	Head, Heart, Health, Hands
HEW	Health, Education and Welfare
HRAF	Human Relations Areas Files

IEP	individualized educational plan
IQ	intelligence quotient
IRA	International Reading Association
IRI	informal reading inventory (or instruction)
ITPA	Illinois Test of Psycho-linguistic Abilities
JND	just noticeable difference
LD	learning disabled
LEA	local education agency
LESA	limited English-speaking ability
LULAC	League of United Latin-American Citizens
MBD	minimally brain damaged
MMPI	Minnesota Multiphasic Personality Inventory
MMY	Mental Measurement Yearbook
MR	mentally retarded
MSW	Masters in Social Work
NAACP	National Association for the Advancement of Colored People
NCATE	National Council for the Accreditation of Teacher Education
NEA	National Education Association
NIE	National Institute of Education
NIH	National Institutes of Health
NIMH	National Institute of Mental Health
NSF	National Science Foundation
OCR	Office for Civil Rights
OT	occupational therapy
PDK	Phi Delta Kappa
Ph.D.	Doctor of Philosophy
PKU	phenyiketonuria
PMR	profoundly mentally retarded
PPVT	Peabody Picture Vocabulary Test
Psy.D.	Doctor of Psychology
PT	physical therapy
PTA	Parent/Teacher Association
RANN	Research Applied to National Needs
R & D	research and development
REM	rapid eye movement
RFP	request for proposal
RN	registered nurse
RNA	ribonucleic acid
RT	reaction time
SD	standard deviation
SEA	state education agency
SES	socioeconomic status
SMSA	standard metropolitan statistical area
SPSS	Statistical Packages for the Social Sciences
SQ	social quotient
SR	stimulus-response
TAT	Thematic Apperception Test
TMR	trainable mentally retarded
USOE	U. S. Office of Education
WAIS	Wechsler Adult Intelligence Scale
WASP	White Anglo-Saxon Protestant

SPECIAL AND ALTERNATIVE PROGRAMS

In today's society, schools that offer a single traditional program are not serving the needs of all of their students.

Modern board members will spend more time discussing alternative and special programs proposed by school administrators. Many of those programs will have their genesis in federal and state mandates.

Because many of the programs are controversial, it is important that board members act with proper information and understanding. In the sections that follow a number of special and alternative programs, and the promises and problems of those programs, will be examined.

The Need for Special and Alternative Programs

It is estimated that fully one-third of the students in schools today require some sort of alternative or special program. Although many educators would argue that all students are special, certain students have been labeled or classified as exceptional children. An exceptional child is one who deviates significantly from other children on some dimension, e.g., hearing, intelligence, behavior, to a degree resulting in inability to profit from general education without certain adaptations in what is presented or how it is presented. Among those children are students who experience mild learning problems such as inability to read or language handicaps. Other special cases are the visually impaired, emotionally disturbed, physically handicapped, the chronically ill, the disruptive, and those students suffering from specific disabilities such as the autistic and aphasic. Still a third class exists: students who are academically gifted, artistically talented, or experiencing special conditions during the normal pattern of growth and development.

Special needs children have been identified by the United States Office of Education as children who fall into the following twelve major categories:

Mentally Retarded	Hard-of-Hearing
Speech Impaired	Multiple Handicapped
Orthopedically Impaired	Specific Learning Disabilities
Visually Handicapped	Seriously Emotionally Disturbed
Deaf	Other Health Impaired
Deaf-Blind	Gifted or Talented

The culturally different and emotionally deprived can also be identified as children with special needs. Disruptive students are yet another group with special needs. In addition, children of separation and divorce are a group who must receive special attention in the 1980s.

Board members are responsible for seeing that needs are diagnosed, new materials and programs developed, instruction differentiated, and organizational patterns structured for special needs students. They are also responsible for being knowledgeable about all federal, state, and local legislation and legal and executive mandates affecting special needs students. The board member must also be aware of organizations and agencies available to help these students and keep abreast of new research and programs for students with special needs.

Labeling of Special Needs Students

Children in public schools have been categorized in a number of ways including age, sex, I.Q., grade, achievement levels, ethnic membership, and numerous other criteria. Categories are used to organize school programs and as a basis for differentiating treatment. The courts have not objected to the use of categories or classifications for special needs students. They have only challenged the way certain classifications were made.

The use of labels, both formal and informal, for special needs children may create problems of low self-esteem and achievement in those who may be treated differently than normal students by teachers and peers. The administrator has a special responsibility to see that all special needs students are treated with respect and dignity and that a label will not prohibit a student from opportunities that are available to other children.

Another problem associated with labeling is that labels carried by children from noneducational agencies may not correspond to those used by the school. For instance, a "juvenile offender" labeled by the courts may be an "emotionally disturbed" student at school.

A final problem with labeling of special needs students is students who carry multiple labels such as "educationally mentally retarded-delinquent" or "learning disabled-disadvantaged." In such cases, it is often difficult to determine the relative potential of the specific components of the classification.

See Table 5.2 for definitions of various classification categories for exceptional students.

Table 5.2 Definitions of Various Classification Categories for Exceptional Students

Trainable Mentally Handicapped	A moderately mentally handicapped person is one who is impaired in intellectual and adaptive behavior and whose development reflects his reduced rate of learning. The measured intelligence of a moderately handicapped person falls approximately between 3 and 4 standard deviations below the mean (51-36 on the Stanford Binet, and 54-40 on the Wechsler), and the assessed adaptive behavior falls below age and cultural expectations.
Severely Mentally Handicapped	A severely mentally handicapped person is one who is impaired in intellectual and adaptive behavior and whose development reflects his reduced rate of learning. The measured intelligence of a severely handicapped person falls approximately between 4 and 5 standard deviations below the mean (35-20 on the Stanford Binet, and 39-25 on the Wechsler), and the assessed adaptive behavior falls below age and cultural expectations.
Profoundly Mentally Handicapped	A profoundly mentally handicapped person is one who is impaired in intellectual and adaptive behaviors and whose development reflects his reduced rate of learning. The measured intelligence of a profoundly handicapped person falls approximately five standard deviations below the mean (below 25 on the Stanford Binet), and there is limited or no adaptive behavior.
Educable Mentally Handicapped	An educable mentally handicapped student is one who is mildly impaired in intellectual and adaptive behavior and whose development reflects a reduced rate of learning. A student's performance on an individual psychological evaluation which indicated an approximate intellectual ability between 2 and 3 standard deviations below the mean (68-52 on the Stanford Binet, and 69-55 on the Wechsler, plus or minus 5).
Students with Communicative Disorders	Students with a communicative disorder may have trouble speaking, understanding others, or hearing the sounds of their world. They may have difficulty saying specific sounds or words, using words correctly, using the voice correctly, or speaking clearly and smoothly. Some students are unable to make muscles needed for speech work adequately. Other students may have a hearing problem that prevents them from understanding the

teacher and others around them. Some students need help in learning words and in understanding how to put them together into sentences. To be considered for speech, language, or hearing therapy services, the student should be referred to the speech, language, and hearing clinician for testing, with written permission from parent or guardian. After all testing (speech, hearing, language, and any other as appropriate), a staffing committee meets to discuss the student's problem and to decide how best to help the student.

Hearing Impaired Students

Students who are born with a severe hearing loss (70 dB or greater in better ear in speech frequencies), or who acquire a loss before learning language and speech, are considered deaf by state Department of Education definition. These students will be unable to hear language and speech unless they receive special education instruction. To be considered for enrollment in the Hearing Impaired Program, the student must have a medical evaluation which would include a general physical examination and an evaluation by an ear specialist (otologist) and complete hearing evaluation by an audiologist. After all testing is completed, a staffing committee meets to discuss the student's problem and to decide how best to help the student.

Specific Learning Disabilities

A student with specific learning disabilities has a disorder in one or more of the basic psychological processes involved in understanding or in spoken and written language. These may be manifested in disorders of listening, thinking, reading, talking, writing, spelling, or arithmetic. They include conditions which have been referred to as perceptual handicaps, brain injury, minimal brain dysfunction, dyslexia, developmental aphasis, etc. They *do not* include learning problems which are due primarily to visual, hearing, or motor handicaps, mental retardation, emotional disturbance, or an environmental disadvantage.

To be considered for placement in a specific learning disabilities program, the student must have average to near average mental abilities, normal visual and hearing acuity, and no evidence of a primary physical handicap. Standardized achievement test scores would indicate difficulty in the basic academic areas of reading, writing, arithmetic, and/or spelling. Specialized test scores would show student difficulty in handling information received by sight and/or by hearing, in language usage and/or in fine motor skills.

Emotionally Handicapped

An emotionally handicapped student is one who exhibits consistent and persistent signs of behaviors, such as withdrawal, distractibility, hyperactivity, or hypersensitivity, which disrupt the learning process.

Emotionally handicapped students show the following behaviors to the extent that they may not be served in the regular school program without at least part-time special placement or consultative services: learning problems that are not due primarily to mental retardation; severe behavior disorders that cannot be controlled or eliminated by medical intervention; inability to build or maintain satisfactory interpersonal relationships with adults and peers.

Physically Handicapped

A student who has a crippling condition or other health impairment that requires an adaptation to the student's school environment or curriculum is considered physically handicapped. The student may have an impairment which interferes with the normal functions of the bones, joints, or muscles to such an extent that special arrangements must be made to provide an educational program.

The student may have a special health problem such as cardiac disorders, diabetes, epilepsy, cystic fibrosis, hemophilia, asthma, leukemia, or nephritis, which would require special arrangements to provide an educational program.

Multi-handicapped students whose primary or most severe disability is a crippling condition or other health impairment may be included in this program.

Gifted

A gifted student is one who has superior intellectual development and is capable of high performance. The mental development of a gifted student is defined by the state Department of Education as greater than two standard deviations above the mean in most tests.

A gifted student usually shows the following behaviors: often he/she will finish assigned work more quickly than the other students; will be searchingly inquisitive and will spend much time reading.

Programs for Special Needs Students

The 1970s saw significant progress in the development of rights and special programs for handicapped students. Although 195 laws specific to the handicapped were enacted between 1927 and 1975, the National Advisory Committee on the Handicapped reported in 1975 that only 55 percent of children and youth were being served appropriately in this country. Sixty-one of the 195 acts were passed between March, 1970 and November, 1975. Public law 93-380 passed in 1974, which expanded provisions of the Elementary and Secondary Education Act of 1965, was the most important of the laws passed. It established a national policy on equal educational opportunity.

The most far-reaching and significant federal act affecting the handicapped was Public Law 94-142, the Education for All Handicapped Children Act of 1975. Public Law 94-142, a virtual "Bill of Rights" for the handicapped, was an amendment to Public Law 93-380. The most important feature of 94-142 was that it included a guarantee of free and appropriate public education of all handicapped students between the ages of three and twenty-one.

Public Law 94-142 with its sweeping provisions has significant legal and instructional implications for school administrators. School administrators must insure that all provisions of 94-142 are complied with by teachers, other administrators, and support personnel. The challenge to build significant programs for students with handicaps must be met by all school administrators and school boards.

Rights of Parents of Handicapped Students

Parents of handicapped students have certain rights that have been guaranteed by state and federal legislation and court decisions.

Parents have a right to attend (they must be notified) staffing meetings when an Individual Education Plan (IEP) is being developed for their child and a right to review any educational records of their children at any time. They also have a right to have their child reevaluated (before the usual three-year period) to determine if their child's special education placement is still appropriate to his or her needs. Parents also have a right to receive special education services from other agencies if their local school system cannot provide such services, and the cost of those outside services must be borne by the local school district. Finally, parents may obtain an independent evaluation if they are dissatisfied with that provided by the local school district or agency. Such independent evaluation, however, will be done at the parents' expense.

Procedural safeguards are strongly enforced for parents of handicapped students by school districts.

Children of Separation and Divorce

Many children enter school today without the security of a two-parent or stable home environment. One in five students in our schools are children of separation and divorce (over eleven million school-age children of divorce). These children have needs that require special attention by school administrators and staffs. The modern board member must contend with a number of issues relating to children of separation and divorce and make crucial policy decisions regarding special procedures for those students. Among those decisions are:

1. Decisions concerning school visits by the noncustodial parent. School administrators might handle this situation in a number of ways, but the most prudent approach would be to ask permission of the custodial parent. Board policy should be clear on how permission is obtained.

2. Releasing a child from school. A board policy should probably only allow release of a child to the custodial parent unless directed otherwise by that parent.

3. Decisions relating to territorial rights of children. Children of parents who separate or divorce may stay in a school after their parents separate and move away from the school district. Such children are often left with a legal guardian, and it is important for administrators to know who that person is and be able to reach him or her. It is also important that the board have a policy statement relating to assignment of children of divorced or separated parents.

4. Access to school records by noncustodial parents. Custodial or residential arrangements do not affect parental access to school records according to the federal Family Education Rights and Privacy Act (FERPA) (U.S. Department of Health, Education and Welfare, Custody and Parent Rights Under the Family Education Rights and Privacy Act, 20 USCA, Section 12328, PL 9438). A school administrator could jeopardize federal funding by denying a parent access to school records.

5. Confidentiality of records comes into play when a noncustodial parent requests certain school records be sent to physicians, attorney, or psychologists. Since both parents have access to a child's records, the rule is that records can be forwarded to either parent.

Other issues faced by administrators include the use of a child's surname, medical emergencies, and financial responsibility. In these cases, common sense dictates action by the administrator. For instance, a child may prefer to be called by one name when legally a name has been changed by adoption. In this case, the administrator may honor the child's request to be called one name while maintaining the legal name in all school records. Medical emergencies should include the school doctor making a decision about treatment rather than a noncustodial parent. Because separations and divorces often include financial problems, it would be prudent for the administrator to provide school funds for students of separated or divorced parents who cannot participate in school functions such as field trips where there is a charge.

The compounding factors of the present-day rate of over 50 percent of all women between the ages of 16 and 65 working; the rise in unmarried-couple households (the number tripled between 1970 and 1980: from 532,000 homes to 1.56 million); the 1.1 million teen-age pregnancies; the 50 percent jump of out-of-wedlock births between 1970 and 1980 (17 percent of all births are illegitimate); and the fact that for every two marriages today, there is a divorce—all directly affect a large number of children today. The dilemma for the administrator is how to give these children the attention they need, provide the special personnel needed to work with them, and help staff members become aware of the special needs of these fragile youngsters.

Programs for Gifted, Talented, and Creative Students

The school board member today is faced with public and school demands that better basic skills programs be developed. Yet, there are numbers of students in schools who quickly move past basic skills. They need an enhanced educational program. These are the estimated three million gifted and talented students who are endowed with academic, artistic, or social talents far beyond the talents of their peers. Gifted and talented students come from all levels of society, all races, and both sexes.

Another area of increasing interest in schools today is that of creativity. Although the study of creativity and the thought processes of creative individuals has been going on for half a century in the United States, only recently have systems and programs been developed to encourage creative thinking in students.

The school administrator today, although faced with demands to improve low achievers' basic skills and to provide for handicapped students, must also provide meaningful programs for gifted, talented, and creative students. A number of instructional models are available to help classroom teachers develop programs for the gifted, talented, and creative. The modern board member must assume the leadership to insure that instructional programs are differentiated for the diverse group of students served. Boards must insist that administrators identify gifted, talented, and creative students and help teachers organize materials and resources to foster a climate of creativity for those students. Board members, administrators, and teachers must all be active participants in nurturing the aptitudes and abilities of gifted, talented, and creative students.

Programs for Economically Deprived and Culturally Different Children

By design, our schools are the melting pot of our society. Court decisions and federal and state legislation have mandated that children of different races and cultures be provided the opportunity to learn with those of other races and cultures. The courts have even gone as far as to mandate that children lacking United States citizenship have a right to free public education.

The right of children to receive special help has been supported by court action and federal legislation. In addition to the compensatory assistance mandated for the handicapped under the Education for All Handicapped Children Act of 1975, the right to compensatory assistance for other groups of children has been supported by the Civil Rights Act of 1964, the Elementary and Secondary Education Act of 1965, and the Bilingual Education Act of 1968.

PREVENTING SEX DISCRIMINATION

The women's movement in the past twenty years has had a great impact on educational opportunities for both sexes. Although the Equal Rights Amendment failed to pass, Title IX, a part of the Educational Amendments of 1972, did much to eliminate sex discrimination in schools. It prohibited discrimination on the basis of sex in educational programs or activities that received federal funds. The Women's Educational Equity Act of 1974 followed. It authorized federal grants to study and develop educational awareness of bias in education and provided curricula and resources to promote greater educational equity for women and girls. A third act under Title II, the Vocational Educational Amendments of 1976, strengthened programs to allow men and women to enroll in training programs for nontraditional occupations and to prepare for combined roles as wage earners and homemakers.

A school board can do much to avoid sex discrimination and foster sex equity. Some strategies include:

1. Finding out from members of groups concerned with sex equity and from colleagues what issues are concerning them about the school program, materials used, or employment practices.
2. Developing plans to insure that girls and boys have an opportunity to enroll in all courses and not allowing sex segregation within those classes.

3. Working with teachers to eliminate sex stereotyping in textbooks and instructional materials.
4. Working within professional administration associations and other groups for sex equality in educational administration.

In 1976 less than one percent of superintendents of schools and less than two percent of senior high school principals were women. In 1982 those percentages had increased slightly but there is still much to be done. The historical data are not promising. For instance, the number of women principals declined from 55 percent in 1928 to 13.5 percent in 1973 and the percent of women school superintendents dropped from nine percent in 1950 to a little over one percent in 1982.

ALTERNATIVE PROGRAMS AND OPTIONAL ALTERNATIVE PUBLIC SCHOOLS

Compulsory attendance laws are now in existence in all fifty states, and students are forced to attend school until a certain age. For about 90 percent of families in the United States, there are no choices for elementary or secondary education. Students are assigned specific schools based on attendance area and are also assigned to specific classes. The choices of programs or options in schools are not many.

The 1960s saw a push for optional schools and alternative programs with examples such as the Parkway Plan (Schools Without Walls) in Philadelphia and the Open Elementary School in South Dakota. The Parkway Plan had students attending classes in office buildings in downtown Philadelphia while the South Dakota plan sought to change elementary programs within existing buildings.

The 1973 *Report of the National Commission on the Reform of Secondary Education* urged school districts to provide a broader range of alternative schools and programs for secondary students. That report had little impact as retrenchment in the late 1970s and early 1980s resulted in fewer alternative programs in schools and a return to more traditional school programs.

Numerous vocational programs, advance placement programs, and many more adult education programs have increased options for high school students in recent years, but those students not fitting those categories still have few choices in programs or school selection.

Alternative schools exist today for pregnant teen-agers (although many choose to continue attending their present school). Also alternative schools have been organized where strict discipline is enforced and basic skills are emphasized. Parents may choose to send their children to these schools as a last resort to suspension or expulsion. Some states have enacted legislation authorizing and providing funds for alternative programs designed to meet the needs of students who are disruptive, disinterested, or unsuccessful in a normal school environment. Such legislation authorizes programs within the school district or in another agency selected by the school board. Finally, alternative schools may exist as centers for the arts or science. Examples are the Harlem School of Dance and the Bronx School of Science in New York City.

Magnet schools have been used as an approach to voluntary desegregation. Located in inner city areas with large numbers of minority students, these schools are designed to offer attractive programs to draw in white students from other areas of the school. Magnet schools were organized under ESAA funding during the 1970s. Unfortunately, in many school districts magnet schools did little to reduce racial segregation. Following critical reports of efforts of magnet schools in late 1979, Congress reduced magnet school funding to thirty million dollars in 1981. The 1982 cut in ESAA funds spells disaster for magnet schools in many school districts where local or state funds are not available to operate such programs.

It must be noted that magnet schools can only reduce desegregation if they are a part of a larger desegregation plan. Voluntary magnet schools can only be a limited remedy to the problems of school segregation. Also, school desegregation does not eliminate other aspects of segregation such as residential and socioeconomic segregation.

Year-round schools and summer schools may be considered as options for some students. Some districts have experimented with schools that operate all year. Children in those schools have the option of vacation time in either fall, winter, spring, or summer. By attending year-round, students can accelerate their progress or broaden their program. Optional summer-school programs also offer students a chance to take extra courses or, in the case of secondary school students, finish high school early. Summer schools can be self-supporting by charging tuition.

The high school has been mentioned most often in the literature as needing reform. Although per-pupil costs have risen, aptitude test scores have steadily declined for high school seniors since 1962. Minimum competency testing has resulted in a greater emphasis on basic skills but has in turn resulted in stale, dull programs for many students. It is not likely in the conservative era of the 1980s that there will be a return to 1960 practices such as free schools, street academics, or learning centers. The reform may come in for higher standards by taxpayers and a movement away from educational excesses of the past.

The need for alternative programs and optional alternative public schools exists more than ever in American education. Private schools are an option available to only a limited number of students. Voucher plans and tuition credit plans offer some hope for making optional programs and schools available but, if implemented, may destroy the option of public school education.

School boards can develop alternative education options by first exerting the leadership necessary to establish a district policy which recognizes the need for alternative programs. This involves teachers, students, parents, and community persons taking part in the establishment of such a policy. Their support can only result from productive dialogue and information about the necessity for alternative programs.

A policy accepted by all elements of the school community should be followed by a plan that can lead to the development and implementation of successful alternative education programs.

Ask for a list and brief description of all special and alternative programs in your school district. Know something of the legal constraints of each of those programs, and don't hesitate to call upon the superintendent or board attorney to help you interpret certain rules and regulations.

Hold your superintendent and his administrators strictly accountable for following all regulations in special and alternative programs, and make sure all board policies are consistent with legal requirements of such programs.

VOCATIONAL PROGRAMS

In the period between 1963 and 1983 vocational education was the fastest growing curriculum area in American education.

Growing out of concerns of parents and students, business and industrial leaders, that most high school students were ill prepared for employment, vocational education became a priority in school districts. A 1980 survey of the National School Boards Association found that a majority of board members and superintendents put vocational education at the top of a list of programs they would like to expand in their school districts. Today, after two decades of expansion of vocational programs, the demand of students for such programs is so high that those requesting such programs are being turned away.

The demand for vocational education began when board members, superintendents, and students realized that a high school diploma was no longer a passport to employment. In the 1950s the federal Manpower Training and Development Act was passed to train unskilled workers who were entering employment. In 1963 only one high school in ten offered training for jobs in industry and one in twenty for merchandising or selling jobs. Through pressures of the U. S. Chamber of Commerce and critics such as Sylvia Porter and Edwin Chase, the movement for developing vocational programs began in the 1960s. Vocational education has grown from an enrollment of four million students in 1963 to almost twenty million students in 1983.

The statistics for vocational programs today are almost staggering. Vocational programs are now available in schools attended by 98 percent of high school students. According to the National Center for Educational Statistics, vocational education is offered in 15,500 public comprehensive or vocational high schools, over 1,400 public secondary-level area vocational centers, 600 four-year institutions of higher education, and 800 public noncollegiate postsecondary institutions. Contrast those figures with those in the early 1960s and one can see the phenomenal growth of vocational programs. For instance, in 1963 there were virtually no technical-vocational centers outside the state of California.

The need for vocational programs has not let up in the 1980s. Today employers are working closely with educational leaders in planning at local and regional levels to insure that curricula developed meet the needs of today's businesses and industries. There is a particular need for relevant materials and coordination to prevent duplication of training efforts between school and businesses. Performance-based training programs are being used in many institutions to better prepare vocational students.

Although the future for vocational education is promising, some issues and problems must be faced by board members. Those include:

1. The rapid development in computer technology in business and the use of robots in industry. We may be training students for jobs that will soon disappear and not be able to train students for highly technical positions.
2. Vocational educational teaching personnel need to improve their own skills. Coming from occupational skills backgrounds, they need training in new methods and techniques.
3. Dependence upon federal and state dollars for vocational programs has left many districts in a position of not being able to adjust with local dollars when those funds are cut. Boards today simply can't afford the high costs of maintaining vocational programs by them-

selves. In addition to personnel costs, expensive equipment and facilities must be provided.

4. Adult students are making up higher and higher percentages of high school students today and many of them are in vocational programs. Adults have unique educational needs and they must be met through creative, well-planned programs.

5. Occupational change has been a way of life for many persons. Adults may switch jobs many times in a lifetime. Vocational education programs therefore must include guidance and career-planning activities. As occupational demands change, vocational curricula must also change. Keeping aware of changes and new programs must be prime tasks of vocational education administrators.

6. Equality between vocational and regular academic programs should receive constant attention by board members and administrators. One program should not be inferior to the other, and a balanced school program should be encouraged throughout the school district. Equality also has to be dealt with in terms of sex-stereotyped careers. Unlocking nontraditional careers for males and females alike should be a priority of all vocational programs.

Study the vocational program offered in the school district. Ask for a briefing by the vocational director or other person in charge of the program. Visit school vocational programs to see what is being accomplished. Make sure those in charge of them deal with the six issues and problems outlined above. Finally, insist on a balanced program of vocational and regular academic course offerings.

ISSUES IN CURRICULUM

Many board members enter office believing the curriculum of most schools is fairly traditional and without controversy. After all, what can be so controversial about how reading, writing, and arithmetic are taught? After a month or two in office, those same board members find that there are many issues about what is taught, how it is taught, what materials are used, how students are grouped, how students are evaluated, reporting systems, testing programs, and the list could go on and on. In the next sections, the more important issues in curriculum you will face will be discussed. Suggestions of questions to ask and research to be conducted by board members will also follow.

Ability Grouping

Grouping or tracking of students can generate considerable controversy, especially from those parents who have children in low-ability groups. There are both pros and cons of ability grouping. Although grouping practices are found in most school districts, often little systematic research has been done by educators before grouping students and organizing classes. Many would argue that the grouping of students benefits teachers, not students. Ability grouping, the putting together of those most equal in estimated learning ability, has been tried, debated, discarded, revived, and debated again throughout the country.

Ability grouping also is called *tracking* or *homogeneous* grouping. *Heterogeneous* grouping allows students of varying abilities, interests, and achievement to interact together in an instructional group.

Recent court cases and legislation have resulted in decisions and regulations barring tracking of elementary and secondary students on the basis of ability or sex. Title IX federal regulations barred grouping practices based on sex of students. For instance, home economics and industrial arts classes must provide equal opportunity for the enrollment of both boys and girls. Sports programs cannot be limited to boys (contact sports are exceptions to this rule). The Federal District Court of Washington, D.C., ruled in 1976 that the practice of ability grouping was unconstitutional because it was discriminatory and resulted in the denial of equal protection of the laws for children of varying racial and socioeconomic background. That decision and others led many administrators to examine grouping practices.

From studies of grouping practices in school systems one can reach a number of conclusions, as follows:

1. Ability grouping is widely practiced in American school districts. In fact, recent studies show over 80 percent of school districts use some form of ability grouping. Ability grouping is systemwide in larger school districts.
2. Ability grouping tends to occur in higher grades more than in lower grades.
3. Students may be grouped homogeneously in one subject area, but it is impossible to group students homogeneously across all subjects in the curriculum. Students who are high achievers in mathematics may not necessarily be high achievers in social studies.
4. Socioeconomic and class differences are increased by tracking students and reduced by nontracking. Evidence from studies and court cases indicates that high socioeconomic groups and mainstream

ethnic groups are overrepresented in high-ability groups or tracks and ethnic minority students overrepresented in the lower groups or tracks.

5. Low achievers include not only those students with low-achievement patterns but children who may be disruptive, emotionally disturbed, or physically handicapped. Often school districts do not distinguish among low achievers as to cause.

6. Ability grouping tends to perpetuate ethnic and racial segregation in schools since many children of minority groups come from lower socioeconomic backgrounds and those students are overrepresented in low-achieving groups.

Ability grouping will certainly cause parental concern in school districts. Parents of higher-achieving students generally strongly support tracking or ability grouping. Most teachers prefer ability grouping of students because it facilitates the carrying out of instruction. Board members must be aware of the implications of ability grouping, especially the legal and educational implications. Although parents of low-achieving students often are not as vocal as those of high-achieving students, those parents have the same rights as other parents. Board members should ask for evaluative information from instructional leaders in the district outlining the effects of district grouping practices on all *students in the district.*

ACCREDITATION AND SCHOOL EVALUATION

Accreditation by a regional accrediting agency involves outside accreditation teams (outside the district) visiting schools to evaluate all aspects of school programs. Accreditation teams use established standards to assess programs and make evaluations about what has already occurred in a school.

A majority of high schools, middle schools, junior high schools, and some elementary schools undergo the accreditation process every five or ten years. If a school is cited for deficiencies or fails to receive accreditation, parents and community persons will pressure the board for immediate action to correct the deficiencies. Not only will poor accreditation reports be embarrassing to the board, but they could result in new board members being elected.

Accreditation of public schools is carried out in some states by state accreditation agencies; e.g., the Missouri State Board of Education is directed by statute to establish requirements for classification and to classify the public schools in Missouri. In states where classification systems are used in an accreditation system, standards are identified that have to be met by all schools in the district. Districts that exceed those standards may receive a higher rating than those simply meeting basic requirements, e.g., AAA rating rather than AA rating.

School Surveys

School surveys, like accreditation visits, view schools externally and look at what has already occurred in schools. They use many of the same standards as accreditation agencies, but usually evaluate the programs only in those areas identified by analysis. A building survey is probably the most common form of survey. Surveys are conducted when needed, and usually rely heavily on the judgment of a panel of selected experts. School surveys, like accreditation visits, usually have a quantitative orientation and focus heavily on structure.

Needs Assessment

Needs assessments, unlike accreditation visits and school surveys, focus primarily on school programs and their clients. They tend to be prescriptive, as opposed to descriptive, and are often conducted internally by members of the organization under review. Needs assessments are just that; they identify problems and tie suggestions to remediation of those problems.

Comprehensive School Evaluation

In order to make effective decisions about school programs, educators must study all phases of school operations. Areas that should be studied in a school district include:

Staff development	Student performance
Parent and community feedback	Teacher effectiveness
Policies and regulations	Program design
Facilities usage	Resource utilization

In most school districts one or more of the above areas should be studied at all times.

Ask to review all of the procedures used for evaluation of programs, buildings, and personnel in your district. If one is not in place, insist on a comprehensive plan for evaluation of all areas of school operations.

Evaluating Instructional Materials — Textbooks

Instructional materials play a central role in the instructional process. Modern technology has produced creative and attractive media for learners, and educators must choose the correct materials needed in their school districts. Since boards often have to approve large expenditures for instructional materials/textbooks, they must be sure that all materials/texts have been formally evaluated. In the era of computers, more and more materials will be in the form of software. The expense for software and machines for software dictates that boards exercise careful judgment. When programs and machines become obsolete overnight, the selection process becomes even more difficult.

Of particular concern to boards today are issues about sex equality and racism in educational materials. Another issue relates to censorship demands by religious and other groups. All boards should have clear-cut policies relating to textbook selection. When objectionable texts or other educational materials are identified, boards should seek broad support for removing or leaving those books or materials. That support is usually solicited through involvement of teacher and citizen review committees and public hearings. If clear-cut policies and procedures for evaluating and reviewing materials/textbooks are not in place, challenges by pressure groups will come often. Many board members have lost elections on the single issue of selection or removal of textbooks or other educational materials.

Accountability — Testing Programs

Another area of potential controversy for board members is that of accountability. The public is demanding better results from school programs, and those outcomes are most often interpreted from test results.

The Scholastic Aptitude Test (SAT) is probably the most familiar to board members because it is administered to almost one million college-bound seniors in American schools each year. Since test scores began a skid in 1963, parents, students, and educators have expressed concern. The drop in high scores also became a convenient missile for critics of the nation's schools.

Many states have implemented minimum competency-testing programs. Minimum competency testing is just what it purports to be—a testing program to measure minimum competencies that all students should have at the end of a school program. Some states have established a minimum competency test as a high-school graduation requirement. Through accountability acts such as the Educational Accountability Act enacted in Florida in 1976, states have set certain standards for all students receiving a high school diploma.

Competency-based testing has led to competency-based educational programs. Some view competency-based education as an excellent opportunity for schools to convert public criticism of education into confidence. Competency-based testing is intended to assure that a student receiving a high school diploma can read, write, compute, and do whatever else the district may ask at a certain level. At the high school level it is supposed to insure the quality of high school diplomas for all schools.

To acquaint board members with types of evaluative measures, the following definitions of tests are offered:

1. Assessment test – A test to determine student achievement or performance levels at some point in time.
2. Norm–referenced – A test that allows the ranking of a student's score in relation to the scores of the students from a sample.
3. Diagnostic – A test to identify specific areas of weakness or strength of achievement of students.
4. Criterion–referenced – A test consisting of items conceptually tied to specific objectives which allows comparison of a student's score to an absolute standard of achievement.
5. Domain–referenced – A test consisting of items tied to a set of objectives that are conceptually interrelated.
6. Minimum competency – A test that measures knowledge and skills that all students are expected to have mastered upon completion of some phase of schooling and that are considered to be useful and essential for everyone.
7. Formative evaluation – Tests given at certain intervals to see if students are making the necessary effort at the appropriate time.
8. Summative evaluation – The final recording of achievement at the end of course work.

Because I.Q. (Intelligence Quotient) test results are used for special placement of students into exceptional programs, board members should be aware that most standardized intelligence tests have cultural bias that accounts for poor performance of many minority students. Standardized individual intelligence tests have been challenged in court when used for placement of students into classes for the "educable mentally retarded" (EMR). Charges that tests were racially and culturally biased have resulted in divided opinion among test experts and federal judges.

Study the various testing programs used in the district. Ask the board attorney to furnish you with a review of court challenges to tests. Check to see if there has been a recent study of evaluation measures used in the school district.

Grading-Reporting Systems

The traditional grading-reporting system in most school districts is one that utilizes some sort of letter grading. The typical pattern is A – Excellent progress, B – Good, C – Fair, D – Poor, F – Failing. Checklists, letters to parents, parent conferences, and point systems (e.g., 90 is passing and 60 is failing) are used to communicate student progress.

Since most grading systems utilize norm-based testing programs, half of the students will always be below average and half above average. Many would argue that such a system discourages a certain faction of our society from furthering its education. A system that would place emphasis on the individual, deemphasize time as a limitation to learning, and utilize diagnostic competency procedures is suggested as an alternative to the traditional norm-based system.

The new system is designed to increase reliability and accountability of educational endeavors by establishing behavioral and criterion-based objectives for each course offered in the school district and relying on measured observable performance and actual growth. The end results are individualized and continuous progress learning.

It may be time for an overhaul of traditional grading and reporting systems used in the district. Performance evaluation measures can be developed that offer greater promise than those found in tra-

ditional systems. It must be noted though that changing grading and reporting systems can be very controversial, so insist that district administrators involve all groups in and out of the system in studying possible alternatives to the system presently in use.

Student Accounting — Pupil Personnel Records

A school board will constantly be provided with reports of student achievement, attendance, discipline, and other data. Those reports are extremely important because they form the bases for many of the critical policy decisions made by the board.

Board members should insist on clear, precise reports. Ask administrators for a summary of each report and for recommendations for program change if needed.

School Lunch Programs

School lunch programs are considered a part of the total school curriculum. The School Lunch Act of 1946 established the federal government as a partner with school districts in providing a balanced lunch for all students. Low-cost foods and milks were provided schools from surplus farm products. Although the federal government and states provided food and funds for school lunch programs, the first instance of providing underprivileged children low-cost or free meals in schools was begun by the Children's Aid Society in New York City as early as 1853.

Administration of school lunch programs is not an easy job. Health and nutrition experts must be hired as well as lunchroom workers and food preparers. Some districts contract out food services to the private sector while others utilize school centers to prepare food for that school and in some cases surrounding schools.

Inservice training for food service personnel is essential to prepare them for providing nutritious meals to great numbers of students. Personal health, safety, and hygiene should be emphasized in all school lunch programs.

A school lunch program can be a headache to board members if there is poor administration of that program. School lunches are a big budget item because of the number of personnel involved and the cost of food and equipment. Make sure your superintendent is on top of the school lunch program. Ask for frequent reports from the superintendent and his/her chief administrator of the lunch program about its operation.

Pupil Transportation Service

School budget funds for transportation are one of the major expenses in public education today. Students have been transported to school at public expense for years, if they lived great distances from a school. Compulsory attendance laws meant more children than ever were attending school.

Recent developments, such as consolidation of schools and bussing for racial integration, have increased the number of children riding school buses.

Some districts own their own buses while others contract with private companies to transport students.

Since students riding buses are under the direction of the school, it is important that good bus drivers be employed and that safety be emphasized.

Board members will often have to approve the use of buses for field trips and deal with changes in boundaries, routes, and schedules for school buses. Bus time should be considered part of the total educational experience of students so boards should monitor closely the total operation of pupil transportation.

School Health Services

School health services include health, instruction, healthful living, and health service, such as physical, psychological, and dental examinations, vision and hearing testing, and height and weight measurement. Prevention of disease is an important aspect of school health services, and boards can require immunization of students prior to their entering school.

Sex education and drug education have become important aspects of health programs in schools. Mental health programs are also being emphasized in today's schools.

School nurses, psychologists, psychiatrists, and public health personnel are all being used in school systems today. Large districts may be able to have full-time health personnel while small districts can join together and employ regional specialists.

Boards must adopt policies that require evaluation of funds for school health just like all other programs found in the district. Some state laws provide for health personnel and programs above the normal funds provided for educational programs or use a weighted scale to provide additional funds.

Counseling Services

Guidance programs are found in most schools in the country. Counselors and other types of personnel help provide counseling services to students. Pupil counseling may be on academic, vocational, and personal problems.

Other professionals who work with counselors in helping students include:

Psychometrists. These personnel both administer tests and make interpretations and diagnoses.

Psychologists. Psychologists administer tests and provide group and individual therapy.

Psychiatrists. Psychiatrists provide help to students with deep-seated problems.

Attendance Personnel. Once known as truant officers, these persons help enforce compulsory school attendance laws by working with students, teachers, and parents to correct causes of poor attendance at school.

Social Worker or Visiting Teacher. These personnel facilitate home-school communication. They work with students and parents.

Classroom Teacher. Teachers are in closer contact to students than any other school personnel and spend some of their time counseling students. Advisor-advisee programs exist in some schools, allowing teachers to work in formal advising and counseling activities with students.

Many of the services discussed such as school lunch programs, health services, transportation, and guidance may seem like services that should be provided by other institutions. Unfortunately, the school is the last institution available to help students with many of the physical, health, and other problems found in the modern world. A student who is hungry, ill, unhealthy, or can't transport himself or herself to school cannot learn. We must, therefore, assume the responsibility for providing help for those students in our schools.

NEW PROGRAM PRESSURES

School administrators and boards are faced with new pressures today to offer new programs for students in schools. Two of the most important programs suggested are programs for disruptive students and career education.

Since a great proportion of the time of building administrators and teachers is related to classroom behavior, school personnel are constantly seeking ways to deal with student discipline. Alternative schools for disruptive youth where discipline is extremely strict are now found in school districts. Another program for disruptive youth is "inschool suspension" (a student is suspended from regular classes but must attend a special class within the school building). Various other intervention programs are law education and classroom management.

Career education is another program concept that has received considerable attention in schools. Students need career information to make judgments about future training and potential employment. Changing job opportunities and a rapidly advancing technology have made career planning difficult for many students.

The early 1980s saw a challenge by fundamentalist religious groups of the teaching of evolution in schools. "Creationism" or "Scientific Creationism" which emphasized the divine origin of man was suggested as an additional part of the science curriculum. Court decisions soon indicated that the teaching of creationism violated the doctrine of separation of church and state. Religious groups have not given up on this issue or on the reintroduction of prayer in schools. Indeed, on the last issue President Reagan in 1982 called for a constitutional amendment that would allow prayer in public schools.

Finally, gifted and talented students are receiving increased attention in school districts today. Back-to-basics programs and minimum competency testing programs have resulted in an imbalance of curriculum for underachievers while those creative, gifted, and talented youth lacked attention. The 1980s will see more programs and attention given to above-average students in our schools.

CURRICULUM AND INSTRUCTION TERMS

Board members will be exposed to a number of terms used in curriculum and instruction. The following glossary should be helpful to you as you study the various school programs in the district:

Curriculum

affective   A term describing behavior or objectives of an attitudinal, emotional, or interest nature. It is discussed in the *Taxonomy of Educational Objectives: Handbook II, The Affective Domain* by David Krathwohl and others.

behavior objectives
This term describes an instructional intent in such a way that the post-instructional behavior of the learner is projected, i.e., what the learner should do, or be able to do, at the conclusion of an instructional sequence.

cognitive
An adjective referring to learner activities or instructional objectives concerned with *intellectual* activities and discussed in *The Taxonomy of Educational Objectives: Handbook I, The Cognitive Domain* by Benjamin S. Bloom and others.

course of study
A guide prepared by a professional group of a particular school or school system as a prescriptive guide to teaching a subject or area of study for a given grade or other instruction group.

criterion
This word usually refers to the measure used to judge the adequacy of an instructional program. Ordinarily, it would be a test, broadly conceived, of the program's objectives.

curriculum
A structured series of intended learning outcomes.

lesson plan
A teaching outline of the important points of a lesson for a single class period arranged in the order in which they are to be presented; it may include objectives, points to be made, questions to ask, references to materials, assignments, and so forth.

psychomotor
This refers to learner activities or instructional objectives relating to physical skills of the learner, such as typing or swimming.

resource unit
A collection of suggested learning and teaching activities, procedures, materials, and references organized around a unifying topic or learner problem; it is designed to be helpful to teachers in developing their own teaching units.

scope
The extent or range of content or objectives (or both) covered by a course or curriculum.

sequence
The order in which content (or objectives) is arranged in the curriculum.

subject
A division or field of organized knowledge, such as English or mathematics.

syllabus
A condensed outline or statement of the main points of a course of study.

teaching unit
The plan developed with respect to a particular classroom by an individual teacher to guide the instruction of a unit of work to be carried out by a particular class or group of learners for a period longer than a single class session.

Instruction

analogous practice	This term describes the responses made by the learner during the instructional sequence that are comparable, but not identical, to those called for in the instructional objective.
appropriate practice	This expression refers to opportunities provided the learner during the instructional sequence to respond in a fashion consistent with that described in the instructional objective. (See *Analogous Practice* and *Equivalent Practice*.)
constructed response	This refers to a learner's response, either to criterion test items or to material in the instructional product, wherein he is obliged to make a response which he, himself, must generate, as opposed to choosing between responses that have been generated for him. For instance, when a student is obliged to write a short essay, this would be an instance of constructed response. Short "fill-in" answers to questions are also classified as constructed responses.
contingency management	This generally refers to classroom schemes that are based on the learner's receiving some kind of positive reinforcement for particular learning attainments. For example, in some cases the child can secure coupons for achieving certain instructional objectives, the coupons later being redeemable for rewards the child wishes to receive.
discipline	This term can be used in a variety of ways, but for most teachers it refers to the procedures by which classroom control and order are maintained.
en route behavior	The behavior(s) that the learner acquires as he moves through an instructional program from his original entry behavior to the desired terminal behavior.
entry behavior	Sometimes referred to as prerequisite behavior, this describes the learner's behavioral repertoire as he commences the instructional program.
equivalent practice	This refers to responses made by the learner during the instructional program that are *identical* to those called for in the instructional objectives.
knowledge of results	This expression refers to a scheme by which a learner is provided with information regarding the adequacy of his responses. Sometimes called "feedback" or "corrective feedback," knowledge of results is provided whenever the learner can find out whether his responses are appropriate or inappropriate.
negative reinforcer	A stimulus that, when *removed* from a situation, increases the probability of the response that it follows. For example, a teacher might find that releasing a child from some aversive situation (staying after

school) would increase the likelihood of a particular response of the child. (Negative reinforcement is not to be confused with punishment.)

perceived purpose   Promoting the child's realization of the worth of a particular subject he is studying or an objective he is attempting to accomplish.

positive reinforcer   A stimulus which, when *added* to a situation, increases the probability of the response it follows. For example, a teacher might find that verbal praise would increase the student's tendency to perform a particular classroom action.

punishment   An aversive act that occurs after a particular response and is designed to diminish the frequency of the response it follows.

selected response   In selected responses the learner chooses among alternatives presented to him, as when he selects multiple-choice responses, discriminates between true and false statements, and so on.

task analysis   The ordering of instructional objectives or en route behaviors to facilitate the attainment of instructional goals.

terminal behavior   The behavior that the learner is to demonstrate at the conclusion of the instructional program. What is terminal behavior in one program may, of course, be the initial behavior for a subsequent program.

Board members must be careful to review every new program suggested for the district. Too often, boards adopt "the solution of the day" and a careful study of the impact of new programs is not considered. Pull-out programs often result in more problems than they solve. Finally, every new program should fit the established goals of the district and must not create an imbalance in the curriculum.

6

Financing Schools

The decade of the 1970s witnessed the greatest reform in school finance in more than half a century. Between 1970 and 1980 over half of the states enacted substantial changes in the manner in which revenues for school operations were generated.

The two most important reform measures in school finance were 1) District Power Equalizing, the principle that every school district in the state, regardless of wealth, has the same dollar resource per pupil as any other district, and 2) Full State Assumption, the removing of the taxing power of local school districts with the state assuming all responsibility for raising and distributing revenues for schools.

The implications for school boards of both of the finance reform measures are immense. In the equalization measure, poorer school districts, or those unwilling to support schools adequately, would be subsidized by wealthier school districts. All students, regardless of where they live, would receive the same level of schooling. The Serrano decision in the California Supreme Court in 1971 and other state court cases, along with equalization legislation, have really said to school boards, "You and your voters don't have the discretion to choose to spend more or less than an established level for schools."

The Full State Assumption of school financing shifts the total burden of raising money for schools from school districts to the state. The reasoning behind such a move is that local school boards must rely primarily on ad valorem property taxes for revenue while the state has a variety of taxes, e.g., sales taxes, income tax, gasoline tax, etc., available to tap as sources of revenue for schools. With urban areas

165

decaying, property taxes have been reduced considerably. Also rural areas with a low property tax base also have had trouble raising sufficient taxes for schools. With full-state funding, city and rural districts could have as much funding as property-rich districts. This also means persons in property-rich districts would be subsidizing schools in less-wealthy areas. Perhaps the biggest concern of board members is that decision making follows the dollar. In other words, decisions about schools will be made in state capitols rather than at the local level.

The die may have already been cast in American education for control of schools to shift from local to state levels. Many states, before and after the Serrano case, instituted minimum funding laws to insure equalization of funding in school districts. Slowly, states are assuming a greater share of the funding of school programs. In this chapter you will examine board policy relating to preparing an annual budget, learn the language of a budget, review sources of revenue for schools, examine the shifting of the burden of supporting schools from the local to the state level, learn how a budget is constructed, look at possible trends in school finance, and learn many of the financial terms used.

BOARD POLICIES RELATING TO ANNUAL BUDGET

As a board member, you will be responsible for reviewing policy statements relating to the preparation of the annual budget. Some boards establish a Board Budget Commmittee to oversee the preparation of a budget. Other boards act as a committee of the whole to get at the task of budget preparation.

Boards actually are responsible for school budgets but rely on the school superintendent and district planning groups to prepare a "working budget" for their initial consideration. Negotiations with teachers and state legislation may extend the budget preparation process, thus delaying a final budget until the last moment. That is why boards begin budget preparation early in the fall. A budget should emerge before the end of the fiscal year (uniformly, June 30).

What should a board member look for in policy statements regarding budget and school finances? First, a statement relating to the fiscal year and budget committee reports. A sample follows:

TITLE: FISCAL YEAR – BUDGET COMMITTEE REPORTING

The fiscal year shall begin on the first day of July. The Budget Committee shall report during that month of each year an estimate of the income available for current expenses for the fiscal year and shall at the same time recommend to the Board appropriations to be made for expenditures of the year in accordance with those estimates.

Second, a statement relating to approval of the budget. See the following sample.

TITLE: APPROVAL OF ANNUAL BUDGET

At the beginning of each fiscal year, the Board of Education shall receive and consider budget recommendations of the Budget Committee and shall approve an annual budget for the school system for the ensuing fiscal year.

Third, a statement such as the following regarding expenditure of funds:

TITLE: EXPENDITURES OF FUNDS

No report or resolution shall be adopted by the Board calling for the expenditure of money unless it states specially the fund from which the appropriation is to be made and is accompanied by the certificate of the Treasurer that there is a balance in such fund available for such expenditure.

Fourth, requirements for increasing appropriations during the year and for inter- and intra-fund transfers. Two examples of policy statements regarding these areas follow:

TITLE: INCREASING APPROPRIATIONS

A two-thirds vote of the entire Board shall be required to approve a recommendation to increase any of the appropriations originally made in the annual apportionment of funds.

TITLE: INTRA-FUND TRANSFERS

Intra-fund transfers of monies from one account to another may be made without prior Board approval provided, however, that each transaction shall not involve an amount of money exceeding twenty-five thousand dollars – ($25,000.00).

Fifth, a provision for a statement explaining proposal for increasing or reducing board funds. An example of a policy statement for such a provision follows:

TITLE: NEW PROPOSALS – FISCAL NOTE REQUIRED

Whenever the Superintendent of Schools or his staff recommends for approval a proposal to the Board of Education or any of its committees requiring new or increased expenditures of Board funds or requiring reduced Board funds, there shall be incorporated therein or attached thereto an explanatory statement and an estimate of the amount of additional or reduced funds required by said proposal.

And sixth, statements regarding the selection of depositories for board funds. Examples follow:

TITLE: ANNUAL SELECTION OF DEPOSITORIES

The treasurer shall annually solicit proposals from banking institutions in the City of _____ who are interested in becoming legal depository for Board funds for the ensuing fiscal year. Each proposal should list the financial services that the bank would provide the Board if it were to receive the Board's deposits.

The Board shall annually select one or more banking institutions as its depository and shall enter into a written contract with such depository prior to the start of the fiscal year.

As a board member, thoroughly familiarize yourself with all policies, procedures, and regulations regarding the school budget. Collectively, you and other board members are ultimately responsible for managing the taxpayers' money and, even more important, providing the proper level of support necessary for student learning in the district. Get involved in the budget process from the first day of service on the board.

LEARNING ABOUT SCHOOL FINANCE

In addition to knowing about board policies relating to school finance, board members should be active in *seeking* support for schools. Since funds for schools come from federal, state, and local sources, board members should familiarize themselves with how funds from those sources are raised and distributed. In the next sections we shall look at all aspects of school finance beginning with the most important concern of funding resources for education.

AVAILABILITY OF FINANCIAL RESOURCES

Finding resources for education looms as the single greatest problem for schools in the 1980s. Although money can't correct all the ills of public education, an absence of adequate funding can lead to crowded school buildings, an inadequate and narrow curriculum, poorly quali-fied teachers, and less-than-adequate learning conditions for students. School finance represents a highly emotional issue in American educa-tion, and one that will see significant change in the near future.

Prior to this decade, public support of education has never been a serious problem. Historically, the public has given schools a major share of tax-dollar revenues. However, the effects of infla-tion during the 1970s, an increasing public interest in educational outcomes, and a long-term outlook for more resources needed for schools in the future has brought into question the obligation of the public in supporting schools. The rationale for such support, then as now, was the need for an enlightened citizenry to partici-pate in the democratic process called for by our Constitution.

Over a one-hundred-year period there evolved a pattern of educa-tional finance that was a joint state and local effort. During the past twenty years the federal government has also become a major partner in the financing of public education so that a ratio of 50 percent local, 40 percent state, and 10 percent federal support might be "average" for school districts in the United States in the mid-1980s. Such figures are deceiving, however, as many school districts have a much greater dependence on one of these three sources. In general, during the 1970s state aid to local schools increased while local efforts to finance schools decreased. During the 1980s it appears that both local and federal aid to school finance will diminish. Whether states will be capable of pick-ing up the "slack" created by this decline of support remains uncertain at this time.

In the following sections each level of contribution to the finance of schools—federal, state, and local—is analyzed. By far the most criti-cal issue related to school finance is whether property taxes can con-tinue to serve as the primary basis of school operating revenue. The disparity among school districts and the real tax burden on those own-ing property makes "property" a questionable source of revenue for the remainder of this century.

Federal Contributions

In earlier chapters of this guide it was shown how the federal role in education has grown during the past one hundred years. From support of the "general welfare," the federal role has increased its scope to in-clude "categorical" aid to education for a number of purposes. In short, education has become one means by which the national government implements policy and guarantees constitutional liberties.

It is important to note that in all states the state government, usually through the state board of education, is responsible for prescribing rules covering all contracts or agreements made with federal agencies by tax-supported public schools. There has never been a time when federal aid to education was forced upon either state or local education agencies. Rather, the federal government has used aid to local and state agencies to assist in meeting legal requirements or to initiate new programs where funding was available.

For the immediate future, it appears that the federal contribution to education will be curtailed. As a funding trend, a strong possibility is that states will continue to be given more discretion in the use of federal dollars through a so-called "block grant" program rather than the costly "categorical" aid programs of the past.

State Contributions

Prior to 1923, state contributions to local education efforts in the public schools were irregular. Historically, the property tax had been the source of most public school revenue. This source, established in a time when the nation was primarily an agricultural economy, began to evidence disparity shortly after the beginning of the twentieth century. City districts had greater taxing power and, therefore, were able to offer a higher quality education program for their students than rural areas. In 1923 George Strayer and Robert Haig conceptualized a "foundation program" that would increase the likelihood that all students could receive a quality education. Such foundation programs were implemented in the various states over a thirty-year period and today form the backbone of state contributions to public education.

In the 1980s states have become the dominant partner in the funding of public schools. Raising revenue through a variety of sources such as state income taxes, state property taxes, gasoline taxes, and gambling taxes, the states disperse funds to local school districts in three forms: general appropriations, categorical units, and equalization grants. The outlook for the immediate future is for the state role in the financing of public schools to continue to grow.

While each of our fifty states acts in a unique manner to support local education efforts, the allocation of funds falls into two dominant patterns: flat grants and equalization programs. Flat grants tend to give each local district a uniform amount according to some criterion such as the number of pupils, number of teachers, or other uniform measure. Sometimes such grants reflect variations in unit costs according to need. Two common formulas are ADA and ADM which are shown here:

$$ADA = \frac{\text{sum of no. children present each day}}{\text{no. days in the school year}}$$

(average daily attendance)

$$ADM = \frac{\text{sum no. children present + sum no. children absent each day}}{\text{no. days in school year}}$$

(average daily membership)

In contrast to flat grants, equalization grants allocate money to local districts in inverse proportion to local taxpaying ability. This "wealth equalizing" approach to funding establishes a minimum floor or foundation for every child in each district. Examples of methods used to establish this cost differential include:

Weighted student approach. In thirty-three states the allocation of funds is directly dependent on the number of students, with some type of weighting factors "cranked" in to insure equality.

The teacher unit. Eleven states use the teacher as the critical unit for allocation of funds. In these states, a ration of pupils to teachers is established by the legislature and used to pay a major portion of teacher salaries.

The classroom unit. Six states use a "teacher plus" formula in which basic support services are calculated in addition to teacher salaries to guarantee a foundation of support.

Sources of Local Contributions

Almost all of this nation's school districts receive funds to operate from the federal, state, and local level. Local districts can receive funds directly (in accordance with state policy) or as "pass-through" funds which are distributed by the state education agency. Local districts do receive educational dollars from a variety of federal agencies including the Department of Education, Department of Labor, Department of Defense, Department of Agriculture, and the Office of Economic Opportunity. Examples of federal programs that supply funds to the local school district include: Education of the Handicapped Act, Elementary and Secondary Education Act (Titles I, II, IV-C, VI, and VII), Vocational Education Act (Amended PL 95-40), and the School Lunch Act. Overall, local school districts receive about 10 percent of their operating funds from these sources, although some districts receive a much higher proportion from federal sources.

Local districts also receive state monies as outlined in the previous section. These general, categorical, special, and equalization grants comprise about 50 percent of most local operating funds, although this figure can be much higher in some parts of the United States.

Finally, local school districts receive between 30 and 50 percent of their operating funds directly from local sources of revenue. While a trend in the past decade has been to use local sales taxes to "ease the burden," better than 90 percent of this local revenue results from the taxation of property (See Figure 6.1).

The property tax that supports local education efforts is known as an "ad valorem" tax because it consists of an assessment of a tax rate upon a tax base, with the tax base expressed in value terms (dollars) instead of unit terms (acres). It is a proportional tax in that the tax rate (with notable local exceptions) is uniform regardless of the size of the base. The steps to establish a local property tax for schools are simple: 1) define the boundary of the area to be taxed, 2) determine the value of the property for tax purposes, 3) establish a tax rate, and 4) develop a collection procedure.

In most states the legislature sets a limit on the tax rate for local property. This rate is usually expressed in mills (a mill is one-tenth of a cent) allowed to be applied to the assessed value of the property. Most states also set a minimum millage required of the local district in order to be eligible to participate in the state fund sharing. State law may also allow discretionary tax mills to be assessed for special purposes such as capital outlay (building programs) or discretionary purposes.

Finally, local school districts raise money for the development and operation of school programs through instruments of indebtedness called bonds. Bonds allow local school districts to borrow money for present operational needs while at the same time obligating taxpayers to repay the amount with interest in the future.

Borrowing money is a serious business for a school district. Bonds must be approved by local school boards and, in most districts, voted upon favorably by the taxpaying public. States set limits on the borrowing power of districts, and their borrowing capacity is "rated" by financial institutions. If the public approves a bond program, a local school district must still find a lender. Public bidding for school bonds is commonplace, but it has become increasingly difficult in recent years for school districts to gain public approval to indebt the school district and the taxpayers in the district.

Two major types of bonds are used by public schools: term bonds and serial bonds. Term bonds are issued for a definite period of time, and during this period only interest is paid by the district. The term bond may be accompanied by a "sinking fund" in which the district systematically builds up monies for repayment at the end of the obli-

Figure 6.1

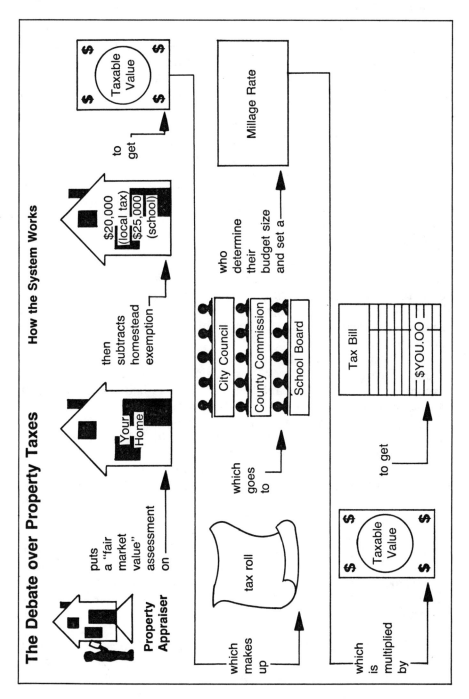

gation period. In the case of a serial bond the district repays on schedule and payments include both principal and interest.

Find out exactly what the sources of revenue are for your district from each of the sources mentioned in the previous sections—federal, state, and local. What percent of the total amount of revenue does each represent?

As a political person (and you are one in the best sense of the word), be prepared to lobby for funds from each source.

And what of foundation money and funds from the private sector? Many boards actively seek such funds. Shouldn't yours?

BUDGETS AND FISCAL RECORD KEEPING

A sound budget is both a financial plan and an educational plan. The budget, to be useful as a tool for decision making, must connect the income element and the expenditure element with educational goals. Budgets are not simply a tabulation of anticipated receipts and disbursements.

The purpose of classifying expenditures through a formal record-keeping procedure is to provide a basis for grouping and analyzing expenditures. It is important to know what is being purchased, the destination of a purchase, and the timing of a purchase. Fiscal record keeping allows us to identify authorizations, determine what is owed, keep special accounts separate, and provide a basis for reporting to the public and auditing.

Budget development is a year-long activity in most school districts. Early in the fall school districts utilize planning committees to work up projected budgets for the following year. These projections undergo a review in light of anticipated revenues, and a "working budget" emerges in the spring. An item that may delay the finalization of the working budget into an official budget is the teacher salary schedule. Usually, this schedule is projected by early spring but negotiations may drag on into April, May, or later. A final revised budget is determined once this major item (about 75 percent of the budget is for salaries) is known. The completed budget is formally adopted by the board as part of a public process following scheduled hearings.

School systems throughout the United States use a fairly uniform coding system in budgetary matters. Budget series numbers are assigned to indicate the "destination" of a budget item; e.g.:

Administration: 100 Series
  110. *Salaries*
    110-a. Board of Education
    110-b. Board Secretary's Office
    110-c. Treasurer's Office
    110-d. School Elections

Usually, for the sake of convenience and clear communication, a major budget series is simplified to only primary categories such as:

1. Administration
2. Instruction
3. Attendance, Health, Security
4. Transportation
5. Plant operation
6. Plant maintenance
7. Fixed charges
8. Community services
9. Capital outlay

School districts also use "object codes" to indicate what service or commodity is being received as the result of an expenditure. These codes are numbered from 0 to 1000 in increments of 10 to allow the addition of items as they are procured. An example of object codes would be the following:

010 Regular salaries
020 Temporary or overtime salaries
030 Supplies
040 Contracted printing/publishing
050 Rental
  –
  –
  –
990 Officer contingency fund

Finally, school district budgets contain funds that are special in nature and often designated by a state accounting system. Examples of items from a general operating fund budget would be:

Fund 01– Incidental fund
Fund 04– Debt service fund
Fund 05– Teachers fund
Fund 12– Lunchroom fund
Fund 15– Free textbook fund

Since budget development in most districts is an ongoing process, school administrators will not be expected to develop a new budget proposal from "scratch" each year, but will be asked to review the previous year's budget and project the coming year's needs. Except in the smallest districts, this process is centralized and will mean a review of a computer printout and some decision making in discretionary areas.

Using budget construction worksheets, principals will project a desired budget and, collectively, these school projections become the first draft of a district budget. In its final form the school-level budget displays items according to series number, object code, and cost.

During the late 1960s a formal program called PPBS was developed to assist school leaders in analyzing budgets according to their intended programmatic purposes. PPBS, or Planning, Programming, Budgeting System, helped districts focus on goals and objectives, looked ahead to future years, assisted leaders in reviewing alternatives, and provided a cost/benefit analysis for planners. PPBS consisted of four basic steps to be followed by a district:

1. PLANNING
   a. School staff, students, and community residents are surveyed regularly to collect data for educational decision making.
   b. Data collected are analyzed and summarized into statements of the community's educational needs.
   c. Priorities of identified needs are established.
   d. Statements of district goals and objectives are generated for all areas of educational need.
2. PROGRAMMING
   a. A Program Structure allowing for the organizational examination of objectives and activities is developed by the district.
   b. Specific objectives are generated, consistent with district goals and objectives, at all levels of the program structure.
   c. Alternative sets of activities for accomplishing the various program objectives are described and analyzed on a multiyear basis.
   d. The optimum set of activities is selected from the alternatives on the basis of comparative estimated effectiveness and cost.
   e. Deficient or innovative programs are subjected to greater analysis.
   f. Deficient or innovative priority programs are subjected to more detailed analysis.
3. BUDGETING
   a. Costs of achieving program objectives via the selected set of activities are examined.

    b. Funding priorities are established, based on district needs.

    c. Specific programs providing greatest achievement for most reasonable cost in *priority areas* are selected for implementation.

    d. Expected results and costs of each program for the coming year are reported to the public.

    e. The public, or its representatives, authorizes the intended allocation of funds for the achievement of the results described for the district programs.

4. SYSTEM EVALUATION

    a. Achievement of program objectives and funds expended for each program are documented and analyzed.

    b. Achievement and cost data analysis for each program become input to the Planning and Programming functions for subsequent years.

    c. Achievement and cost data for each program are reported to the public.

    d. Program achievement and cost data, plus continuing analysis of the community's educational needs, result in revision of objectives, program structure, and the district's curricular programs.

PUBLIC SCHOOL FINANCE IN THE 1980s AND BEYOND

As we approach the mid-1980s, it is apparent that our method of financing public school education is failing. For over a decade school districts have had difficulty in passing millage levies and securing monies from school bonds for capital improvements. A more recent trend is a number of fiscal failures by local school districts that have resulted in closed or curtailed school programs. While much of this stress is found in peripheral areas of American education, the symptoms and the causes of failure are general to most public school districts: a property tax base that is too narrow to support an ever-demanding educational program.

During the 1980s fiscal distress will be found in two types of school districts: sparsely populated rural areas where a full local effort is simply not sufficient and large urban districts that suffer from municipal overburden. While the small local districts may be helped by changes in minimum foundation programs, cooperative service ventures with other small districts, or even consolidation programs, no such hope is on the horizon for major city systems that educate nearly one-fourth of this nation's public school children.

FINANCIAL TERMS

The modern school board member will be exposed to many terms used in school finance. The following definitions should serve as a handy reference to new and old board members alike:

account	A descriptive heading under which are recorded financial transactions that are similar in terms of a given frame of reference, such as purpose, object, or source.
accounting	The procedure of maintaining systematic records of events relating to persons, objects, or money; and summarizing, analyzing, and interpreting the results of such records.
accounts receivable	Amounts owing on open account from private persons, firms, or corporations for goods and services furnished by a local education agency (but not including amounts due from other funds or from other governmental units). Although taxes receivable are covered by this term, they should be recorded and reported separately in the Taxes Receivable account.
accrual basis	The basis of accounting under which revenues are recorded when earned or when levies are made, and expenditures are recorded as soon as they result in liabilities, regardless of when the revenue is actually received or the payment is actually made. See also Current Expense, Estimated Revenue, and Expenditures.
administration	Those activities that have as their purpose the general direction, execution, and control of the affairs of of the Local Education Agency that are systemwide and not confined to one school, subject, or narrow phase of school activity.
aid, state	Grants by the state to local (country or district) school administrative units for the support of an educational program.
allot	To divide an appropriation into amounts for certain periods or for specific purposes.
amortization of debt	(a) Gradual payment of an amount owed according to a specified schedule of times and amounts. (b) Provision for paying a debt by means of a sinking fund.
apportionment formula	A mathematical formula for computation of the amount of state aid for which a local school district may be eligible. It usually takes into consideration the school district's ability to raise a designated amount of money from a uniform tax effort toward financing a minimum guaranteed dollar amount of revenue per pupil.

apportionment of school funds	The division and distribution of money for school purposes by a central agency, such as a state, to its subordinate units according to a predetermined basis.
appraisal	Act of making an estimate of value, particularly of property, by systematic procedures that include physical examination, pricing, and often engineering estimates. Also the value established by estimating.
appraised value	The value established by appraisal.
appropriation	An authorization granted by a legislative body to make expenditures and to incur obligations for specific purposes.
assessed valuation	An official valuation of property, or income, for the purpose of taxation.
assessment	(a) The process of making the official valuation of property for the purpose of taxation. (b) The valuation placed upon property as a result of this process.
assessment, special	A compulsory levy made by a local government against certain properties to defray part or all of the cost of a specific improvement or service which is presumed to be of general benefit to the public and of special benefit to the owners of such properties.
audit	The examination of records and documents and the securing of other evidence for one or more of the following purposes: (a) determining the propriety of proposed or completed transactions, (b) ascertaining whether all transactions have been recorded, (c) determining whether transactions are accurately recorded in the accounts and in the statements drawn from the accounts.
average daily attendance, ADA	The aggregate days' attendance of a given school during a reporting period divided by the number of days school is in session during this period. Only days on which the pupils are under the guidance and direction of teachers should be considered as days in session. The average daily attendance for groups of schools having varying lengths of terms is the sum of the average daily attendances obtained for the individual schools.
average daily membership, ADM	The aggregate days' membership of a school during a reporting period divided by the number of days school is in session during this period. Only days on which pupils are under the guidance and direction of teachers should be considered as days in session. The average daily membership for groups of schools having varying lengths of terms is the sum of the average daily memberships obtained for the individual schools.
balance sheet	A formal statement of assets, liabilities, and fund balance as of a specific date.

bond	A written promise, generally under seal, to pay a specified sum of money, called the face value, at a fixed time in the future, called the date of maturity, and carrying interest at a fixed rate, usually payable periodically. The difference between a note and a bond is that the latter usually runs for a longer period of time and requires greater legal formality.
bond discount	The excess of the face value of a bond over the price for which it is acquired or sold. The price does not include accrued interest at the date of acquisition or sale.
bond premium	The excess of the price at which a bond is acquired or sold, over its face value. The price does not include accrued interest at the date of acquisition or sale.
bonded debt	That portion of the indebtedness of a unit of government (state, county, school district) represented by outstanding bonds.
budget	A financial plan that embodies the educational program, proposed expenditures, and the sources of revenue to support the program for a given period. There are different kinds of budgets, such as the annual budget, long-term budget, capital budget, departmental budget, and building budget. The term of the budget may vary from one to two years or longer.
budget calendar	In budgeting practice, a guide for identifying responsibilities and dates associated with the budget-making process.
budget, capital	A budget that contains a projection of the capital improvement expenditures of a school district and the methods by which such expenditures will be financed. The capital budget commonly covers multiple years, in contrast to the current budget, which usually extends for one year only.
budget classification	Budget summary forms prescribed by most states classify expenditures and revenues by defined categories and subcategories. Some of the typical expenditure categories include capital outlay, debt services, fixed charges, general control, instruction, maintenance of plant, operation of plant.
budget document	The instrument used by the budget-making authority to present a comprehensive financial program to the appropriating body. The budget document usually consists of three parts. The first part contains a message from the budget-making authority together with a summary of the proposed expenditures and the means of financing them. The second consists of schedules supporting the summary. These schedules show in detail the proposed expenditures and means of financing them together with information as to

past years' actual revenues and expenditures and other data used in making the estimates. The third part is composed of drafts of the appropriation, revenue, and borrowing measures necessary to put the budget into effect.

budget process
: Method or methods by which the budget plan is initiated, prepared, adopted, and administered. Includes the persons and procedures involved in carrying the budget from the planning stages to the end of the fiscal period.

capital outlay
: An expenditure that results in the acquisition of fixed assets or additions to fixed assets which are presumed to have benefits for more than one year. It is an expenditure for land or existing buildings, improvements of grounds, construction of, additions to, or remodeling of buildings, or initial, additional, and replacement of equipment.

cash
: Currency, checks, postal and express money orders, and bankers' drafts on hand or on deposit with an official or agent designated as custodian of cash; and bank deposits. Any restriction or limitations as to its availability should be indicated.

cash basis
: The basis of accounting under which revenues are recorded only when actually received, and only cash disbursements are recorded as expenditures.

cash discounts
: An allowance received or given by vendors for payment of invoices within a stated period of time.

categorical aid
: Educational support funds provided from a higher governmental level and specifically limited to (earmarked for) a given purpose; e.g., special education, transportation, or vocational education.

chart of accounts
: A list of all accounts generally used in an individual accounting system. In addition to account title, the chart includes an account number which has been assigned to each account. Accounts in the chart are arranged with accounts of a similar nature; for example, assets and liabilities.

check
: A bill of exchange drawn on a bank payable on demand; a written order on a bank to pay on demand a specified sum of money to a named person, to his order, or to bearer out of money on deposit to the credit of the maker. A check differs from a warrant in that the latter is not necessarily payable on demand and may not be negotiable; and it differs from a voucher in that the latter is not an order to pay. A voucher-check combines the distinguishing marks of a voucher and a check; it shows the propriety of a payment and is an order to pay.

clearing accounts
: Accounts used to accumulate total receipts or expenditures either for later distribution among the accounts

to which such receipts or expenditures are properly allocable, or for recording the net differences under the proper account. See also Revolving fund, Prepaid expenses, and Petty cash.

contingent fund   Assets or other resources set aside to provide for unforeseen expenditures, or for anticipated expenditures of uncertain amount.

contracted services   Services rendered by personnel who are not on the payroll of the Local Education Agency including all related expense covered by the contract.

controlling account   An account usually kept in the general ledger in which the postings to a number of identical, similar, or related accounts are summarized so that the balance in the controlling account equals the sum of the balances of the detailed accounts. The controlling account serves as a check on the accuracy of the detailed account postings and summarizes the expenditures in relation to the budget estimates.

cost accounting   That method of accounting that provides for the assembling and recording of all the elements of cost incurred to accomplish a purpose, to carry on an activity or operation, or to complete a unit of work or a specific job.

cost benefit   Analyses that provide the means for comparing the resources to be allocated to a specific program with the results likely to be obtained from it; or, analyses that provide the means for comparing the results likely to be obtained from the allocation of certain resources toward the achievement of alternate or competing objectives.

cost center   The smallest segment of a program that is separately recognized in the agency's records, accounts, and reports. Program-oriented budgeting, accounting, and reporting aspects of an information system are usually built upon the identification and use of a set of cost centers.

cost effectiveness   Analyses designed to measure the extent to which resources allocated to a specific objective under each of several alternatives actually contribute to accomplishing that objective, so that different ways of gaining the objective may be compared.

cost, pupil   The annual cost of operating the school computed on the basis of the pupil as the unit, the "pupil," however, being variously defined as "pupil in average daily attendance," "pupil enrolled," "pupil in average daily membership," "full-time equivalent," etc.

cost unit   The unit of product or service whose cost is computed.

current   The term refers to the fiscal year in progress.

current expense	Any expenditure except for capital outlay and debt service. Current expense includes total charges incurred, whether paid or unpaid.
current loan	A loan payable in the same fiscal year in which the money was borrowed.
debt service	Expenditures for the retirement of debt and expenditures for interest on debt, except principal and interest of current loans.
deficit	The excess of the obligations of a fund over the fund's resources.
depreciation	Loss in value or service life of fixed assets because of wear and tear through use, elapse of time, inadequacy, or obsolescence.
direct costs	Those elements of cost that can be easily, obviously, and conveniently identified with specific activities or programs, as distinguished from those costs incurred for several different activities or programs and whose elements are not readily identifiable with specific activities. are not readily identifiable with specific activities.
disbursements	Payment in cash. See also Cash.
double entry	A system of bookkeeping that requires for every entry made to the debit side of an account or accounts an entry for the corresponding amount or amounts to the credit side of another account or accounts.
effort, financial	A numerical index designed to show the financial effort a local school district is making to support its educational program. Various indices may be employed, such as taxes raised locally per expenditure pupil unit, tax rate on full property valuation, and the tax rate for net current expenditure.
employee benefits	Compensation, in addition to regular salary, provided to an employee. This may include such benefits as health insurance, life insurance, annual leave, sick leave, retirement, and social security.
encumbrances	Purchase orders, contracts, and salary or other commitments which are chargeable to an appropriation and for which a part of the appropriation is reserved. They cease to be encumbrances when paid or when actual liability is set up.
entry	The record of a financial transaction in its appropriate book of accounts. Also the act of recording a transaction in the book of accounts.
equalization	The process whereby the state government allocates funds to school districts taking into consideration their ability to raise tax money from their local resources; it usually involves guaranteeing that a

specified minimum dollar amount per unit (classroom unit, pupil) will be raised by uniform levy on the taxable property of the district. In the amount it fails to do so, the state makes up the difference as an equalization payment.

equipment
: An instrument, machine, apparatus, or set of articles which (a) retains its original shape and appearance with use and (b) is nonexpendable; i.e., if the article is damaged or some of its parts are lost or worn out, it is usually more feasible to repair it than to replace it with an entirely new unit.

equity
: Equity is the mathematical excess of assets over liabilities. Generally this excess is called fund balance.

estimated revenue
: If the accounts are kept on an accrual basis, this term designates the amount of revenue estimated to accrue during a given period regardless of whether or not it is all to be collected during the period; if the accounts are kept on a cash basis, the term designates the amount of revenues estimated to be collected during a given period.

evaluation
: The process of ascertaining or judging the value or amount of an action or an outcome by careful appraisal of previously specified data in light of the particular situation and the goals and objectives previously established.

expenditures
: Charges incurred, whether paid or unpaid, which are presumed to benefit the current fiscal year.

federal revenue
: Revenue provided by the federal government. Expenditures made with this revenue should be identifiable as federally supported expenditures.

fidelity bond
: A bond guaranteeing the Local Education Agency against losses resulting from the actions of the treasurer, employees, or other persons of the system. See also Surety Bond.

financial accounting
: The recording and reporting of activities and events affecting the money of an administrative unit and its program. Specifically, it is concerned (1) with determining what accounting records are to be maintained, how they will be maintained, and the procedures, methods, and forms to be used; (2) with recording, classifying, and summarizing activities or events; (3) with analyzing and interpreting recorded data; and (4) with preparing and initialing reports and statements that reflect conditions as of a given date, the results of operations for a specific period, and the evaluation of status and results of operation in terms of established objectives.

fiscal period
: Any period at the end of which a Local Education Agency determines its financial condition and the

results of its operations and closes its books. It is usually a year, though not necessarily a calendar year. The most common fiscal period for school systems is July 1 through June 30.

fixed assets   Land, buildings, machinery, furniture, and other equipment which the Local Education Agency intends to hold or continue to use over a long period of time. "Fixed" denotes probability or intent to continue use or possession, and does not indicate immobility of an asset.

fixed charges   Charges of a generally recurrent nature that are not readily allocated to other expenditure categories. They consist of such charges as: school board contributions to employee retirement, insurance and judgments, rental of land and buildings, and interest on current loans. They do not include payments to public school housing authorities or similar agencies.

flat grant   A grant of money from state or federal governments to local school districts without regard to the districts' ability to raise funds from their own tax sources.

foundation program   A school finance term used to describe the minimum program of education which will be guaranteed in each school district from local and state funds. It is usually designated in law as a given expenditure in dollars per classroom unit, per pupil, or per teaching unit.

full-time equivalency   The amount of time for a less than full-time activity divided by the amount of time normally required in a corresponding full-time activity. Full-time equivalency usually is expressed as a decimal fraction to the nearest tenth.

function   An action that contributes to a larger action of a person, living thing, or created thing.

fund   An independent accounting entry with its own assets, liabilities, and fund balances. Generally, funds are established to account for financing of specific activities of an agency's operations.

general control (administration)   Consists of those activities that have as their purpose the general regulation, direction, and control of the affairs of the school district, that are systemwide and not confined to one school, subject, or narrow phase of school activity.

general fund   Used to account for all transactions that do not have to be accounted for in another fund. Used to account for all ordinary operations of a Local Education Agency.

general ledger   A book, file, or other device in which accounts are kept to the degree of detail necessary, that summarizes the financial transactions of the Local Education Agency. General ledger accounts may be kept for any group of items of receipts or expenditures on which an administrative officer wishes to maintain a close check.

grants-in-aid
Contributions made by a governmental unit to a Local Education Agency but not related to specific revenue sources of the respective governmental unit; i.e., general, or if related to specific revenue sources of the governmental unit, are distributed on some flat grant or equalization basis. Grants-in-aid are made by intermediate governments, state governments, and the federal government.

gross income
Revenues before deducting any expenses: an expression employed in accounting for individuals, financial institutions, and the like. Also, gross revenue, or incidental revenue of a manufacturing or trading enterprise.

imprest system
A system for handling disbursements whereby a fixed amount of money is set aside for a particular purpose. Disbursements are made from time to time as needed. At certain intervals, a report is rendered of the amount disbursed, and the cash is replenished for the amount of the disbursements, ordinarily by check drawn on the fund or funds from which the items are payable. The total of cash plus unreplenished disbursements must always equal the fixed sum of cash set aside.

indirect expenses
Those elements of cost necessary in the provision of a service that are of such nature that they cannot be readily or accurately identified with the specific service. For example, the custodial staff may clean corridors in a school building that is used jointly by administrative, instructional, maintenance, and attendance personnel. In this case, a part of custodial salaries is an indirect expense of each service using the corridors. However, it is impossible to determine readily or accurately the amount of the salary to charge each of these services.

indirect services
Services that cannot be identified with a specific program. All support services programs are indirect services of instruction programs.

instruction
Consists of those activities dealing directly with or aiding in the teaching of students or improving the quality of teaching. These are the activities of the teacher, principal, consultant, or supervisor of instruction, and guidance and psychological personnel.

interest
A fee charged a borrower for the use of money. See also Debt Service.

internal auditing
Activities involved with evaluating the adequacy of the internal control system: verifying and safeguard-

ing assets; reviewing the reliability of the accounting and reporting systems; and ascertaining compliance with established policies and procedures.

inventory
: A detailed list or record showing quantities, descriptions, values, and, frequently, units of measure and unit prices of property on hand at a given time. Also, the cost of supplies and equipment on hand not yet distributed to requisitioning units.

investments
: Securities and real estate held for the production of income in the form of interest, dividends, rentals, or lease payments. The account does not include fixed assets used in Local Education Agency operations.

invoice
: An itemized list of merchandise purchased from a particular vendor. The list includes quantity, description, price, terms, date, and the like.

journal
: The accounting record in which the details of financial transactions are first recorded.

journal voucher
: A paper or form on which the financial transactions of the Local Education Agency are authorized and from which any or all transactions may be entered in the books. By means of the journal voucher, the budget may be put into operation and expenditures made to meet authorized obligations. Journal vouchers are also used to set up revolving funds and petty cash funds, and for authorizing all entries in the bookkeeping system for which no other authorizations, such as deposit slips, invoices, etc., are available. A form of journal voucher is a memorandum in the school board minutes.

ledger
: Contains all the accounts of a particular fund or all those detail accounts that support a particular General Ledger account. See also General Ledger.

leeway
: The amount of local tax resources that is regularly available to a school district but is not included in the district's required contribution to the apportionment formula or foundation program.

levy (verb)
: To impose taxes or special assets. (noun): The total of taxes or special assessments imposed by a governmental unit.

liabilities
: Debt or other legal obligations arising out of transactions in the past which are payable but not necessarily due. Emcumbrances are not liabilities; they become liabilities when the service or materials for which the encumbrance was established have been rendered or received.

loans
: See Bond, Current Loan, Long-Term Loan, and Short-Term Loan.

local education agency (LEA)
: An educational agency at the local level that exists primarily to operate schools or to contract for educa-

tional services. Normally, taxes may be levied by such publicly operated agencies for school purposes. These agencies may or may not be coterminous with county, city, or town boundaries. This term is used synonymously with the terms "school district," "school system," and "local basic administrative unit."

long-term loan
A loan that extends for more than five years from the date the loan was obtained and is not secured by serial or term bonds.

maintenance of plant (plant repairs and repair and replacement of equipment)
Those activities that are concerned with keeping the grounds, buildings, and equipment at their original condition of completeness or efficiency, either through repairs or by replacements of property (anything less than replacement of a total building).

management information system
A network of communication channels (voice, digital, etc.) that acquires, retrieves, and redistributes data used in managing the educational process and in supporting the individual and collective decision-making process.

net expenditure
The actual outlay of money by the Local Education Agency for some service or object after the deduction of any discounts rebates, reimbursements, or revenue produced by the service or activity.

net income
The balance remaining to the Local Education Agency after deducting from the gross revenue for a given period all operating expense and income deductions during the same period. See Revenues.

noncategorical
A term usually applied to revenue and means revenue from any or all sources that is not identifiable with specific expenditures; i.e., it is general fund revenue which loses its identity as it is expended for objects relating to many service areas.

object
The commodity or service obtained from a specific expenditure.

obligations
Amounts that the Local Education Agency will be required to meet out of its resources, including both liabilities and encumbrances.

operation of plant
Consists of the housekeeping activities concerned with keeping the physical plant open and ready for use.

overhead costs
Those elements of cost necessary in the production of an article or the performance of a service that are of such a nature that the amount applicable to the product or service cannot be determined accurately or readily. Usually they relate to those objects of expenditures that do not become an integral part of the finished product or service, such as rent, heat, light, supplies, management, supervision, and other similar items.

permanent school fund	Money, securities, or land that have been set aside as an investment for public school purposes of which the income, but not the principal, may be expended. These funds have been derived, in most cases, from the sale of state land set aside by the federal and/or state government, rents and royalties, and from surplus revenue returned to the state by the federal government. In some instances, there may be endowment funds for individual schools. There may be nonexistent funds, also, which are legally recognized as an obligation.
petty cash	A sum of money set aside for the purpose of paying small obligations for which the issuance of a formal voucher and check would be too expensive and time-consuming. Also, a sum of money, either in the form of currency or a special bank deposit, set aside for the purpose of making change or immediate payments of comparatively small amount. See also Imprest System.
planning-programming-budgeting-evaluation system (PPBS)	A structured procedure for determining policy in the allocation of resources for accomplishment of priority programs; it emphasizes long-range planning, analytic evaluative tools, and economic rationality in setting goals and objectives and in the determination of programs.
posting	The act of transferring to an account in a ledger the detailed or summarized data contained in the cash receipts book, check register, journal voucher, or similar books or documents of original entry.
prepaid expenses	Expenses entered in the accounts for benefits not yet received. Prepaid expenses differ from deferred charges in that they are spread over a shorter period of time than deferred charges and are regularly recurring costs of operation. Examples are prepaid rent, prepaid interest, and unexpired insurance premiums. An example of a deferred charge is unamortized discount on bonds sold.
program	A plan of activities and procedures designed to accomplish a predetermined objective or set of allied objectives.
prorating	The allocation of parts of a single expenditure to two or more different accounts. The allocation is made in proportion to the benefits that the expenditure provides for the respective purposes or programs for which the accounts were established.
pupil activity fund	Financial transactions related to school-sponsored pupil activities and interscholastic activities. These activities are supported in whole or in part by income from pupils, gate receipts, and other fund-raising activities. Support may be provided by local taxation.

purchase order

A written request to a vendor to provide material or services at a price set forth in the order; used as an encumbrance document.

purchased services

Personal services rendered by personnel who are not on the payroll of the Local Education Agency, and other services that may be purchased by the Local Education Agency. See also Contracted Services.

real estate

Land, improvements to site, and buildings; real property.

rebates

Abatements or refunds.

receipts

This term means cash received. See Revenues.

receipts, non-revenue

Amounts received that either incur an obligation that must be met at some future date or change the form of an asset from property to cash and therefore decrease the amount and value of school property. Money received from loans, sale of bonds, sale of property purchased from capital funds, and proceeds from insurance adjustments constitute most of the non-revenue receipts.

receipts, revenue

Additions to assets that do not incur an obligation that must be met at some future date and do not represent exchanges of property for money.

receiving and disbursing

Accepting and paying out funds. It includes the current audit of receipts, the preaudit of requisitions or purchase orders before the order is placed to determine whether the amounts are within the budgetary allowances, and to determine that such disbursements are lawful expenditures of the school or Local Education Agency.

refund

A return of an overpayment or overcollection. The return may be either in the form of cash or a credit to an account.

register

A record for the consecutive entry of a certain class of events, documents, or transactions, with a proper notation of all of the required particulars. The form of register for accounting purposes varies from a one-column to a multicolumnar sheet of special design whereon the entries are distributed, summarized, and aggregated usually for convenient posting to the accounts.

reimbursement

The return of an overpayment or overcollection in cash.

repairs

The restoration of a given piece of equipment, of a given building, or of grounds to original condition of completeness or efficiency from a worn, damaged, or deteriorated condition. See also Maintenance of Plant.

replacement of equipment

A complete unit of equipment purchased to take the place of another complete unit of equipment which is to be sold, scrapped, or written off the record, and serving the same purpose as the replaced unit in the same way.

requisition   A written request to a purchasing officer for specified articles or services. It is a request from one school official to another school official, whereas a purchase order is from a school official (usually the purchasing officer) to a vendor.

reserve   An amount set aside for some specified purpose.

revenues   Additions to assets that do not increase any liability, do not represent the recovery of an expenditure, do not represent the cancellation of certain liabilities without a corresponding increase in other liabilities or a decrease in assets, and do not represent contributions of fund capital in food service and pupil activity funds.

revolving fund   A fund provided to carry out a cycle of operations. The amounts expended from the fund are restored from earnings from operations or by transfers from other funds so that it remains intact, either in the form of cash, receivables, inventory, or other assets.

salary   The total amount regularly paid or stipulated to be paid to an individual, before deductions, for personal services rendered while on the payroll of the Local Education Agency. Payments for sabbatical leave are also considered as salary.

school plant   The site, buildings, and equipment constituting the physical facilities used by a single school or by two or more schools sharing the use of common facilities.

school site   The land and all improvements to the site, other than structures, such as grading, drainage, drives, parking areas, walks, plantings, play courts, and playfields.

securities   Bonds, notes, mortgages, or other forms of negotiable or nonnegotiable instruments.

serial bonds   Issues redeemable by installments, each of which is to be paid in full, ordinarily out of revenues of the fiscal year in which it matures, or revenues of the preceding year.

shared revenue   Revenue that is levied by one governmental unit but shared, usually in proportion to the amount collected, with another unit of government or class of governments.

short-term loan   A loan payable in five years or less, but not before the end of the current fiscal year.

sinking fund   Money that has been set aside or invested for the definite purpose of meeting payments on debt at some future time. It is usually a fund set up for the purpose of accumulating money over a period of years in order to have money available for the redemption of long-term obligations at the date of maturity.

special fund
: Any fund other than the general fund.

special revenue fund
: Used to account for money appropriated or granted for special purposes. Uses and limitations are specified by the legal authority establishing the fund and, generally, the resources of this fund cannot be diverted to other uses.

stores
: Supplies, materials, and equipment in store-rooms subject to requisition.

subsidiary accounts
: Related accounts that support in detail the summaries recorded in a controlling account. See also Clearing Accounts.

supply
: A material item of an expendable nature that is consumed, worn out, or deteriorated in use; loses its identity through fabrication or incorporation into a different or more complex unit or substance.

surety bond
: A written promise to pay damages or to indemnify against losses caused by the party or parties named in the document, through nonperformance or through defalcation; for example, a surety bond given by a contractor or by an official handling cash or securities.

surplus
: The excess of the assets of a fund over its liabilities; or if the fund also has other resources and obligations, the excess of resources over obligations. The term should not be used without a properly descriptive adjective unless its meaning is apparent from the context. See also Unappropriated Surplus.

systems analysis
: Activities involving the search for an evaluation of alternatives that are relevant to defined objectives, based on judgment, and, whenever possible, on quantitative methods; the development of data processing procedures or application to electronic data-processing equipment.

tax anticipation notes
: Notes (sometimes called "warrants") issued in anticipation of collection of taxes, usually retirable only from tax collections, and frequently only from the tax collections anticipated with their issuance. The proceeds of tax anticipation notes or warrants are treated as current loans if paid back from the tax collections anticipated with the issuance of the notes.

tax assessment and collection
: Activities concerned with assigning and recording equitable values to real and personal property, assigning a millage rate (dollars yield per thousand dollars), and receiving yield in a central office.

tax rate
: The amount of tax stated in terms of a unit of the tax base.

(a) To determine the tax rate:

$$\frac{\text{total taxes to be raised: } (\$50,000)}{\text{total assessed valuation: } (\$2,500,000)} = .02$$

(b) To express the tax rate:
as a percent of the assessed value; as 2 percent of $2,500,000.

as dollars and cents per $100 or $1,000 of assessed value; as $2.00 per $100 or $20.00 per $1,000.

as mills per dollar of assessed value; as 20 mills per $1.00; a mill is 1/10 of a cent, or $.001.

trade discount	An allowance usually varying in percentage with volume of transactions, made to those engaged in certain businesses and allowable irrespective of the time when the account is paid. The term should not be confused with "cash discount."
transfer voucher	A voucher authorizing posting adjustments and transfers of cash or other resources between funds or accounts.
travel	Costs for transportation, meals, hotel, and other expenses associated with traveling on business for the Local Education Agency. Payments for per diem in lieu of reimbursements for subsistence (room and board) also are charged here.
trial balance	A list of the balances of the accounts in a ledger kept by double entry, with the debit and credit balances shown in separate columns. If the totals of the debit and credit columns are equal or their net balance agrees with a controlling account, the ledger from which the figures are taken is said to be "in balance."
unappropriated surplus	That portion of the surplus of a given fund that is not segregated for specific purposes.
unencumbered balance of appropriation or allotment	That portion of an appropriation or allotment not yet expended or encumbered; the balance remaining after deducting from the appropriation or allotment the accumulated expenditures and outstanding encumbrances.
unexpended balance of appropriation or allotment	That portion of an appropriation or allotment that has not been expended; the balance remaining after deducting from the appropriation or allotment the accumulated expenditures.
unit cost	Expenditures for a function, activity, or service divided by the total number of units for which the function, activity, or service was provided.
voucher	A document authorizing the payment of money and usually indicating the accounts to be charged.

warehouse inventory adjustment	Amounts reflected as a deficit as a result of an audit or count of items held in a stores or warehouse inventory.
warrant	An order drawn by the school board to the Local Education Agency treasurer ordering him to pay a specified amount to a payee named on the warrant. Once signed by the treasurer, the warrant becomes a check payable by a bank named on the warrant by the treasurer.

Read over and study the above terms because you will hear them over and over again during your term on the board. Keep a tab in this section of The School Board Primer *and refer to it anytime you hear unfamiliar school finance terms.*

CHAPTER 7

Business Aspects of a School System

The operation of schools today is not only a business, but a big business. Business management of schools is a complex operation. Effective management must be provided in school districts, and school boards are responsible for seeing that good management practices occur in all aspects of school business.

The problems of retrenchment, inflation, high interest rates, and increasing governmental mandates have focused attention on the operation of schools. No other agency of government receives as much public scrutiny as the public schools. In most districts budget and bond programs must be submitted for voter approval. Often other agencies of government must review district budgets before they can be operational. State legislatures often put restrictions on how school funds are raised and spent. Legislatures mandate strict accountability measures. Whether it is because schools are so close to the people, or such large expenditures of tax dollars go to schools, business practices of schools are always under review by the public and the media.

As a board member, you must not only be sure that strong board policies relating to business practices are in place, but that the administrative team and teaching staffs follow those policies. Boards should hold the superintendent and his or her staff strictly accountable for overseeing all business practices in the district. Competent staffs must be hired to administer all aspects of the school programs including record keeping, reporting, and auditing of those programs.

A number of factors have contributed to the complexity of business management of school districts. The proliferation of federally financed programs made necessary the hiring of additional staff for record keeping and reporting. Broader insurance and benefits programs for teachers require more bookkeeping by administrative staffs. Court-ordered bussing and racial integration of schools have necessitated reporting and record keeping unheard of before in school districts. Finally, the broadening of school programs in vocational, adult, and special education areas has added to the responsibilities of business administrators in school districts.

In this chapter we will review the major business affairs of schools including transportation, staff personnel, food services, purchasing, managing equipment and supplies, insurance programs, and building utilization. In addition, we will examine management systems used in school districts to improve business practices.

ADMINISTRATIVE STAFF REQUIREMENTS

Although staff requirements for business operations are dependent upon the size of the district, two key persons are the Assistant Superintendent for Business and the Assistant Superintendent for Personnel. They may hold other titles such as director or coordinator. In very small districts the two positions may be consolidated under the leadership of one person.

Where the two positions exist, the following responsibilities are usually assigned:

Assistant for Business	**Assistant for Personnel**
Plant Maintenance	Manpower Planning
Transportation	Recruitment and Selection
Food Services	Development and Evaluation
Purchasing	Negotiation and External Relations
Accounting and Payroll	Certification
Fund Management	Personnel Services
Auditing and Reporting	

In large school districts there may well be a Deputy Superintendent for Management. That person would be responsible for coordinating the various managerial services necessary for the operation of a school system. Those functions include those performed by the Office of Administrative Support Services, Purchasing, Food Services, Transportation, Warehouse, Book Bindery, Data Management Services, Personnel Services, and Fiscal Management Services.

The Administrative Support Services will usually be headed by a top-level administrator who will be responsible for providing non-instructional support to schools and administrative facilities in the areas of plant operations, including custodial and stationary engineer services, architecture and engineering, maintenance and construction, grounds maintenance, real estate services, and printing and publication services.

Personnel needs for carrying out the business affairs of a school district must be based on the objectives of the organization and the size of the school district. Good planning will help board members and district administrators deal with economic developments and hold personnel costs down.

Recruitment, selection, placement, and evaluation of personnel are all critical elements of a district plan for business personnel. Many of the policies relating to personnel may be subject to negotiation or civil service requirements, but boards can still insist on hiring only the most highly qualified person for each position. Evaluation policies are particularly important because they allow a school system to maintain quality control of business personnel within the organization. A personnel development system should be in operation in each district to insure that all personnel receive the training needed to function productively in the system.

Know who the key persons are who run the business operations of the district. Ask the superintendent to analyze staff needs for business operations and to recommend changes in staff if necessary. You can't get involved in administration as a board member, but you can insist on an efficient business operation in the district.

Food Service

Food service programs in most districts have grown into a major operation. Coordination of food services is usually the responsibility of a Food Service Director. That person is often a dietitian or a person trained in food preparation.

The person in charge of food services must not only direct the planning of menus and preparation of food but administer the purchase of lunchroom supplies and equipment. Food service workers must also be hired and lunchroom management monitored.

Most districts use a variety of federal surplus food commodities and provide free or low-cost meals to students in need. Strict record keeping must be maintained and reporting procedures followed.

It is essential that the district coordinator of food services have a good background in business and personnel relations.

Transportation

Transportation costs in many school districts have increased dramatically because of consolidation of schools and bussing of students to achieve racial integration. Many districts transport thousands of students daily to and from schools even without court-ordered bussing.

School districts may own their own buses and hire their own drivers, maintenance personnel, and bus garage, or may contract with private firms to transport students. In city systems many students provide their own transportation or walk to school.

The bussing of students to achieve racial integration added an additional burden to already tight budgets in most districts. One district busses students 80,000 miles a day using 16,000 gallons of gasoline per day. At $1.25 per gallon that adds up to a yearly cost of $3,600,000 in fuel costs alone. The additional buses needed, maintenance, insurance, and personnel add even more costs. Those funds cannot be used for instruction.

Boards today in many areas are faced with reduced budgets, yet must maintain high-cost transportation systems when under court mandate. Taxpayers don't really sympathize with boards asking for more transportation funds even if the district is under court order.

As fuel costs go up for both school operations and bussing, boards will face difficult decisions as to what budget items to cut to compensate for those additional fuel costs.

Ask to see the latest transportation study done in your district. Compare costs of district-owned buses versus private contracting for transportation. Look for ways to reduce transportation costs since every dollar saved can be used to better the instructional program.

Purchasing and Managing Equipment and Supplies

All school supplies, material, and equipment must be received, stored, and distributed in the most efficient way possible. School supplies must be readily available to teaching and other personnel in the districts. Warehouse and distribution centers must be provided and a trained staff to monitor and distribute equipment and supplies. Even though equipment and supplies make up a small portion of the school district budget, strict accounting procedures must be in place to insure that supplies and equipment are available when needed and that there is an efficient record-keeping system in place.

The following are suggested as guidelines for purchasing policies in a school district:

- A single staff person should be responsible for purchasing activities in the district
- A district-wide inventory system should be in place to prevent hoarding and provide an adequate picture of what supplies and equipment are available
- Standard forms should be developed and used in the district.
- Purchase requests should be initiated by the person who will be the eventual user of materials and supplies
- Policies for submitting requests for equipment and supplies should be explained to all staff members
- All state statutes and local policies relating to limitations on dollar amounts of goods that can be purchased without bids should be strictly followed. Competition bids should be required for all purchases exceeding a total purchase of more than $500.

The selection of equipment is a continuous process in most school districts. Quality standards should be established for each piece of equipment. Wherever possible, standard equipment should be considered for use. A list of standardized items should be circulated to all personnel and strong justification given for selecting any items not on the list.

The following are suggested criteria for selection of equipment:

- Equipment should be purchased at the lowest cost consistent with quality and utilization.
- The educational value of the equipment should be established. Equipment that does not contribute substantially to the educational program has no place in the school system.
- Workmanship and quality of equipment should be evident as well as strength and durability.
- Ability of the vendor to service a product should be taken into consideration when purchasing any piece of equipment. Vendors should be checked for reliability and integrity before being selected to do business with the school district.

• Safeguards for protection of funds should be provided through specific and clearly worded contracts and agreements.

Review all policies relating to purchasing and managing equipment and supplies. Look into leasing of equipment rather than purchasing.

Warehouse and Distribution

School systems may have a central warehouse for the receiving, storing, and distribution of goods. The warehouse should be staffed with warehousemen, equipment operators, and repairmen.

The function of a Warehouse and Distribution Division in a school district is to provide services as follows:

1. Receive, store, and distribute educational supplies, foodstuffs for the lunchrooms in schools, and raw materials to be used by the Maintenance Division.
2. Repair musical instruments and office machines.
3. Make all deliveries and pickups of equipment, supplies, mail, textbooks, and raw materials.

Maintenance

A Division of Maintenance in a school system is staffed with skilled mechanics in the various building trades, building trades foremen, maintenance supervisors and building laborers, and a maintenance supervisor.

A maintenance division is responsible for providing skilled labor for repairs, maintenance, and attending to all Board of Education buildings and facilities.

School Plant Management

The primary aim in the operation of a school building is to provide for pupils and teachers the optimum environment for learning.

The school plant is defined as the buildings, grounds, facilities, and equipment of the school. Billions of dollars are spent annually in the building and maintenance of schools. Managing the utilization of these facilities, equipping them, and administering the maintenance of these facilities are major responsibilities of school boards.

Very few boards today are planning new facilities. Most of the attention is in providing for more efficient use of buildings or phasing out of school buildings. An effectively planned school plant should facilitate a planned educational program. Space utilization becomes an important function in the world of declining resources, high energy costs, and continued inflation. Non-utilized or poorly utilized space results in waste. Boards must insure that space is well used and that space assignments reflect the best educational use of available space.

Equipment purchase is governed by district policy, but the principal and his staff must consider the educational specifications for equipment and determine its purpose or use. Principals must develop a procedure for ordering certain equipment and work with staff in assigning priorities for various needs.

Maintenance refers to routine periodic services that keep a school operating. Painting, repairs to desks and equipment, and keeping the school plant clean are all concerns of the principal. A pleasant building that facilitates learning is dependent upon the supervision of custodians but also upon the general "set" of the school. Where students and teachers respect the school and each other, you will generally find a school free of trash in the halls and graffiti on the restroom walls. The principal can set the tone for the school by effective leadership. Developing a good instructional program and effective pupil personnel procedures can do much to build school spirit and high morale. Where there is a healthy school spirit and high morale, the building reflects that atmosphere.

Good school plant maintenance is critical. Poor maintenance or cutting corners can result in rapidly deteriorating plants and wasted dollars for replacement costs.

School Security

Security of school buildings has become an administrative problem of enormous proportions in today's world. The cost of replacing broken windows in schools is about the same amount as spent for textbooks in American schools. Losses because of theft and vandalism cost school districts millions of dollars annually.

Assaults on students, arson, theft, and vandalism are problems faced daily by school administrators. The school principal must deal with each school-related crime. Time spent on this nonproductive task takes time away from the other important duties of the principal. Preventing theft or vandalism can only be accomplished through a well-thought-out security program and boards should insist that such a program is in place. The superintendent must take the initiative in developing such a program by involving students, parents, local law enforcement officials, and other members of the community. That leadership responsibility cannot be delegated to subordinates.

BOARD POLICY ON USE OF SCHOOL PROPERTY

School buildings may be used for many purposes other than instruction. Schools may be centers for voting, emergency shelters, town meetings, and even for church organizations. School property may be used for public meetings, discussions, and other social, civic, or educational policies provided such activities do not interfere with the primary operation of the public schools.

Although school buildings are most often used for single or short-range meetings, the adopting of the community-school concept in many districts has meant that school buildings are in use each afternoon and evening through the year. Community schools offer a variety of social, recreational, and educational services to all persons in the community.

Board policies relating to the use of school buildings should include the following provisions:*

1. Since school buildings are public property, they should be made available to the public as freely as is consistent with state laws and board policies.
2. In granting community use of school buildings, the Board of Education shall at no time surrender its control of such property.
3. Public school buildings should be open after school hours for such purposes as have a district educational value or will benefit the community. The question of whether a proposed use meets those criteria should be determined by the superintendent.
4. Applications for use of school buildings should be granted with the understanding that the Board of Education reserves first claim on all school property. Cancellations of permits may be ordered whenever necessary, with or without due notice.
5. The responsibility for the issuance and cancellation of permits,

---

*It must be noted that the following are suggested policies. Some states may have regulations that may not allow some of the activities suggested.

and any changes thereto, should be vested in the superintendent or his designee.

6. Where an organization or individual uses a school building for successive days, any furniture or equipment that must be moved should be reinstalled before the start of the regular school program.

7. Religious instruction or worship services should not be allowed on public school property [Note: Some boards may allow churches to meet for a temporary period in school buildings when a church building burns or a church is under construction or repair].

8. Minors should not be allowed to contract with the board for use of school buildings.

9. Fund-raising groups should not be allowed the use of a school building for any function unless the function is for the immediate aid of the school itself.

10. The board may rent school buildings to any individual or organization for a performance, exhibit, entertainment, or any similar function given for commercial or private interest.

11. Political groups or organizations may rent school buildings for political meetings, speeches or debates, union meetings or elections. Care should be exercised that opposing political interest groups have equal opportunity to rent buildings.

12. No group or individual should be allowed to conduct activities on school property when such activities may cause damage to board properties or facilities.

13. All applications for the use of school premises should be made to the principal or administrator in charge of the school to be used. No meeting or activity should be scheduled on school premises without the knowledge and approval of the principal or building administrator in charge. A special board form should be used for all applications for use of school facilities.

14. The applicant and all individuals and organizations using school buildings should be jointly and severally liable for any injury or damages thereto arising from such use. Individuals or groups using school buildings should be responsible for the supervision of the activity and the conduct of the persons present and will indemnify and hold harmless the board and its employees from all losses, claims, demands, and liabilities arising from such organization's use of the building.

15. Meetings or activities scheduled at schools after regular daytime school closing hours should generally not begin earlier than 7:00 P.M. and should not extend beyond 10:00 P.M. unless special permission is granted.

16. The number of nights a school may be used without charge should

be limited. Not only should there be a regulation relative to the number of nights a building may be used, but a charge should be made to cover cost of utilities and the salary of the custodian needed to get the building back in order after an event.

17. The use of intoxicants on school property should be prohibited.
18. If a school cafeteria is used for refreshments, the Director of Food Services may require that the applicant use the services of the cafeteria manager.
19. Gymnasiums or swimming pools should not be used by nonschool organizations or groups. Tennis courts or athletic fields may be used if such use does not interfere with the needs of school groups or organizations. City recreation departments may be granted use of swimming pools upon agreement with the board. Lifeguards should always be present at pools during their use. Many districts have reciprocal agreements with city and county agencies for use of recreational facilities.
20. Special policies should be adopted regarding the use of school buildings or grounds on national or school holidays.
21. Parking on school grounds and smoking in schools should be regulated by board policies. All safety rules mandated by state, city, and board should be enforced.

Make sure board policies regarding the use of buildings are consistent and fair. You will hear many special pleas for the use of school buildings during your term on the board. Having clear-cut policies can avoid much grief.

PROTECTION OF SCHOOL PROPERTY

School districts have an enormous investment in buildings and equipment and taxpayers should be guaranteed that that investment will be protected. To protect against vandalism and theft, districts should take the following precautions:

1. An inventory of school property should take place annually.
2. Exterior and interior lights should be used in all school buildings.
3. Exterior locks on school property should be changed annually if possible. The number of keys should be strictly controlled.
4. A trained Security Director should be hired and security officers

used to patrol schools after hours. If the district is small, security should be contracted out to a private agency or working agreements with the local police department should be developed.

5. Boards should have a strict policy of prosecution of all persons caught vandalizing school property. Vandal damage should be reported immediately and repaired as soon as possible.
6. School safes should be emptied nightly of all funds and school files locked in vandal-proof files.
7. A specific person should be responsible for securing all buildings at the end of working hours.
8. All school property should be marked with identification numbers.
9. Boards should publicize vandalism costs to taxpayers. Citizens should be encouraged to report any suspicious activities at school sites.
10. Restitution from offenders and parents should be sought and the punishment made known to the public.
11. Alarm systems should be installed in all school buildings. Protective screens or window guards should be used and fences installed around schools.
12. If possible, have someone live on school grounds, especially where there are large property areas, e.g., a police officer housed in a mobile home on school property.

If a comprehensive security program is not in place in your district, insist that one be implemented. Costs of such a program far outweigh the costs of repairing vandalized school buildings.

INSURANCE PROGRAMS

School districts are constantly faced with the fact that catastrophe may strike employees and buildings. As with individuals, boards must protect the school district against such losses. Local districts find protection through various kinds of insurance programs.

The board may choose to insure through regular private or state-operated insurance programs, or by self-insurance in which the district assumes its own risks through a reserve fund. One other alternative, although not a satisfactory one, is to have no insurance. Only large districts can afford to have a self-insurance program. Other districts must choose a private or governmental plan.

School districts are usually insured against losses due to fire, property damage (liability), bodily injury, burglary or theft, and automobile or bus accidents.

Insurance costs have risen dramatically in urban districts where a large number of schools are located in crime-prone areas.

It is important that one person be designated by the board to be responsible for administering the district's insurance program. In small districts, the superintendent or an assistant superintendent is usually charged with that responsibility. The school insurance administrator's position should include inventorying and appraising all school property to determine values, and providing for the restoration or replacement of school properties in case of loss. The district administrator should also be responsible for selecting an agent-of-record to handle the insurance program. That agent would work with all local agents holding policies when insurance claims are filed.

The school superintendent should monitor closely the administration and operation of the district insurance program. Usually board policy statements regarding insurance only deal with the type of insurance program a district utilizes, e.g., self-insurance, public or private, and who is in charge of such a program. As conditions change in insurance (which often happens), the superintendent should keep the school board fully informed of district responses to those changing conditions.

CENTRAL OFFICE MANAGEMENT

The central school office is the hub of a modern school system. Not only are key administrators such as the superintendent housed in that building, but communication systems and important records are contained there.

Since boards usually meet in the district office building, that building is visited by many of the citizens of the community. As a meeting place, conference center, and office for important school administrators, the central office must be a warm and inviting place for parents, students, and community persons.

The district office employees should be highly trained and courteous individuals. Regular inservice programs should be offered those persons to help them maintain a high degree of effectiveness.

BOND PROGRAMS

Boards of Education are authorized by state law in most states to issue bonds (subject in most cases to approval of the voters) for school construction and repair of facilities. In some states nonschool agencies are authorized to issue bonds for school construction. Some boards make expenditure for capital outlay (buildings) from current bonds. Most boards, however, must borrow funds over a long period of time to spread payments out over a period of years.

Boards of Education today are spending more time closing buildings or repairing them rather than building new ones. However, some districts are still constructing new schools.

Most states have bond limits that restrict the amount of indebtedness a board can incur. School bond issues must also be submitted to a state agency (usually the state board) for approval.

As enrollment continues to decline in most school districts, and funds continue to be restricted, fewer bond programs are being proposed by boards. Of those proposed, only a very small proportion of bond issues are approved by the voters. Boards today are seeking relief from the state for repairing buildings, converting them, and building new facilities. One promising trend is for districts to convert old buildings to offices and to rent, lease, or sell them to private businesses. Boards must exercise caution though in selling off buildings that may be needed in the future. The costs of replacing existing buildings would far exceed the original cost of construction of those facilities.

No bond program, or construction or repair program utilizing existing funds should take place without a school plant survey. Today boards should examine closely program needs and tie those needs directly to building needs.

Types of School Bonds

Serial bonds are bonds that mature annually over the life of the issue, usually in smaller amounts in the first years of maturity and in larger amounts during the last years. Interest and principal payments are combined during the life of the issue.

Serial–Redemption Sinking–Fund Bonds are a variation of the serial bond. This type of bond is callable and obligations are paid off in serial order as quickly as the accumulations of a continuing levy permit.

Straight Bonds are bonds that provide that the principal is payable in a lump sum at the expiration of the term of the bond. Such bonds require the building up of a sinking fund over the period of the bond, e.g., twenty years, to pay the entire principal at once.

In today's bond market boards are facing high interest rates and inflexibility on the part of bondholding companies. Bondholders just don't want to deal with fixed interest rates unless those rates are extremely high.

Bonds that are most attractive to the market are general obligation bonds that have a prior claim on the general funds of the issuing body or are secured by an unlimited tax.

Revenue certificates that are payable exclusively from the proceeds of a particular tax, e.g., one-half cent of a sales tax, and have been earmarked for a particular use (air-conditioning, gymnasiums, etc.) are sometimes used by school boards. City or county governments make wide use of revenue certificates because they, unlike school boards, have income other than local tax income, e.g., revenue sharing, state cigarette taxes, fees, etc. Interest rates on revenue certificates are usually higher than interest rates on bonds with the same maturities because revenue certificates are not as well secured as bonds.

CLOSING SCHOOLS — THE BOTTOM LINE

Good business practice in a school district sometimes means a board must close a school because factors such as enrollment, location, and the age of a building preclude its use as a center for student learning.

All boards today are faced with financial constraints which are debilitating in terms of educational programs and facilities. Facing the "cold reality" of declining resources and higher costs, boards today must make decisions as to the closing of one or more facilities. A careful cost-benefit analysis must be made to select the particular facility that should be phased out. Buildings that are operating at below the average efficiency of all the facilities in the district simply can't continue to operate.

Before a board makes a decision to close a school (and after generating much public heat from the community in which the school is located), a building-by-building cost analysis and comparative study must be completed. Factors considered in the cost analysis of a building are the amount of capital outlay funds necessary to restore the building to minimum standards, electricity and heating costs, insurance costs, and custodial costs.

The possible use of a facility is a major consideration. Can the building be converted to an office building or should it be written off and the property sold? Should the building be sold, leased, or left to remain idle? To let a school remain idle is probably the least desirable alternative. Vacant buildings are open invitations to vandalism. They also rapidly deteriorate and require higher insurance protection.

Partial leasing or short-term leasing of a building may be an alternative, especially if you might need to reopen the building five years later. Governmental agencies have been good customers for school leasing. Day-care centers, programs for the elderly, and recreational programs have been placed in old school buildings.

The American Association for School Administrators (AASA) has suggested an excellent facilities usage criteria test for closing schools. If a board can answer yes to each of the following criteria, a school should probably be closed.

Closing the school would mean:

1. Keeping students relatively close to their neighborhoods.
2. Keeping students from crossing major physical barriers.
3. Maintaining a similar socioeconomic, racial, and ethnic mix.
4. Closing the school with the lowest enrollment.
5. Closing the oldest school with a weak academic performance record.
6. Closing the least educationally flexible building.
7. Closing the "high cost" maintenance/capital outlay building.
8. Closing a building that can be recycled.
9. Closing the building that requires the least additional cost of district-wide transportation.
10. Closing the building most in keeping with the recommendations of the Special Task Force on Buildings.

Emotions run high in districts where boards must close schools. Boards won't blunt the emotions but can survive the criticisms often leveled at them for closing buildings by insisting that a careful cost analysis be made of each building in the district and applying the ten criteria suggested by AASA.

MANAGEMENT SYSTEMS USED IN SCHOOL DISTRICTS

School-Based Management

School-based management moves a number of policy and budgeting decisions from the district level to the school building level. School-based management operates on the assumption that all those involved in that local school should participate in making those decisions.

School-based management does not mean schools are completely autonomous. Schools have to operate within the framework of the district and the goals and objectives set by the board, administrative staffs, and teachers. It does mean that principals have more control over school operations, particularly the instructional program.

There are five basic principles in school-based management.

1. Funds should be allocated to schools based on the needs of children in the schools.
2. Decisions on how funds for instruction are to be spent should be made at the local level.
3. Specific educational objectives for a school should be set by people associated with the school.
4. Organization of instruction should be determined at the school level.
5. Parents should participate in school decision making.

School councils are usually set up to develop plans for programs, policies, and fund expenditures at the local school level. The school council is composed of the principal, teachers, and parents.

In at least three states—Florida, California, and South Carolina—state legislatures have mandated some form of school-based management. With boards and superintendents maintaining overall responsibility for budget expenditures and operations and fixed costs of so many budget items, there may be little flexibility left in determining how funds may be spent. School-based management does, however, formalize much of what is recognized in educational administration as sound thinking. The individual school is the most appropriate locale in which change and improvement of education may occur.

Comprehensive School Planning

Comprehensive School Planning ties together all aspects of a school or school district into a unified plan for improvement. Those aspects include program revision, staff development, evaluation, building needs, and budget. Comprehensive plans include tasks, timelines, and persons responsible for carrying out tasks.

Systems Theory

Systems theory borrows heavily from the physical and social sciences. It is a holistic approach to school administration because it stresses the independence found in organizations. It explains how changes in one part of the organization affect other parts or the whole of the organization. It is important when examining business practices in a district because it emphasizes the importance of coordinating and relating activities in a school system. By examining all the components of school programs—facilities, materials, funds, teachers, testing, and a host of other variables—deficiencies can be targeted for redesign and bottlenecks or noncontributing conditions can be eliminated. Systems can also help educators build models of preferred conditions for learning.

Four-Day School Weeks

A number of boards have experimented with four-day school weeks especially during the summer months (summer school or special programs). Fuel costs for transportation and air conditioning have led to four-day schedules for school personnel. A number of positive results have come from such programs—the most promising being reduced costs of operation. Student achievement has not suffered nor has efficiency of workers in districts where four-day weeks have been implemented.

Planning, Programming, Budgeting System (PPBS)

PPBS swept the country in the late 1960s and 1970s. PPBS came out of the business community. It draws heavily from the military and from industrial enterprises. Basically, it ties together budgeting with program planning, forcing school leaders to justify all budget requests with program plans.

Program Evaluation and Review Technique (PERT)

PERT is a management technique designed for defining objectives, developing a network design which outlines every task necessary to reach those objectives, and computing a time estimate for reaching the objectives. PERT forces planning and consideration of alternatives. It also assigns responsibility and assesses performance. It does not provide, however, cost information, and this is a shortcoming of the system.

Zero-Based Budgeting (ZBB)

Zero-based budgeting is a system that forces a yearly evaluation of each school program. Rather than taking last year's budget and adding or subtracting dollars for each program area, program planners must start with zero funding each year and justify the need for funds to continue each program.

Management by Objectives (MBO)

Management by Objectives stresses planning and administrative improvement through the setting of objectives to be accomplished at all levels in a school district. MBO allows a school leader to set objectives to be accomplished during the school year and then holds that person accountable for achieving those objectives.

SUGGESTIONS FOR IMPROVING BUSINESS PRACTICES IN SCHOOL DISTRICTS

As stated at the beginning of this section, the operation of schools today is a big business. As retrenchment and declining resources impact our schools, boards must not continue to have school leaders "do business as usual." We've learned that a number of management systems have been borrowed from business and industry as well as the military. We've also learned that one system will not give us all the answers nor will past experiences of growth and innovations help us in an era of decline and an increasingly conservative outlook in education. We can do the following:

1. Design a comprehensive plan for our school district that will tie together all of the important elements of program revision, staff development, evaluation, and budget.
2. Avoid simplistic solutions to major school problems such as closing schools. School leaders need to be aware of hidden costs in closing or opening schools and address the possibility of new uses for school buildings.
3. Address the problem of declining enrollment and reductions in force (RIF) before being faced with a crisis. Responsible approaches must be selected before time runs out. Board members can either retain all schools, facilities, and programs, in spite of great costs or cut programs, staff, and schools. Since the former alternative is unrealistic, the best place to start is to get teachers, parents, students, and administrators to identify criteria to use in closing schools and cutting programs.
4. Develop policies that will facilitate good business practices in the district. Insist that the superintendent hire high-level management

persons and hold them responsible for developing and implementing a cost-effective system of operating every aspect of the school system.

5. Organize the school system budget so that the costs of specific programs can be compared.

6. Analyze the range of possibilities for community contributors to the school system. Utilize business and industrial leaders in the community to help improve business practices and seek help from foundations, labor, and other governmental agencies.

CHAPTER 8

Dealing with Interest Groups

Schools do indeed belong to the people. Of all the American institutions, it is the school that most clearly reflects the shifting expectations, desires, triumphs, and failures of the American character.

Public confidence in our schools is an essential element for the continuation of the educational enterprise. If public confidence and support for schools are to continue, the board must play a major role. Understanding the issues facing American schools, knowing who the interest groups are, learning how to deal with them, and managing the many demands confronting schools are all critical competencies for today's school boards.

TEACHERS' UNIONS AND PROFESSIONAL ORGANIZATIONS

Teachers, like other employees in the private sector, have a right to organize and select leaders to represent them in collective bargaining. Teacher unions have existed at the local level since before 1900. In 1916 four local unions, under the leadership of the Chicago Teachers Association, formed a national organization called the American Federation of Teachers (AFT). AFT became affiliated with the American Federation of Labor (AFL) in the same year.

The teachers' union was usually found where the labor movement was the strongest and that was in the large cities. In the early part of the century, Chicago, New York City, Cleveland, and Detroit locals flourished.

After World War I unions came under attack from school boards and membership, and the number of locals dropped dramatically. During the same period the National Education Association (NEA) grew in membership and strength. School boards preferred dealing with a "professional association" such as an NEA affiliate rather than with a labor union. After World War II the struggle for power between AFT and NEA at national and local levels continued. AFT continued to dominate the larger cities while NEA had its greatest strength in smaller school districts and at the state level.

COLLECTIVE BARGAINING

The modern school board member must be thoroughly knowledgeable about the collective bargaining process. In addition to the possibility of serving as a member of a management negotiating team, the school board member will also have to live up to all the agreements at the bargaining table.

Collective bargaining is a constitutionally guaranteed right of citizens to organize and elect representatives. Early labor legislation such as the National Labor Relations Act of 1935 and the Taft-Hartley Act of 1947 excluded government workers such as teachers from coverage. But as the number of government workers increased (one of five today is a government worker), they demanded a greater voice at the bargaining table. In spite of the growing number of government workers, no legislation was passed by Congress to govern collective bargaining for public employees. A presidential executive order allowed collective bargaining for federal employees with the military exempt, but the fifty states were left to work out plans for regulating labor relations for state and local employees.

Recent state and federal court decisions have upheld the right of state and local employees to engage in collective bargaining. In some states, the state Supreme Court reported that if the legislature did not pass a law allowing public employees collective bargaining rights, the court itself would determine the provisions of collective bargaining. The legislature quickly complied, enacting legislation authorizing collective bargaining rights for all public employees.

Once collective bargaining is authorized, elections are held if there is more than one competing group to represent teachers. After one group has won the election, the school board is required to bargain in good faith with that group.

Rival unions or professional organizations may challenge reorganized bargaining groups. Usually a petition is required with a certain number of certified signatures of teachers before a new election can be held. When there is great dissension, private groups like the American Arbitration Association, or state arbitration organizations such as the Public Employees Relations Board, may be called in to conduct the election.

Certification of the exclusive bargaining representative is only the beginning. Rules have to be worked out between the school board and the bargaining group. Elected bargaining representatives usually gain certain privileges in addition to sitting at the bargaining table. Payroll deductions for members, meeting facilities, use of faculty mailboxes, and school mail service have all been privileges granted collective bargaining organizations.

PARENTAL AND COMMUNITY GROUPS

In addition to formal PTA and parent advisory groups, the board member will often face ad hoc special-interest parent and community groups who may organize for a variety of reasons—to censor textbooks, to get better discipline in the school, to fire certain teachers or administrators, to advocate or fight racial integration, to change the curriculum, alter bussing routes, fight certain businesses in the school attendance area, or to start building projects such as a new football stadium.

Other groups may organize around special interests of their children. These include groups like Band Boosters and Dads' Clubs (who support sports' teams).

In the 1960s parental groups, especially minority groups, in large urban school districts demanded a decentralized administrative structure and community control of schools. Demands ranged from formation of advising committees to locally elected school boards who would share decision-making authority and power with the central or district school board.

In "community control" there is a connotation of legal provision for an elected community school board. In administrative decentralization the school system is divided into areas or zones—smaller units that are often governed by area superintendents. Decentralization does not automatically mean more parent or community involvement. It does mean that district administrators, housed in the local communities, are geographically more accessible to parents.

A 1980 nationwide survey of school districts with student populations of fifty thousand or more indicated that about two-thirds of those districts employed some sort of decentralized model. Decentralized units ranged from as little as two to thirty-two (New York City) and the number of students in the units ranged from as few as 6,000 to 110,000.

With declining enrollment and retrenchment continuing in the 1980s, there may be a trend toward greater centralization. Although the purposes of decentralization include improving school-community relations and reduction of the administrative span of control, the jury is still out in the minds of many educators who point out examples of greater bureaucracy, additional costs, and lack of curriculum continuity in decentralized school districts.

The outlook for continuation of community control is clearer. Disruptions and controversies caused by neighborhood groups trying to elect local school boards and control decision making have led to great resistance on the part of school officials to community control of schools. Moreover, the community control groups many times accommodate a small number of militant groups rather than broadly based community groups. Community participation rather than control seems to hold more promise for real involvement of persons interested in schools.

Some states have legislated that parent advisory groups be organized for each district and/or school. There are few studies available as to the effectiveness of such groups in improving the educational programs of students. The level of participation of minority parents is still lower than that of white parents.

Concerned parents have moved from traditional school organizations such as Parent-Teacher Associations (PTAs) to other organizations concerned with the programs found in local schools. Indeed, the national PTA dropped in membership from a high of twelve million members in the 1960s to half that number in the 1980s.

Parental and Community Interest in School Discipline

In recent Gallup polls discipline has been cited as the major problem facing public schools. About one person in four surveyed cited school discipline as a major problem. In 1981 and 1982 the use of drugs was second to school discipline. It is interesting to note that parents, teachers, and nonparents all cited discipline as the biggest problem facing schools in their communities.

The problem of school discipline has political overtones because the students most likely to be identified as behavioral problems are urban, economically deprived children. Studies also indicate that of students suspended the higher proportion are black students.

Contributing to the problem of discipline in schools has been the great increase in number of single-parent homes, the economic problems facing urban areas, the cutoff of many federal programs designed to reach the urban poor, the failure to re-fund many school programs for disadvantaged and disaffected youth, and the high parent and student mobility in today's society. Aging staffs, remembering past eras of social stability, also are having problems coping with youth who refuse to conform to their standards of behavior. Youth from lower socioeconomic homes also tend to do poorly in school. Lack of achievement leads to frustration and discipline problems.

Parental and Community Interest in School Books

Historically, textbook selection has been a function of professional educators. In recent years parents and other community groups have demanded that they participate in textbook selection and, going even further, asked that certain "offensive books" be removed from libraries and classrooms.

Although no group will be entirely satisfied with decisions made by the school board and school administration on controversial topics, guidelines can be developed to deal with such topics. One obvious strategy is to have meaningful citizen involvement in textbook selection before a controversy begins. After an attack on the selection of books starts, it is difficult to begin or reinstate citizen input.

Citizen involvement must be meaningful, and all interest groups must be heard when examining textbooks. However, a fair balance must be struck between professional judgment of teachers and administrators who work daily with the books and citizens who have interests in textbooks' use in the schools. Citizen censorship would not be beneficial.

The 1980s have seen a growing frustration on the part of many parents and other citizens who have lived over two decades in which schools have been used as instruments of national social policy. Unable to strike back against the Washington administration, those angry persons reach for the one government they can directly control, and that is the school system. School boards must understand that schools can be used by certain groups for their own ends. Charting a steady course in the midst of storms of controversy brought on by groups from the left and the right has to be the responsibility of the school board administrators who function as the buffer between those groups and the students in the schools. The effective board will not simply react, but take the initiative in explaining the school's program to the community and actively involve parents in decisions about books and program offerings. Where a sense of trust of the schools exists in a community, controversial issues can be resolved through compromise between group interests and school interests.

MINORITY GROUPS AND PUBLIC EDUCATION

Blacks have been the single most powerful minority group affecting public education. The 1954 U. S. Supreme Court desegregation decision firmly established schools as instruments of national social policy. No longer were local school districts allowed to maintain racially segregated schools or school staffs.

Black activism has been aided by national organizations such as the National Association for the Advancement of Colored People (NAACP) and the Urban League. Those organizations have had many years' experience of negotiation and litigation in school matters.

Hispanic organizations, representing a substantial number of minority persons, have been less influential than black organizations in effecting educational changes.

Women have been represented strongly in recent years by the National Organization for Women (NOW) and other women's groups working to eliminate sexism in schools.

OTHER ORGANIZED INTEREST GROUPS AFFECTING EDUCATION

The business community has a strong interest in the public schools, primarily as a source for training employees and managers. Local, state, and national Chamber of Commerce groups lobby for certain training programs and for economic education.

At the local level, service organizations such as the Kiwanis, Lions, Rotary, American Legion, and Optimist Club take great interest in schools. Many organizations and clubs sponsor school junior service clubs and contests for students such as essay and oratorical contests. Service clubs want to improve schools, and as such, serve as forums for board members and school administrators to highlight needs or to show off outstanding programs. Many board members and administrators join service clubs and actively participate in community projects.

Nationally, education has come under the influence of charitable foundations such as the Ford Foundation, Rockefeller Foundation, and Carnegie Corporation. Sponsoring research, important studies, and special programs, foundations have precipitated notable changes in American education. Large city systems have also benefited from local industries and businesses that provide foundation grants to those school districts. Many "company towns" have school resources and facilities far beyond comparable towns because of the generosity of the company or industry in that area.

INTEREST GROUPS AND CURRICULUM CHANGE

Since the American educational system is designed to be locally controlled, it is also essentially political. Controversy can be expected in education because of varying opinions about how and what our youth should be taught. The curriculum found in our local educational system reflects the tugs and pulls of various interest groups. Economic education, law education, drug education, sex education, consumer education, and creationism all reflect the wishes of our society. Special programs such as compensatory and minimum-competency testing of students and teachers also reflect a growing concern with the quality of teaching and learning going on in our schools.

When school programs are attacked, the controversy that follows may be healthy since it forces examination of what is taught or should be taught. The modern school board should be well versed in curriculum matters and should be able to defend, or modify, the curriculum if necessary. Where there is good communication between the schools and community, the board can quickly set in motion meetings where proposed curriculum changes can be heard and reacted to in a professional manner by the instructional staff.

Some generalizations can be drawn from an analysis of past controversies relating to pressure for curriculum change:

First, rarely is an entire program or textbook the focus of an attack. Usually, only selected portions are criticized. However, once an attack is begun, usually an entire series of texts comes under criticism as critics generalize their complaints.

Second, initial components may be few, yet they tend to secure public support by identifying their interests with the "average American." The "American way" is often used in the rhetoric of right-wing groups.

Third, although critics sometimes represent diverse interests such as labor unions and the Chamber of Commerce, church groups, and the Ku Klux Klan, they frequently ally themselves in efforts to remove textbooks or change an offending curriculum.

Fourth, often board members, administrators, and curriculum developers find themselves embroiled in a controversy which they neither expected nor were properly prepared to cope with.

Because schools in America are uniquely local responsibilities, nearly everyone has some views on how they should be run. Until the second half of the twentieth century, most adults had their last education at the high school level and tended to stay in the same towns in which they were educated. The sense of ownership in schools was great. Greater mobility, many more adults pursuing post-high-school education, the reduction in neighborhood schools brought on by bussing and consolidation of schools, greater private school enrollment, all have contributed to the feeling that "schools belong to somebody else!" Since educators have always been viewed with some suspicion by the public, the problem of fostering a positive identification of parents and other community persons with the schools has become acute in the past decade. Such lack of identification contributes to an atmosphere of detachment and distrust and leaves administrators and teachers with little support when attacks on the school program occur.

National Curriculum Projects

In the 1950s the threat of communism and a growing nationalism contributed to the development of national curriculum projects to improve intellectual training in schools. The early focus was on science and mathematics, areas that many felt were weak in our schools. Critics such as Arthur Bestor, a Professor of History at the University of Illinois, and others felt there had to be a national thrust in curriculum development if we were to improve school programs and face up to the Russians who were emphasizing intellectual development, especially in the sciences.

The first move was the formation of the National Science Foundation (NSF) which funded efforts to build new physics and biology programs (Physical Science Study Committee-PSSC and Biological Sciences Curriculum Study-BSCS). The launching of the Russian sputnik in 1957 expanded such efforts, and more funding for curricular reform came with the passage of the National Defense Education Act (NDEA).

In 1963 the National Science Foundation began to fund national curriculum projects in areas other than science and mathematics. Their first effort in 1963 was *Man, A Course of Study* (MACOS). That program immediately came under violent attack from right-wing organizations and church groups (aided by sympathetic congressmen who cut off aid to NSF) because of controversial material found in the program. By 1975, MACOS had become so controversial that it became the last major project completed under NSF funding. The BSCS Human Sciences Curriculum was developed by NSF about the same time, but, like MACOS, was never disseminated.

We are well aware in the 1980s that such efforts as those of the National Science Foundation were not enough to effect curriculum reform. In fact, in the early 1980s we have seen a new call for reform in mathematics and science curricula. The emphasis today, as it was in the 1950s, is the need to keep up with the gains made by the Soviet Union in mathematics and science education.

Board members today cannot hope to wait for nationally directed curriculum writing projects. Revision and strengthening of curriculum must come at the local level. Even at the height of the development of elementary and secondary national science and mathematics programs, a small percentage of schools actually implemented those programs. Even more startling is the fact that twenty years later most of these programs have disappeared from the curricula of schools. Scientists and other intellectual interest groups have run head-on into the American phenomenon of local control of schools. We do not have a national system of education nor can we gain any consensus on a national purpose of education even on such an issue as meeting the challenge of the Russians in technical fields.

THE FUNDAMENTALIST RIGHT

Not since the anti-Communist witch hunts of the 1950s have we seen such violent attacks on American education and other institutions as that of fundamentalist church groups in the 1980s. The leading fundamentalist right group, the Moral Majority, gained prominence in the conservative landslide election of 1980.

The major target of fundamentalist right groups is what the Christian fundamentalists label "secular humanism." Humanism is an attitude that recognizes the dignity of man, but to fundamentalists represents an attempt to glorify man over God. With funding coming from wealthy right-wing conservatives and a diverse field of right-wing political and religious groups, the antihumanist campaign gained great strength in the early 1980s. Unfortunately, the main battleground for the right-wing groups has been the public schools. Textbooks, teachers, teaching methods, and programs such as sex education and human relations have come under violent attack by right-wing groups. For instance, in 1980 a group of citizens burned forty copies of the book, *Values Clarification,* in the city parking lot of Warsaw, Indiana.

To give the board member an insight into the extent of the attack on humanistic education, the following is a partial list of humanistic programs, terms, agencies, and foundations identified by antihumanistic groups as those to look out for and protest in school curricula:

Terms
Academic Freedom
Acceptance
Accountability
Achievement Motivation
    Program
Active Listening
Actualization
Adlerian Therapy
Affective Domain
Affective Teaching
Agents of Change
Alternate Economic Systems
Alternative Behaviors
Alternative Lifestyles
Analysis
Anthropology
Armenianism
Attitude
Attitudinal Behavior
Awareness

Behavior
Behavior Modification
Behavioral Objectives
Behavioral Outcomes
Behaviorism
Beliefs, Deeply held
Black Studies
Body Language

Capping Off
Careers Education
Carnegie Foundation
Center for War-Peace Studies
Change Agent
Child-Centered Learning
Child Development
Choosing Freely
Citizenship
Client-Centered Therapy
Clinician
Common Good, For the
Communicating
Communication Skills
Community Education
Community Schools
Computerized Instruction
Conditioning
Conflict
Confluent Education

Conjoint Therapy
Consciousness
Consensus
Coping
Counseling, Group
Creative Expression
Creative Life Management
Creative Listening
Creative Thinking
Creative Writing
Creativism
Criticism
Culturally Deprived

Decision-Making
Deeply Held Beliefs
Democracy
Democracy, Participatory
Diagnostic Approach
Diagnostic Clinician
Disconnectedness
Discovery Method
Discussion Groups
Domain, Affective
Drug Education

Emotional Growth
Emotions
Encounter Groups
Enlightenment
Esalen Institute
Ethics
Ethnic
Eupsychian Network
Experimental Program
Expression, Non-verbal

Fabianism
Facilitator
Family Life Education
Feedback Mechanism
Feelings
Ford Foundation
Foundations:
    Carnegie
    Ford
    Kettering
    Mott
    Rockefeller
Free Schools

Gaming Techniques (e.g. Mood Masks, Amnesia, Chairs, One-Way Glasses, Dear Granny Letters)
Gestalt Therapy
Global Community
Global Economy
Global Man
Global Perspective
Global Resources
Good of the People, For the
Group Consensus
Group Counseling
Group Criticism
Group Discussion
Group Dynamics
Group Facilitator
Growth, Human
Growth, Self

Hawaii
Hawaii Master Plan
Helping Relationships
Human Development
Human Dynamics
Human Growth
Human Potential
Human Relations
Human Resources
Human Sexuality
Human Themes
Humanism
Humanistic
Humanities
Humanized Learning

IALAC (I Am Lovable and Capable)
Identity
Illuminati
I-Message
Individualized Instruction
Inductive Method
Innovative Program
Inquiry Method
In-Service Training (for Teachers, Administrators, etc.)
Interact
Interaction
Interdependence
Internalization
Interpersonal Relations

Journals (Private or Surveillance)

Kettering Foundation

Laboratory Method
Learning Clinician
Learning How to Learn
Learning through Inquiry

Magic Circle
Mastery Skills
Measurable Objectives
Measurable Outcomes
Mental Health
Messianic
Middle Schools
Modular Scheduling
Moral-Free Teaching
Morals, Teaching without
Mott Foundation
Multi-Cultural Studies
Multi-Ethnic Studies

NEA Peace Studies
Nihilism
Non-Directive Therapy
Non-Traditional Roles
Non-Verbal Expression

Objectives, Measurable
Occult
Open Classroom
Open Concept Classroom
Open Design Classroom
Operant Conditioning

Parent Effectiveness Training (PET)
Parenting
Peace Studies (NEA)
Performance Budgeting
Planning, Programming & Budgeting System (PPBS)
Prescriptive Teaching
Preventive Mental Health
Private Journals
Problem-Solving
Programmed Instruction
Progressive Education
Psychometrist
Psycho-Drama
Psycho-Politics

Psycho-Therapy

Questing

Racism
Reality Therapy
Receiving
Reinforcing
Relativism, Scientific
Relevant Curriculum
Responding
Risk-Taking
Rockefeller Foundation
Role-Playing
Roles, Non-Traditional

School Health Education Studies
    (SHES)
Schools Without Failure
Schools Without Walls
Scientific Relativism
Secular
Secular Humanism
Self-Acceptance
Self-Actualization
Self-Adjustment
Self-Analysis
Self-Awareness
Self-Concept
Self-Criticism
Self-Evaluation
Self-Examination
Self-Growth
Self-Help
Self-Hood
Self-Identity
Self-Image
Self-Judgment
Self-Morality
Self-Understanding
Sensory
Sex Education
Sex Information in Education
    (SIECUS)
Sharing
Situation Ethics
Social Development
Social Growth
Social Interaction
Social Problems
Social Values
Socio-Drama

Socio-Grams
Stereotyping, Sex
Street Schools
Surveillance Journals
Synthesizing

T-Group
Taxonomy
Teacher Effectiveness Training
    (TET)
Therapy, Adlerian
    Client-Centered
    Conjoint
    Gestalt
    Non-Directive
    Reality
Third-Force Psychology
Three-Tier Curriculum
Transactional Analysis
TA for Tots
TA for Kids
TA for Teens
Transfer Leadership
Trust

Understanding
Utopianism

Values
Values Clarification
Values Continuum
Values, Social
Valuing

Weltanschauung (World View)
Western Behavior Sciences Institute
Will of the People
Witch Craft
Whole Child Development
World Goodwill
World Overview
World View

Agencies/Foundations
Carnegie Foundation
Education Development Corp.
Esalen Institute
Ford Foundation
Harris Institute for Transactional
    Analysis
Health, Ed. & Welfare (HEW)

Institute for Personal Effectiveness
    in Children
Kettering Foundation
Mott Foundation
National Education Ass'n. (NEA)
Nat'l. Institute of Ed. (NIE)
Nat'l. Institute of Mental Health
Nat'l. Science Foundation (NSF)
Nat'l. Training Laboratories (NTL)
Office of Education, U. S.
Rockefeller Foundation
Western Behavioral Sciences
    Institute

Curriculum Areas
Language Arts
English Communications
Social Sciences
Art
Sociology
American History
World History
Anthropology

But Don't Be Surprised If Human-
    ism Surfaces in:
Home Room
Careers Education
Physical Ed. Classes
Home Economics
(Some teachers have even held small-
    group Sensitivity Training Ses-
    sions in their home in the even-
    ings.)

    Clearly, from the above list, one can see the scope of the labeling process used by the fundamentalist right. Very little is not suspect. The school administration and board must defend school programs and topics that have been taught for years without controversy. An attack on a particular program or topic by a minister in the t.v. pulpit on Sunday night can bring a rash of calls to the principal on Monday morning. The use of the media and direct mailings by fundamentalist right groups have been most successful in arousing local groups to challenge school programs. Again, board members and school administrators must have the skills needed to protect teachers from intimidation and resist the forces attempting to dictate narrow interpretations of the curriculum.

Teaching Creationism and Evolution

The creation/evolution controversy is one that is alive in our schools today.* Court cases rivaling the 1925 Scopes trial have focused attention on belief systems about the origin and development of living things.

Creationism, generally defined, states that all things were created by God basically as they now exist. Creationism also supports the premise that there are purpose and order in the universe and opposes the idea that chance plays any part in the order of things.

Evolutionists subscribe to the premise that God may have begun the whole process by creating matter and life but that changes in living and nonliving things result from the operation of their inherent potentialities and are not subject to control of any supernatural power. Some theistic evolutionists maintain that God not only began the process but continues to direct the changes that eventually evolved into the universe we know now. Their position is very close to creationist beliefs.

The issue in schools is whether both creationism and evolutionism should be taught students. Very few creationists want to forbid teaching evolution. Their main concern is that creation theory be taught and presented accurately and that evolution be taught as a theory and not a fact.

Other Church-State Issues Affecting Curriculum

Although creationism is espoused by religious groups, it is less a religious issue than a philosophical one. Other church-state issues have had a greater impact on the curriculum of public schools.

The First Amendment to the Constitution which states in part, "Congress shall make no law respecting an establishment of religion or prohibiting the free exercise thereof," and later the Fourteenth Amendment which extended the prohibitions against Congress to the states, have been the bases for a number of important U. S. Supreme Court decisions relating to church-state issues in education. Among the most important court decisions are the following:

Pierce v. Society of Sisters, 1925, affirmed the right of parents to send their children to nonpublic schools.

---

*On January 5, 1982, a U. S. federal judge in Arkansas ruled that the Arkansas creationism law was unconstitutional. The judge ruled that "it was simply and purely an effort to introduce the biblical version of creation into the public school curricula."

Emerson v. Board of Education, 1947, approved publicly financed bussing for Catholic school youngsters in states that had no constitutional prohibition against such expenditures.
McCollum v. Board of Education, 1948, prohibited church representatives from coming into public schools to provide religious instruction.
Zorach v. Clauson, 1952, allowed released time for public school youngsters to attend religious classes away from the school grounds.
Engel v. Vitale, 1962, and *Abington Township School District v.
   Schempp,* 1963, invalidated official prayers and Bible readings
   in public schools.
Board of Education v. Allen, 1968, upheld the practice of public schools
   to loan secular textbooks to parochial school students.
Lemon v. Kurtzman; Early v. Di Censo, ruled against several forms
   of public aid to church schools including reimbursement for teacher salaries, textbooks, and other instructional materials.
Wisconsin v. Yoder, 1972, supports the Amish in their refusal to obey
   compulsory attendance laws.
P.E.A.R.L. v. Nyquist, invalidated tuition grants for parochial school
   pupils, tax benefits, grants for state-mandated services, and grants
   for maintenance of parochial school buildings.
Meek v. Pittenger, 1975, declared as unconstitutional states providing
   nonpublic schools with services such as counseling and testing,
   hearing and speech therapy, and services for exceptional, disadvantaged, and remedial students.

In 1965 Congress passed the Elementary and Secondary Education Act, which authorized huge expenditures for school children,
including parochial and other nonpublic school children. Several
states had already provided aid to nonpublic schools in the form of
textbook loans, and ESEA opened a Pandora's box of new court decisions relating to the rights of states or school districts to provide aid
to nonpublic schools for textbooks and other supplies. Court decisions
upheld the right of public funds to be used for textbooks for nonpublic
schools based on the premise that textbook loans served a secular function in parochial schools.

Four areas of aid seem to have passed the constitutional test in the
courts. They are the loaning of secular textbooks to nonpublic schools;
the providing of transportation for nonpublic school students by states
and school districts; the providing of auxiliary services such as speech,
hearing, and psychological diagnostic services for nonpublic students
if they meet the tripartite test of purpose, effect, and excessive government entanglement; and shared time where parochial and public

school students take "value free" courses such as mathematics and language arts in both parochial and public school buildings.

ESEA, Title I, has opened the door for public special education services to be provided for nonpublic school children by mandating that public schools provide such services. Often, districts have provided services for speech and hearing in special vans and other mobile units which park at the front doors of nonpublic schools. The "skating around" the issue of church-state relationships such as the liberal interpretation of ESEA guidelines and of court decisions has opened the door to many services for nonpublic school students that they would not ordinarily have enjoyed.

Religion in Schools

Bible reading and prayer in schools have received constant attention with calls each year for a constitutional amendment allowing such practices. The 1948 McCollum decision has stood up over the years as the U. S. Supreme Court consistently rejects appeals that would allow religious exercises in schools. At the same time that religious exercises have been banned in schools, the right of students to miss school for religious holidays has been upheld.

Although teachers cannot teach religion, they can teach about religion. The distinction between the two is not always evident, but the courts have upheld the right of schools to offer courses in religious studies if done so with a historical approach and if equal treatment is given all religions.

In a culturally diverse country such as the United States local tradition has guided school boards and administrators in allowing relationships between the schools and local churches. There are no national standards relating to what should be taught solely by the schools, the church, or by parents. Often, board members may find a homogeneous community, that has long been engaged in practices that reflect a single set of values, torn apart when a certain student or parent challenges those practices in court.

Board members must not only be aware of court decisions affecting church-school relationships and their impact on curricular decisions, but also know something of the values and standards of the community served by their school. The modern board member can expect to be caught in controversies relating to church-state issues and may well be a participant in court suits before his or her career is over.

We must not forget that there are nonpublic schools which serve school children. Indeed, there are almost 18,000 private schools in the

United States enrolling almost five million students or approximately 10 percent of all students enrolled in this country. Of the nonpublic schools, 85 percent are church-related—61 percent are Catholic and 9 percent Lutheran.

LAW AND THE CURRICULUM

A major force in the 1980s has been the efforts of the American Bar Association, local bar groups, law enforcement officials, and judicial officers to implement law-related education in our schools. Today every state has some sort of law-related education going on in its schools, ranging from one course at the high school level to well-developed programs funded by government and private sources. Many states have legislated that a law curriculum be implemented at all levels of schooling. Developing a respect for the law is the major purpose of law education in the schools.

The fact that youth between the ages of ten and eighteen account for almost one-half of the serious crimes in this country is reason enough for the inclusion of the study of law in the K–12 curriculum. Discipline problems, the breakdown of the family structure, and drug-related problems have increased youth contacts with the law.

Law education programs in schools have continued to grow and flourish thanks to the support they have received from members of the judiciary, law enforcement officials, and the business community. Law education, unlike sex education, has received almost total support from the public.

School boards have found increased parental support of the school program when law-related studies have been introduced in schools. The modern board member should be knowledgeable about legislation relating to law education and be able to participate in the drafting of a policy to include such a program in schools.

CORPORATE INFLUENCE ON THE CURRICULUM

In many states consumer or economic education has been mandated for school children. Various interest groups including Chambers of Commerce, consumer groups, and business and industry leaders have been responsible for the campaign to educate children about business and commerce. Although the goals of all of those groups are to produce knowledgeable and healthy consumers and producers, some educational leaders see more indoctrination than education occurring—especially when corporations and trade associations shower classrooms with educational materials that link their products and names with all that is good, true, and beautiful.

RESTORING CONFIDENCE IN SCHOOLS

In spite of the many special-interest groups focusing on schools, school reform has been disappointing. The national curriculum projects in science and mathematics and attempts at socially integrating all students have produced shallow results. Interest groups today, whether formal groups such as teachers unions or groups organized around special causes, many times represent only narrow interests.

Parents are often apathetic about what goes on in schools. They are aroused only when special-interest groups raise issues that may affect their children. Armed with little information about an issue except what is provided them by the interest group, such parents are easily led and may appear before the board as well organized and deeply interested in an issue.

Youth today, according to a recent survey by the *Wall Street Journal*, are less inspired by social issues than students of the past. High school students of the 1960s and 70s were considered a special-interest group with considerable clout. The Tinker case, establishing students' rights of protest in 1969, and other court decisions were evidence of students exerting pressure as a group to change the educational system. By 1981, however, students expressed a greater concern with material than with social goals. The mood of the 80s with high school students is one of pragmatism. Students living the good life want to maintain or exceed their present style of living. Career choices are those that will lead toward the highest income.

Faced with apathetic parents, students less inspired by social issues, interest groups making unprecedented demands of schools, and schools turned abruptly from a growth industry to a declining one, public schools are heading into a difficult era. The public has discovered, contrary to American myth, that the schools cannot accomplish every function asked of them.

Changing social/economic conditions in the 1980s clearly demand a new administrative approach in dealing with the many needs of our schools. School improvement will depend upon administrative leaders organizing available resources in a manner that will produce maximum learning for all students.

Rather than viewing special-interest groups as enemies with alien goals, boards should reach out to these groups and form a partnership with them that will establish common priorities and collaboration in attaining common goals.

The school and community should cooperatively ascertain the educational needs of the community. Administrators need to develop a systematic method of assessing community needs and opinions on public education matters. Surveys, questionnaires, and public meetings can be used to solicit views from parents and other citizens. Some school districts have used newspapers to solicit ideas and even "grade" the school system on the job it is doing. Bridges should be established with minority groups. Administrators can get invited to meetings of local ethnic and racial groups. Cultural programs can be offered at school and bilingual publications can be used.

The schools need continuously to interpret the school program and the activities of the school to the community. The school administrator and his teachers should set up direct communication links with parents and the community. Successful techniques include using a school and district newsletter, public meetings, call-in radio shows, open-house meetings at schools, and visits to community centers.

Formal and informal advising committees should be developed to find out what the community expects of the schools. It is important in all sessions with parent and community groups that no educational jargon be used. Also meetings should be scheduled at times convenient to persons in the community.

The board member should know who the formal and informal interest groups are in the community. Since basic educational policy is not always determined by the interaction between official power-holders and representatives of competing formal interest groups, the administrator should know who the "power structure" is in the community. Power leaders, "movers and shakers," rarely get involved directly as members of interest groups or elected officials yet wield great influence in educational matters. Knowing who these persons are and how to reach them may be a critical professional skill for the modern school administrator.

Boards should organize parent and community volunteer programs in the schools. The more adults feel they are a part of the schools, the less likely they will be to criticize them.

The National Coalition for Parent Involvement in Education (NCPIE) is an alliance of major educational associations that has as its major goal the improvement of children's education by promoting practices that increase the involvement of parents and other citizens in the educational process as it occurs in the public schools, home, and community.

NCPIE published an annotated bibliography in 1981 that includes thirty-five studies, each of which indicates that parent involvement in schools improved student achievement.

Communicating with Students

Boards and school administrators must become more active in dealing with students. Principals and other administrators should spend time on school campuses talking with students. In addition, regular "rap sessions" should be scheduled with students.

Boards often acknowledge student achievement and performance at board meetings. Scholarship winners, athletic teams, musical groups, and student government groups are often recognized by special board resolutions. But what of the students who may not fit those categories? How can boards communicate with those students? How can boards communicate with all students?

Perhaps the best method of communicating is to set in motion regular meetings with students not only in the regular board room but at school sites during the school day. Forums, discussions, appearances at assemblies, and simply having lunch with students at schools are ways of interacting with them. Other methods of communicating include newsletters to students (we seem always to aim newsletters to parents) and working through groups like the Student Council. Surveys can also go out to students to elicit their views and ideas on major issues facing the board.

Special-interest groups representing every cause known to mankind will make an appearance before your board during your term in office. Since you represent all of the children of all of the people, you cannot allow yourself to become a captive of any one group. In our democratic society everyone has a right to be heard. A good board will have policies that will allow for direct, meaningful, and orderly communication with all persons and interest groups.

CHAPTER 9

Making a Difference —
Improving School Systems

Most board members are appointed or elected to office with the idea that they will seek to improve the school system they will represent. Simply wanting to improve the school system is not enough. The board member must know about the evaluation process, be able to develop standards by which to measure school programs, be knowledgeable about methods of improving administrator and teacher performance, know about organizational structures and how to improve organizations, be able to set in motion a needs assessment process, and, finally, know how to use information from a needs assessment to develop a long-range comprehensive program for school improvement. In this chapter ways of improving your school system will be discussed so that you can indeed *make a difference.*

IMPROVING THE INSTRUCTIONAL
PROGRAM

In any school system decisions have to be made daily on how and when children will learn. Based on these decisions, learning materials and activities are generated to assist that learning.

In today's schools the instructional program must serve a variety of learners including the handicapped. The board and superintendent are responsible for carrying out a broad program, but it is the curriculum workers in the district who must implement the kinds of instructional programs appropriate for all learners.

Instructional programs are not just the result of happenstance. They have their geneses in societal expectations, appropriate knowledge to be mastered, and the needs of learners.

Boards are responsible for seeing that a balanced instructional program based on identified needs of students, knowledge to be learned, and societal needs and expectations is made available to all students in the school district. The superintendent is charged with selecting instructional leaders with the skills needed to accomplish that task.

The skills needed by today's instructional leaders are many. They include conducting a needs assessment, designing a program improvement plan, and conducting program evaluation. Board members should be familiar with all three of these skill areas because they represent critical points in improving the instructional program.

Conducting a Needs Assessment

Needs assessment is a technique used to match current status with desired goals. The discrepancies between stated goals and present conditions become identified needs. The instructional leader must choose the right source for input data. Students, parents, teachers, administrators, and community persons all may be sources of data. The right kinds of questions must be asked and suitable questionnaires be developed to carry out the needs-assessment process. All curricular and instructional planning should be preceded by a needs assessment. It must be noted that the professional administrator is not lost in the process of carrying out a needs assessment. The needs-assessment data are not always value-free and cannot automatically replace the judgment of a competent administrator.

The needs-assessment framework, or outline, is flexible to the degree that the questions asked in the assessment should match the mandate for change or improvement. A typical needs-assessment approach to inform school officials would include the following:

1. General Information
    a. Location of school district
    b. Demographic characteristics of immediate area
    c. Natural resources of region
    d. Commercial–industrial data
    e. Income levels of area residents
    f. Special socioeconomic considerations
2. General Population Characteristics
    a. Population growth patterns

   b. Age, race of population
   c. Educational levels
   d. Projected population
3. School Population Characteristics (Ages 3–19)
   a. School enrollment by grade level
   b. Birth rate trends in school district
   c. In-migration, out-migration patterns
   d. Race/sex/religious composition of school district
   e. Years of school completed by persons over 25 years of age
   f. Studies of school dropouts
4. Programs and Course Offerings in District
   a. Organization of school programs
   b. Programs' concept and rationale
   c. Course offerings
   d. Special program needs
5. Professional Staff
   a. Training and experience
   b. Awareness of trends and developments
   c. Attitudes toward change
6. Instructional Patterns and Strategies
   a. Philosophical focus of instructional program
   b. Observational and perceptual instructional data
   c. Assessment of instructional strategies in use
   d. Instructional materials in use
   e. Decision-making and planning processes
   f. Grouping for instruction
   g. Classroom management techniques
   h. Grading and placement of pupils
   i. Student independence
   j. Evaluation of instructional effectiveness
7. Student data
   a. Student experiences
   b. Student self-esteem
   c. Student achievement
8. Facilities
   a. Assessment of existing facilities and sites
   b. Special facilities
   c. Utilization of facilities
   d. Projected facility needs
9. Summary of Data

The utility of the needs assessment is that it measures the relative progress of a school toward its goals rather than some absolute standards. Needs assessments generally involve the faculty and staff in the gathering and analysis of data, thereby providing a medium for the principal or superintendent in establishing professional communication. Needs assessments can also be used, at a later date, as a baseline for evaluation of program development.

The needs-assessment process should precede any program change. If a proposal for program change comes to the board before a needs assessment has been conducted, the board should reject the proposal.

Program Development Plan

School planning is a critical area that often fails to incorporate the essential purpose of the institution. To be effective, school planning must be both purposeful and comprehensive. Planned change, reflected by the school development plan, is the link between conceptual systems and areas of applied problems.

For the school leader, the development of a comprehensive program development plan is the culminating activity after a series of events. Such a plan comes only after goals and philosophy have been clarified. The plan should allow the conducting of a broad-based needs assessment. It should be built upon the identification of major program concepts that will guide planning. From these prerequisites come a program of action and the resources required to implement the components.

The result of a formal program development plan is an overall management system that does the following:

Selecting instructional programs requires skills and knowledge on the part of school leaders. The established criteria that can be used in selecting instructional programs are as follows:

The first consideration in the selection of instructional programs has to be the purposes for which the instructional program is being planned. Whether it is the objectives stated for a particular lesson in a classroom, or the general educational goals for a school or district, planning occurs on the basis of the purposes defined. As stated early in this text, the authors believe good instructional programs must adequately reflect the aims of the school or agency from which they come. At the school level, the faculty, students, and parents need to define comprehensive educational goals, and all curriculum opportunities offered at the school should be planned with reference to one or more of those goals.

Second, a good instructional program must provide for continuity of learning experiences. Students should progress on the basis of their achievement, not on the basis of how much time they have spent in the program. Instructional programs that are planned over several years lend themselves to better vertical progress. Continuity of learning experiences with a program dictates that a relationship between disciplines be established. Core or interdisciplinary programs allow students to see purpose and meaning in their total instructional program.

Third, all principles of learning need to be drawn upon in selecting an instructional program. Programs that rely solely on operant conditioning as a psychological base for teaching neglect the important theories of Arthur Combs, Jean Piaget, and others. All those associated in education understand the difficulty of putting psychological principles into practice. A careful analysis of new programs can reveal the psychological bases of those programs.

Fourth, programs selected should make maximum provision for the development of each learner. Any program selected should include a wide range of opportunities for individuals of varying abilities, interests, and needs. Each child is characterized by his or her own pattern of development. Youngsters are curious, explorative, and interested in many things. An instructional program must promote individual development rather than making students conform to a hypothetical standard.

Fifth, an instructional program must provide for clear focus. Whether a program is organized around separate subjects such as history or science, or around related subjects such as social studies, it is important that the one selecting the program know which dimensions to pursue, which relationships of facts and ideas should stand out, and which should be submerged. The problem for those who are reviewing programs is to decide which element of the program is the center of organization. Instructional programs may be organized around life problems, content topics, interests, or experiences. In selecting instructional programs, however, the organizing focus must also be examined to see which topics are emphasized, which details are relevant, and which relationships are significant.

And finally, a good instructional program should be well planned and must include a built-in process for evaluation. Steps need to be defined that would include a periodic assessment of the success of the program and a continuous process for reviewing and updating it.

Evaluating School Programs

Many facets of a school program can be evaluated, including its objectives, its scope, the achievement of students, quality of teaching, and equipment and materials used. Informal evaluations may be accomplished by simply talking to students, teachers, and parents about the program or through written opinion surveys. Formal evaluations may include examining students' achievement, checking whether stated objectives were met, or through the use of other criteria such as number of students gaining employment or number of students exceeding national norms on college entrance tests.

Purposes of Evaluation

The general purpose of evaluation is to improve the educational program by facilitating judgments about its effectiveness based on evidence. Specific purposes include:

1. To make explicit the rationale of the instructional program as a basis for deciding which aspects of the program should be evaluated for effectiveness and what types of data should be gathered.
2. To collect data upon which judgments about effectiveness can be formulated.
3. To analyze data and draw conclusions.
4. To make decisions that are based on the data.
5. To implement the decisions to improve the instructional program.

There are many sources of data for evaluating an instructional program. Figure 9.1 illustrates some of these sources.

Figure 9.1   Sources of Data for Evaluating an Instructional Program

1. *Background of the curriculum change*
   Where did the impetus come from for change?
   Who spearheaded the effort?
   When did it get underway?
   What specific events or activities were involved?
2. *Process of the curriculum change*
   Who was involved?
   How many participated?
   Who coordinated the efforts?
   Who sponsored the efforts?
   How long a period of time was involved?
   What kinds of activities did participants engage in?
3. *Nature of the curriculum change*
   What are the objectives of the new curriculum?
   What was changed?
   Who decided what changes should be made?

What criteria were employed in deciding to make the changes?
What kind of learning theory underlies the changes?
4. *Results of the change*
How widespread is change today?
What is the present direction of the change today?
How is the change being evaluated?
What plans are presently available regarding the future of the change?
5. *What research has been done on the change* (Study of studies: include abstracts)
How much research has been done?
Where was the research done?
Who did the research?
How available and how trustworthy are the data?
What does the research show?
What problems have been identified in the research thus far?
What conclusions are apparent from the research done?

Figure 9.2 provides the board member with even more questions that might be asked before curriculum decisions are made.

Figure 9.2 How Many of These Questions Were Answered *Before* You Made Your Last Curriculum Decision?

- Should you build your *own* curriculum or adopt one that's already well developed?
- Are learner behaviors specified in terms of instructional objectives?
- How do you define *goals* and *objectives*?
- Which is the more *economical*—your current curriculum or one of the new instructional systems?
- Will *replacement* and equipment costs make adoption prohibitive?
- Do the new instructional materials really fit your students' *needs*?
- Do the teaching methods include *discovery* or inquiry?
- Are the salesman's *claims* completely accurate?
- Can the new materials be used with *"disadvantaged"* children?
- What about *process* versus content?
- What about *personnel*, time, and space?
- Will special kinds of multimedia *hardware* be needed?
- Should teachers use only a *textbook*?
- Will the new elementary curriculum "match" your secondary program?
- Will the new curriculum be *flexible* enough for your teachers' individual styles?
- How do the alternative models compare in terms of cost?
- Do local *budget* restrictions eliminate any consideration of certain curricula?
- What *advertising* claims can be refuted after using one of these units?

- How much *evaluation* time can your staff save by using an information unit?
- Is the prospective new program really based on *well-researched* learning theories?
- Are methods for *individualizing* provided?
- What about *individual* differences, levels of abilities, readability, etc.?
- How was *content* selected and how is it organized?
- What are the anticipated *cognitive*, affective, or psychomotor outcomes?
- What kind of staff *training* will be necessary?

What about curriculum change? Who is involved in making curriculum changes? Is it one administrator or a broadly based group of teachers and administrators?

Key Definitions in the Evaluation Process

Board members will hear many evaluation terms used in presentations before the board. The following terms will prove useful to members of the board:

content validity	The degree to which a measuring device is judged to be appropriate for its purpose; for example, the degree to which it is congruent with a set of instructional objectives.
correlation	The tendency for corresponding observations in two or more series to have similar positions.
criterion-referenced measurement	Measurement designed to assess an individual's status with respect to a particular criterion or standard of performance, irrespective of the relationship of his performance to that of others.
criterion validity	Characteristically, the degree to which a particular measure, such as a test of intellectual ability, correlates with an external criterion such as subsequent scholastic performance in college.
distractors	These are the alternatives or wrong answers in a multiple-choice or comparable test item.
formative evaluation	The evaluation of an instructional program before it is finally completed; that is, the attempt to evaluate a program in order to improve it.

item analysis	Any one of several methods used in revisng a test to determine how well a given item discriminates among individuals or different degrees of ability or among individuals differing in some other characteristic.
item sampling	The procedure of administering different forms of a test (characteristically, shorter forms) to different individuals, thereby reducing the time required for testing.
norm-referenced measurement	Measurement designed to assess an individual's standing with respect to other individuals on the same measuring device.
percentile (centile)	The point in distribution of scores below which a certain proportion of the scores fall. For example, a student scoring at the seventieth percentile on a test would have exceeded the scores of 70 percent of those taking the test.
reliability	The accuracy with which a measuring device measures something; the degree to which a test measures consistently whatever it measures.
standardized test	A test for which content has been selected and checked empirically, for which norms have been established, for which uniform methods of administering and scoring have been developed, and which may be scored with a relatively high degree of objectivity.
summative evaluation	The final evaluation of a program in which the results of the program are characteristically compared with results of comparable programs in order for selection to be made among competing instructional programs.
validity	The extent to which a test or other measuring instrument fulfills the purpose for which it is used.

The terms presented in Figure 9.3 also will prove useful to members of the board.

Figure 9.3 The Evaluation Process

PRE-EVALUATION

Educational Goals	These are statements of the ultimate aims of the educational process and describe conditions as they should be at the end of any portion of the pupil's educational experience. These statements will necessarily be general, lumping together large segments of pupil behavior into generally accepted categories.
Present Conditions	This description of conditions as they exist prior to any particular portion of the pupil's educational experience should be couched in the same terms as the EDUCATIONAL GOALS so that the two are directly comparable.

EVALUATION

Educational Need	"Evaluation" as such begins when an educational need is identified and defined. The term "educational need" refers to some deficiency, gap in required competency, or absence of desired behavior revealed by the comparison of PRESENT CONDITIONS with EDUCATIONAL GOALS. In some models this is referred to as the "problem."
Purpose	The purpose (sometimes called "goal") is based upon the need and states the nature of the change that will be necessary to satisfy the educational need.
General Objective (one or more for each purpose)	General objectives derive from the PURPOSE and state more specifically the desired changes which are considered to be directly related to achievement of the PURPOSE. The general objective defines a behavioral area of concern and at least implies the specific behaviors to be altered.
Specific/Behavioral Objectives (one or more for each general objective)	These follow directly from the GENERAL OBJECTIVE and precisely define the behaviors to be altered. The statement should define the anticipated outcome of a given process and should be stated in terms of observable behaviors. It should also point directly to the method by which the behavior will be measured and the criteria by which success or failure will be determined.
Baseline Data (one or more for each SPECIFIC OBJECTIVE)	Baseline data are derived from measures of the specified behavior *prior* to the beginning of any attempt to alter that behavior. These data describe in precise terms the PRESENT SITUATION and should substantiate at least one aspect of the EDUCATIONAL NEED. That is, they should indicate the extent of the deficiency, the magnitude of the gap in required competency, or the absence of the desired behavior.
Activity or Treatment	This statement should spell out the activities to be undertaken in an effort to alter the behavior defined in the SPECIFIC OBJECTIVE. Ideally, the rationale underlying the activity and relating it to the desired changes should also be given here.
Comparison Data (one for each BASELINE DATA)	The measures from which the comparison data are derived should be the same as or directly comparable to the measures upon which BASELINE DATA were established.
Analysis (one for each pair of BASELINE DATA and COMPARISON DATA)	This statement should spell out in detail the manipulations (e.g., graphic, arithmetic, statistical, etc.) that will be used in the interpretation of the data. There should be enough—and only enough—information to enable any other knowledgeable evaluator to draw comparable data and subject them to the same analysis.

POST-EVALUATION

Conclusions   The conclusions based upon the analysis will reflect (1) whether or not the activity was effective in
accomplishing the SPECIFIC OBJECTIVE and (2)
the extent to which the accomplishment of that objective contributed to the alleviation of the EDUCA-
TIONAL NEED.

---

*Is there a formal process for evaluating school systems in the dis-
trict? Does the board receive regular information about the effectiveness of school programs?*

ORGANIZATIONAL IMPROVEMENT

Organizational Structure

The concern with organizational structure and improvement in schools
and school districts has led to studies of school structures and various
plans for organizational improvement. Borrowing heavily on research
from business and industry, educational leaders have studied all aspects of scientific management of schools. Some of the concepts borrowed from business and industry include administrative efficiency,
specialization and standardization of work, and increased productivity from efficiency of operation.

As retrenchment continues in public education, the whole area of
scientific management of schools becomes more important. How to
make organizations "leaner" and more efficient will occupy much of
the time of school leaders in the 1980s.

Systems Theory

By the early 1970s the myriad of influencing variables in schools, as
represented by the various organizational processes, found focus in
general systems theory. Systems theory, a product of the physical sciences, provided the concept of interdependence in organizations and
explained why changes in one part of an organization could affect
other parts or the whole of the organization.

Organizational Development

Perhaps the high watermark in the study of organization processes
is the concept of Organization Development (O.D.), a planned and sus-
tained effort to apply behavioral science for system improvement.

The process of Organization Development consists of data gathering, organizational diagnosis, and action intervention. The fulfillment of the O.D. program is, in a real sense, changing the way a school works. There are three elements of organization (processes) that appear important for changes: the roles people play, the goals of the organization, and the operational procedures in place.

Organizational Relationships

While the study of organization structure and process has proved a convenient lens for viewing administration, another focus has been the relationship of persons within organizations. Approached from a number of variables such as communication, individual needs, morale, motivation, and small group work, the study of organizational relationships has enriched the study of administration and provided some clues about why organizations function.

It was, in fact, a study of efficiency that ushered in the human relations area of organizational analysis. At the Hawthorne plant of Western Electric Company during the 1920s researchers were attempting to determine the relationship between illumination and production. The chief investigator, F.J. Roethlisberger, was surprised to find that production increased with every change in the experimental condition; whether illumination was increased or decreased, productivity went up. A mysterious force, later labeled the "Hawthorne Effect," was noted and eventually determined to be a human attitudinal factor.

The school, as any other organization, functions through line and staff relationships. By becoming too bureaucratic, a school system can also become unresponsive. Periodic studies of district and school organizations should be undertaken to maximize individual and group effectiveness.

Organization Structure and the Individual

The research into the functioning of organizations in the United States has been comprehensive and continues today. Balancing the needs of the organization with the needs of the individual has been the subject of much study over the years. We do know that for organizations to function effectively, there has to be a congruence between the needs of healthy individuals and the demands of formal organizations. As pressures on schools continue because of shrinking resources, school leaders will need to understand better how school organizations work. They will also need to know how to make them work more efficiently.

IMPROVING ADMINISTRATIVE PERFORMANCE

Since school boards must rely on school administrators to implement policies, there is much concern about the quality of administrative leadership. Improving administrative performance from the superintendent to the school-level administrator has become a priority item in most school districts in the country.

Much of the research and writing in recent years has focused on the administrator as a "manager." Under pressure from state legislatures and state departments of education to make schools more efficient, school leaders have turned to business to find ways of training school personnel for leadership positions. Because of declining resources and enrollment in most areas, principals are being called on to manage resources with the greatest possible expertise.

Many of the management tools mentioned earlier such as MBO, PERT, and PPBS are being utilized at the school level. School principals can use these management tools effectively to maximize the attainment of goals set for the school. These tools facilitate planning and decision making about the utilization of allocated resources.

Budgeting techniques are especially important to the school principal. Because school costs have been rising faster than the growth of the economy, every dollar spent or saved is important. Many school costs are "fixed," that is, they are tied to certain classifications such as teacher salary schedules. Other costs vary and it is those variable costs that principals must efficiently control.

One management tool used effectively in schools is zero-based budgeting. Zero-based budgeting forces the administrator to prepare a new budget each year. A school program is subject to zero-based budgeting when there is a resource/cost-effective relationship. Cost effectiveness is translated into dollars by analyzing stated program objectives with the resource costs needed to attain them. Zero-based budgeting forces a review of each school program by requiring that all programs be assessed and their costs justified each year.

In addition to budget preparation, the principal is responsible for managing staff, school program, plant, resources, student attendance, and student transportation. Staff management responsibilities include making decisions and keeping records regarding absences, benefits, and travel. Principals have to make sure teachers and support staff are on duty and performing required tasks. Teacher absenteeism has become a major problem in many school districts. To reduce teacher absences, special incentives have been offered such as paying teachers for unused sick days. School administrators are spending countless hours finding substitutes and covering classes on short notice.

Unauthorized student absences appear to be increasing in many districts. Absenteeism is an administrative problem second only to student discipline, especially in urban schools. Since average daily attendance (ADA) is used to calculate distribution of funds, it is no wonder that school principals are under constant pressure to keep attendance rates up.

Student transportation is a district responsibility, but the school principal must provide information on student routes, deal with bus discipline problems, and manage the pickup and delivery of students at the school site. Increased bussing for school integration and consolidation of schools have contributed to increased demands upon the principal's time.

Managing the school plant is another task of the school principal. High fuel and maintenance costs have resulted in a push to conserve energy and reduce expenditures for repairs. Although principals would rather deal with the instructional program than broken window panes, because of increased vandalism over the past decade, they find themselves too often dealing with the latter. A number of procedures have been suggested for keeping down vandalism, such as fences erected around the building, regular police patrol after school hours, changing school locks periodically, security checklists by custodians and other staff, evening use of facilities by community groups, and immediate repair of vandal damage.

Although many would see school principals as simply business managers, the principal is much more. He or she is the instructional leader of the school. Instructional leadership cannot be delegated to others. It can be shared with teachers, assistants, and department leaders or team leaders. The effective school principal, then, must process the knowledge and skills necessary to carry out the school's instructional program and assume an active leadership role in instructional improvement. (See Figure 9.4)

Figure 9.4   Skills and Competencies for Administrators

Political Skills	Understanding change in schools
	Sensitivity to decision boundaries
	Knowledge of new budget language
	Awareness of community power structures

Instructional Skills	Conducting program evaluation
	Implementing behavior management systems
	Organizing an inservice plan
	Recruiting and evaluating teachers
	Designing a program development plan
	Conducting a needs assessment
Interpersonal Skills	Managing committee meetings
	Small group and one-to-one conferencing
	Practicing active listening
	Developing learning climates
	Conducting public relations
Technical Skills	Transportation and student safety
	Scheduling and registration procedures
	Preparation of a budget
	Maintenance of records
	Physical plant management
	Office management

CHANGE IN SCHOOL ENVIRONMENTS

Educators have spent over twenty years in the intensive study of change in school settings only to be reduced to thoughtful uncertainty. It seems "the more things change, the more they remain the same." Still, it is important for the new board member to have some understanding of the change process if only to avoid the "china shop syndrome."

Several key lessons have been learned that are of value to the new board member. First, change occurs in stages and different members of a school faculty participate in different stages. As a rule, about 15 percent will initially try an idea and another 35 percent will follow. It is best to place the effort to change with these persons and not the 50 percent trailing reluctantly. Second, demonstration of change is better than talk about change. Third, involvement in change and knowing about change is the result of creative "stealing" rather than invention. To borrow an idea is also faster than to produce an original one, and time is a scarce resource in school work.

In the 1980s and beyond, change will probably not be as frequent as in the past, and most change will be refinement rather than an installation of new ideas or practices. It will be to the new administrators' advantage to slow change down so that error can be recognized prior to the development of major problems. With fewer resources, mistakes will loom larger in the next two decades in schools. Figure 9.5 is presented for the reader's study and use in determining the probability of successful change in schools.

Figure 9.5   Educational Innovations Probability Chart

Educational Innovations Probability Chart

Higher Risk ← → *Lower Risk*

	Higher Risk				Lower Risk
Source of Innovation	Superimposed from outside	Outside agent brought in	Developed internally with aid	External idea modified	Locally conceived, developed, implemented
Impact of Innovation	Challenges sacrosanct beliefs	Calls for major value shifts	Requires substantial change	Modifies existing values or programs	Does not substantially alter existing values, beliefs or programs
Official Support	Official leaders active opposition	Officials on record as opposing	Officials uncommitted	Officials voice support of change	Enthusiastically supported by the official leaders
Planning of Innovation	Completely external	Most planning external	Planning processes balanced	Most of planning done locally	All planning for change done on local site
Means of Adoption	By superiors	By local leaders	By Reps	By most of the clients	By group consensus
History of Change	History of failures	No accurate records	Some success with innovation	A history of successful innovations	Known as school where things regularly succeed
Possibility of Revision	No turning back	Final evaluation before committee	Periodic evaluations	Possible to abandon at conclusion	Possible to abort the effort at any time

Role of Teachers	Largely bypassed	Minor role	Regular role in implementing	Heavy role in implementation	Primary actor in the classroom effort
Teacher Expectation	Fatalistic	Feel little chance	Willing to give a try	Confident of success	Wildly enthusiastic about chance of success
Work Load Measure	Substantially increased	Heavier but rewarding	Slightly increased	Unchanged	Work load lessened by the innovation
Threat Measure	Definitely threatens some clients	Probably threatening to some	Mild threat resulting from the change	Very remote threat to some	Does not threaten the security or autonomy
Community Factor	Hostile to innovations	Suspicious and uninformed	Indifferent	Ready for a change	Wholeheartedly supports the school

Shade the response in each category which most accurately reflects the condition surrounding the implementation of the school. If the "profile" of your school is predominately in the high risk side of the matrix, substantial work must be done to prepare your school for change.

IMPROVING TEACHER PERFORMANCE

As with improvement of administrator performance, boards do not have a direct hand in the improvement of teacher performance. However, the board does set policies for inservice training programs, provide budgets for teacher evaluation and improvement, and participates in collaborative programs with universities and teacher education centers. Because teachers are the professionals closest to learners, school boards have a special obligation to insure that the most competent teachers be hired. The board also has an obligation to provide resources so that teachers can continually update skills and teaching practices. Finally, the board has an important obligation to see that effective methods of teacher evaluation are used.

Most districts negotiate the types of evaluative instruments and procedures to be used with teacher groups. One result of such negotiation has been the adopting of such innocuous instruments that little valuable data about teacher performance are gathered. Most certainly, where such a situation exists, the principal must supplement his or her data with hard data gathered from other sources. One valuable source is direct observation of staff in performance of duties. Other sources of hard data include student achievement, absenteeism on the part of teachers and students, and student and parent interviews.

A number of school districts have developed assessment centers to screen candidates for teaching and administrative positions. The assessment centers utilize a number of techniques including: an analysis of college transcripts, formal interviews, completion of essay tests on educational topics, tests of verbal and quantitative ability, and personality tests. Although the assessment centers are organized to insure that teachers and administrators meet minimum standards, the completion of assessment center activities often "screens out" marginal candidates.

Misconduct by teachers and administrators can lead to revocation of teaching certificates. Such loss of certificate leads to dismissal. Misconduct by teachers or administrators with students, e.g., sexual misconduct, assault, falsification of reports, and theft, are the major causes for revocation of certificates.

Principals represent the leadership group most responsible for selection and evaluation of school personnel. In an era of accountability and liability, today's principal must be knowledgeable and skilled in selecting and evaluating the teaching and support personnel needed to carry out the school program.

Ask to look at instruments used to evaluate teachers in the district. Insist that the board adopt a policy that includes a strong evaluation system and an assistance program for all teaching and administrative personnel.

IMPROVING BOARD AND SUPERINTENDENT RELATIONS

One can hardly leave the subject of change in the settings in which schools operate without examining changes in school boards. In recent years minorities have found voices and articulated demands to boards, and their leaders have become board members. Increasing numbers of women are being elected to school boards. Women have emerged as highly skilled board members who can make tough decisions under fire.

The classic view of local school boards was that of policymakers who pretty well determined the direction of schools. Today boards find themselves in a decreasing role as policymaker and engaged more in mediating the way policy is being applied to the local school system from outside agencies such as the courts and legislative bodies.

Of increasing concern is the method of selecting board members and superintendents. The politicizing of both groups (much of which was brought on by active teacher unions) has led to the need for finding new ways to improve the working relationship between the school board and the superintendent.

Whether board members are elected or appointed, they try to respond to a tradition of being nonpolitical in the partisan sense. In fact, the role of the board member is one of the last opportunities to rise above petty politics and to remain apart from political demands—at least that's the way it used to be. Today, as pressure groups converge on boards and controversy tends to be commonplace, board members have become more realistic about a political role.

Today appointed boards often find themselves at odds with an appointed superintendent. Where boards and superintendents are elected, there seems to be even more chance of confrontation. What can we look to in the 1980s as ways to get boards and superintendents to work together for the common good? The following are suggestions:

1. A board and superintendent must communicate not only formally, but informally. A board member and superintendent may not like each other but they can talk about school problems.
2. The error of youth is to believe intelligence is a substitute for experience, while the error of age is to believe experience is a substitute for intelligence. Often experienced board members don't want to listen

to new board members or a new superintendent or new board members and superintendents view "oldtimers" as "dinosaurs."

3. School boards have always considered it worthy to work for the unanimous vote, to establish consensus, and to promote a team atmosphere. Such boards have little precedence for dealing with dissent, controversy, and the hot issues of today. Boards are relatively unskilled as "managers of change and diversity." Boards and superintendents must have inservice training in how to deal with controversy. Listening skills, group dynamics, and group management are but a few of the topics that should be addressed in such inservice sessions.

4. Boards and superintendents today are not really planning for change but simply reacting to the steady hammer-beat of one demand after the other. Becoming proactive rather than reactive will require boards and superintendents to develop long-range comprehensive plans for their school districts. Rather than meeting time after time to deal with trivia, boards and superintendents should concentrate on the long haul rather than the immediate.

5. "Boards make policies and the superintendent implements them." School board members would probably like a dollar for each time they've heard that statement because they would have a lot of dollars in the bank. What amounts to a truism does not mean that either the board or superintendent acts without the input of students, teachers, parents, and other community members. In today's world it is essential that from development of a policy to its implementation involvement should be sought from all persons impacted by that policy.

COMPREHENSIVE PLANNING FOR SCHOOL IMPROVEMENT

The preparation of a comprehensive plan for school development represents the culminating activity of a series of events. Such a plan is developed only after the philosophy and goals of the district have been clarified, student and program needs assessed, program concepts agreed upon, and activities to achieve the above have been delineated. It is at that point that a comprehensive plan can be drawn to manage and evaluate progress toward desired ends.

Comprehensive school plans serve two major functions: they enhance the possibility of involvement by persons from the school and community, and they expedite the completion of planned activities. Comprehensive plans can be thought of as having two basic steps that lead to action. First, goals and objectives that define the educational program of the school district are identified. Such directives are rationalized by supportive data drawn from needs assessments or other similar surveys. Second, a program of action and the resources required to implement the various components are identified.

The result of such comprehensive planning is an overall management system that accomplishes the following:

1. What is to be accomplished is clearly spelled out.
2. Communication among all interested parties, especially between the school and the community, is encouraged.
3. There is a maximum utilization of resources within the school district.
4. Information needed for decision making is coordinated.
5. Problems that might prevent the accomplishment of activities are identified.
6. Progress leading to the accomplishment of the plan is monitored.

A number of management tools such as PPBS, PERT, and MBOs can be utilized in developing comprehensive plans. Educators do not have to be experts in the use of all of these techniques, but a general understanding of them and other tools or systems can facilitate planning.

Your district should have in place a comprehensive plan for school development, and each school should have a plan developed for its purposes. The budget should be tied to the comprehensive plan. The board should review the plan yearly, revising it if needed. Questions you might ask about school plans are included in Figure 9.6.

Figure 9.6 Evaluating Your Comprehensive Plan—Questions to Ask*

1. Was there broad-scale, "real" staff involvement, or was the plan written in isolation by the few and rubber-stamped by the many?
2. Was the planning effort launched with the intention honestly to scrutinize the school's efforts and effectiveness, or was planning done as a part of an annual ritual to meet requirements?
3. Was planning conducted in an atmosphere of teamwork and mutuality of effort and concern, or was there evidence of fear of criticism, anti-parallel development, protectionism, politicking, or perfectionism?
4. Was realistic and practical consideration given to the functions of the school, or did the planners leap to the most obvious, easily measured problem statements?

5. Was effort made to generate a set of real alternative actions, or did the planners fasten rapidly on one approach?
6. In deciding on a course of action, was responsibility assumed by all, or was it delegated to only a few?
7. Was there, in the course of planning, continual checking back and forth to assure logic, consistency, relatedness, and continuity among problem(s), goal(s), action strategy(ies), and resource(s), or did the planners "plow through" an outline ignoring cohesion and continuity?
8. Was your school plan developed for actual change and improvement (where warranted or needed), or is it merely a re-hash of what is now being done, put in a format so that it looks like something new and different will occur?
9. If your plan calls for new programming or other changes, was consideration given to what's already been done, or does your plan call for "add-ons" and new responsibilities on top of everything else?
10. In setting timetables and responsibilities, was consideration given to the regularly recurring events in your school (assemblies, parent meetings, parent conferences, holiday observances, school system testing, etc.), or were events just "plugged in" to complete report requirements?
11. Does the plan contain specific steps to be taken at specified times, or does it just say "the staff will do better"?
12. Was there staff consensus on the strategy in your plan, or was it approved by default?
13. Does the action plan reflect "reality" in your school (Are the tasks truly feasible)? Do you have the resources to do them? Is the staff willing to do them? Are you and the staff willing to live with the changes that will accompany performance of the tasks, or is the plan grandiose and overly optimistic?
14. *Finally*, is your plan a guide or roadmap you can follow in succeeding years, or is it just another routine report?

Source: *From *Planning For School Improvement*, St. Louis Schools, 1982. Used with permission.

PROFESSIONAL ORGANIZATIONS FOR BOARD MEMBERS

The modern board member must keep abreast of new developments in education. One of the best ways is to make use of the services of professional organizations. Among the most useful organizations are those listed below:

National School Boards Association (NSBA)

Located at 1055 Thomas Jefferson Street, NW, Washington, D.C. 20007, the NSBA seeks to upgrade and strengthen the performance of school board members throughout the United States. The association publishes its own journal, *The American School Board Journal*, and provides a variety of services to members. In recent years the organization has sponsored special workshops on timely topics such as collective bargaining, and it regularly holds an annual conference.

Association of School Business Officials (ASBO)

Located at 2424 West Lawrence Avenue, Chicago, Illinois 60625, the ASBO serves noninstructional school administrators and representatives of companies that assist schools. Membership is open to other role groups as well. The ASBO publishes a monthly journal, *School Business Affairs*, and provides a variety of other publications to members. A national conference is held annually for those interested in school business management.

The American Association of School Administrators (AASA)

Located at 1801 North Moore Street, Arlington, Virginia 22209, AASA is basically a superintendents' organization, even though membership is open to other roles such as principals, school board members, and professors of educational administration. Organized in 1865, AASA provides a wide range of services to administrators including conferences, workshops, publications, and support for field research. AASA also operates a National Academy for School Executives (NASE) which provides up-to-date workshops on topics of current interest presented by leading authorities.

National Association of Elementary School Principals (NAESP)

Located at 1801 North Moore Street, Arlington, Virginia 22209, the NAESP is an organization designed to aid elementary school principals in their daily work. Membership is open, however, to other professionals and lay persons interested in the administration of elementary schools. The organization publishes an award-winning magazine, *The National Elementary Principal,* and also sponsors an annual convention, various workshops, and a field services division. Professional liability insurance is available to members.

National Middle School Association (NMSA)

Located at Post Office Box 968, Fairborn, Ohio, the National Middle School Association is a recently formed organization (1972) that serves educators interested in the intermediate grades. The NMSA is not an administrators' organization exclusively, being open to all persons on an individual membership basis, but has proven a very useful resource for principals and superintendents seeking assistance in program development at this level. The organization coordinates about twenty-five states units or "leagues of schools" and sponsors an annual conference and workshops.

National Association of Secondary School Principals (NASSP)

Located at 1904 Association Drive, Reston, Virginia 22091, the NASSP is an organization for secondary school principals and various other administrative personnel. NASSP sponsors a wide range of activities for its members including workshops, hot-line services, insurance, travel opportunities, and legal counsel. It also publishes a widely read *NASSP Bulletin* and provides programs through the National Institutes for Secondary School Administrators (NISSA).

Association for Supervision and Curriculum Development (ASCD)

Located at 225 North Washington Street, Alexandria, Virginia 22314, ASCD is a curriculum-oriented organization that serves teachers, supervisors, and administrators through broad-based programming. In addition to publishing its journal, *Educational Leadership*, ASCD promotes inservice opportunities for educators through its National Curriculum Study Institutes (NCSI) which feature authorities on various subjects related to curriculum development and supervision. Through its comprehensive membership, the association also provides a yearbook, monographs on timely topics, and a quarterly newsletter.

Phi Delta Kappa (PDK)

Located at Eighth and Union, Box 789, Bloomington, Indiana 47401, Phi Delta Kappa is a professional fraternity open to men and women in education. This unique organization sponsors local chapters throughout the United States and publishes the most widely read journal in education, the *Phi Delta Kappan*. PDK also is involved in sponsoring limited research projects through its chapters and timely monographs through its Reavis Reading Rooms program.

MAKING A DIFFERENCE

Everyone knows the bad news about school improvement. Resources for school improvement are becoming scarcer these days. Even though we know changes must be made in our school programs, interest in change is not great, and the faith in the possibility of improving school programs is not strong. What can school leaders do under these conditions to seek improvements in school systems—to really make a difference?

There are ways of making a difference in school systems in spite of the fact that many attempts haven't really worked. We know that even though some attempts to improve schools have been unsuccessful, a large number of individual schools have changed for the better. We also know that strategies do exist for improving schools.

Boards and the superintendent can set the tone for high expectations and achievement, and principals and other school leaders can carry that attitude to the school level. Boards can insist on effective administration by school principals. Figure 9.7 provides the board member with useful questions for reviewing administrative leadership in a school.

Figure 9.7 Questions Useful in Review of Administrative Leadership of a School

Administrative

1. How are policy, teacher assignment, discipline methods, and other decisions made?
2. What are administrative attitudes toward students? How do they perceive the relative "power" (respect factor)?
3. What is the degree of support of teachers, and by teachers?
4. What about the accessibility of the administration? Is it approachable?
5. Is there a hierarchy of discipline responses?
6. Does the principal back the faculty in relationships with parents?
7. Do teachers perceive support from above?
8. Where are the valuable resources allocated in the building?
   Toward the "hard" subjects or toward the aesthetic areas?
9. Where are the inter/intra building funds allocated? What are the procedures to determine who gets them?
10. What kind of activities dominate the principal's time? Is she or he visible to staff and students?
11. What minor physical changes have been made by the principal since his or her arrival at the school?

Organizational

1. How is the faculty organized? Chain of command, collegial, ad hoc?
2. How many assistant principals and other administrators are there in the school?
3. How are teachers assigned "duties"? Is there choice?
4. Are there a great many "order" policies like cleanliness, quiet up-the-down-staircase?
5. Are regulations displayed prominently on the walls?

6. Does the building have an institutional appearance, absence of personal items displayed, excessive order?
7. Where is the guidance office located? How are counselors used in the school?

Curriculum

1. Do students have choices in what they study?
2. Is the schedule flexible enough to allow for deviation?
3. Are students placed in rigid "tracks"?
4. What kind of grading system exists? What is the failure and dropout rate?
5. Are there alternatives (substantial) to the academic pattern?
6. Are there numerous electives? Are they accessible?
7. Are there plentiful materials in the room?
8. Is there excessive competitiveness in the school? Star system?
9. Is the curriculum geared to the needs and interests of the students?
10. Are students involved in the planning and implementation of their program?
11. Is there high structure in the classrooms—teaching methods, examination schedules, grade policies, behavior expectations?

Teachers

1. How is the room arranged?
2. Are student art and work displayed?
3. Are bulletin boards up?
4. What is the teacher's relationship with parents?
5. What is the role of the student, teacher in the classroom?
6. What discipline measures are used?
7. What is the teacher's accessibility to students?
8. Does the teacher display socioeconomic prejudices?

THE GOOD NEWS ABOUT SCHOOLS

Since board members often have to deal with the bad news about school improvement and answer questions from parents and other community persons about the effectiveness of schools, you as a board member may need some good news to share about school improvement. The following items may be useful when you find the school system and yourself under attack because "schools don't do enough."*

- In 1950 less than 50 percent of students in the United States graduated from high school. Today that figure is close to 90 percent.
- In 1910 the average 25-year-old American had completed 8.1 years of schooling. Today that total is 12.4 years.

---

*Many of these items are courtesy of the National School Boards Association, your professional organization.

- Since 90 percent of today's adult population attended public schools, the United States' prominence in many fields—space technology, science, medicare, oceanography—is due in large part to the achievement of public high school graduates.
- Elementary school children today do better on standardized tests than they did in the 1960s.
- In 1900 11.3 percent of the United States population was illiterate. Today, it is less than one percent.
- The United States is one of the few countries in the world to provide free, universal public education for all desiring it; in the U.S. more of its fifteen to eighteen-year-olds are enrolled in schools than in any other country in the world.
- The number of students being graduated from U.S. colleges tripled from 1955 to 1980.
- Less than five percent of jobs today are classified as "unskilled," indicating a 97 percent increase in the professional work force from 1940 to 1980.
- Early education programs *do* make a difference. Students who completed early childhood programs combined with in-home instruction showed gains in both school achievement and I.Q.
- Public schools in the United States have reduced energy consumption by 35 percent in the past five years; this is better than any other public institution.
- Reading scores on both comprehension and vocabulary have increased steadily over the past decade for the first three years of schooling.
- In 1950 ten percent of black students were graduated from high school. In 1980 the rate was close to 80 percent.
- The U.S. has done more to help special needs students than any other nation in the world; over three million elementary and high school students have been aided.
- Today's education is a good buy for the tax dollar. The average cost of educating a school youngster today is about two thousand dollars. To care for a young person in a special state or federal program costs about eight thousand dollars a year. To maintain a young person in prison, the cost is about twenty-two thousand dollars a year.

Ask the superintendent and his staff to develop a "good news" list for your school district. Let parents and other community persons know of the good things schools are doing.

CHAPTER 10

Getting Through to People — Leadership and Public Relations

Leadership is simply defined as helping others work toward common goals and purposes. Leadership thus occurs in some kind of group and the leader functions, necessarily, in relationship to members of the group.

Since we know that on the school board only the group decision prevails, it is important to discuss the processes by which individual leadership can be exerted to make the board group work and the school district function. In this chapter you will study the dimensions of leader behavior, learn how to use leadership principles, examine ways to assess school leadership, look at the best way to evaluate the performance of the superintendent, and learn how to use your leadership to improve the way your school system works.

CONCEPTIONS OF LEADERSHIP

Through the years, considerable thought and research have been directed toward understanding leadership behavior, yet leadership remains a rather mysterious concept to most persons reviewing the literature. Far from a lack of information about leadership, the reader is overwhelmed by a wide range of expert opinion and conflicting research reports. Although our definition centers on helping others work toward common goals, you can find over 130 formal definitions of leadership in today's literature. Some of those definitions are shown below to illustrate the breadth of the samples available:

> A leader is best when people barely know he exists. When our work is done, his aim is fulfilled, they will say, "We did this ourselves." Lao-Tzu, *The Way of Life*, 6th century, B.C.

> Love is held by a chain of obligation ... but fear is maintained by the dread of punishment which never fails. . . . A wise prince must rely on what is in his power and not on what is in the power of others. Niccolo Machiavelli, *The Prince*, 1500 A.D.

> Leadership is the art of imposing one's will upon others in such a manner as to command their obedience, their respect, and their loyal cooperation. *G-I Manual*, Staff College, United States Army, 1947.

> Leadership is the ability to get a man to do what you want him to do, when you want it done, in a way you want it done, because he wants to do it. Dwight Eisenhower, 1957.

> Leadership is the human factor which binds a group together and motivates it toward a goal. K. Davis, *Human Relations at Work*, 1962.

> Leadership is the process of influencing the activities of an individual or group in efforts toward goal achievement in a given situation. Hersey and Blanchard, *The Management of Organizational Behavior*, 1977.

Leadership exchange theory focuses on how leaders initially motivate groups to accept their influence, the processes that undergird prolonged exertion of such influence, and the ways in which the leader makes real contributions to group goals. In short, exchange theory seeks to learn and explain how leaders work within their groups to establish and maintain influence. Leadership, by this definition, is an exchange or transaction that occurs (acceptance of influence) when needs are present (until satisfaction is achieved) between the leader and the follower. The following generalizations about leadership in school environments, where multiple group needs are present, are found in the literature:

1. Leadership is a group role ... [The leader] is able to exert leadership only through effective participation in groups.
2. Leadership, other things being equal, depends upon the frequency of interaction between the leader and the led.
3. Status position does not necessarily give leadership.
4. Leadership in any organization is widespread and diffused ... if a person hopes to exert leadership for everybody, he is doomed to frustration and failure.

5. The norms of the group determine the leader.
6. Leadership qualities and followership qualities are interchangeable.
7. People who give evidence of a desire to control are rejected for leadership roles.
8. The feeling that people hold about a person is a factor in whether they will use her or his behavior as leadership.
9. Leadership shifts from situation to situation.

As leadership exchange theory emerges in the 1980s, it becomes clear that the "follower perceptions" of leadership are a critical ingredient for successful leadership practice. If the leader possesses skills or traits that will facilitate group attainment of goals, but is not perceived as possessing those attributes, leadership cannot and will not be exerted. *The authors believe that being visible and directly communicating to follower groups will be a central task of school leadership in the future.* For this reason, understanding patterns or "styles" of leadership is important for a board member seeking to be an effective leader.

STYLES OF LEADERSHIP

Serious studies of leadership style emerged in the 1930s from industry. A critical question for industrial leaders was how to match the organizational tasks of a bureaucracy with the human needs of the worker. Finding a compatible style of leadership to match organizational task requirements presented a research problem that is still being explored today.

Overall, the various conceptions of leadership style suggest a continuum of possible roles. Different models propose a "mix" of variables that influence leadership behavior. Five simple combinations are suggested for the board member's study in Figure 10.1.

Figure 10.1 Leadership Styles

1. "TELLS" Leadership
   A. Seeks unquestioning obedience
   B. Sometimes relies on fear, intimidation
   C. Gives orders
   D. Relies heavily on authority
   E. Sets all goals and standards
   F. Makes all decisions without consulting the group

2. "SELLS" Leadership
   A. Work assignments are allotted to workers

   B. Assignments are sometimes arbitrary
   C. Tries to persuade the group to accept assignments
   D. Seldom builds teamwork
   E. Does not motivate worker involvement
   F. Makes decisions without consulting the group

3. "CONSULTS" Leadership
   A. Does not rely on authority
   B. Develops considerable worker loyalty
   C. Does not hesitate to delegate
   D. Will usually explain "why" a task is to be performed in a certain way
   E. Takes time to inform the group what he or she thinks may be a solution

4. "JOINS" Leadership
   A. Builds teamwork by group involvement
   B. Accepts suggestions from the work group
   C. Treats each worker as an individual
   D. Helps workers achieve their potential
   E. Uses the decision of the group

5. "DELEGATES" Leadership
   A. Turns the decision-making process over to the group
   B. Accepts all group decisions that fit within accepted parameters
   C. Encourages subordinate participation in many activities
   D. Stimulates creative thinking in employees

IMPLICATIONS FOR LEADERSHIP
IN THE 1980s

Research on leadership suggests that true leading results from three factors: having the skills for leadership, being able to match the appropriate skills with the tasks of the group being led, and being seen by the group as a leader. As observed earlier in this book, there is a need for a new style of leadership in the 1980s. School leaders will need to be open and predictable rather than flashy and competitive. School leaders will have to be responsive to the various groups being led. School leaders must possess technical and interpersonal skills. Perhaps most important, school leaders in the 1980s and beyond will need to exhibit a style that acknowledges the political and economic conditions of the immediate environment.

   The 1980s have been an era of decline in most school districts and, where there are resources, a time of prudent management of resources. In most districts board members must "pull in their horns" and deal with limited resources. Leadership styles that are flamboyant will no longer suffice. The cool, deliberating, and predictable board member will be the most successful one. As major problems associated with scarcity impact upon schools, sometimes solutions will not match up with demands. The pie will be shrinking and different slices of that pie will be made at the expense of others. How resources are managed and sound board policies are developed and implemented will determine the success or non-success of boards.

BEING A LEADER

The board member who is to be a leader must work hard to *appear* to be the leader as well as to lead. Board members must think hard about style and image in their role as a leader and pursue both vigorously. The board member must enter service on the board with both momentum and direction while still projecting an image of basic stability.

Self-concept is all important to a board member. Perceptual psychologists have told us that all behavior, without exception, is a function of the behaver's perceptual field at the instant of behavior. Of equal importance in the field of perceptual psychology is the concept of image projection and reception. We know, for instance, that perceptual fields (or vision) are narrowed in a crisis situation. A person in a crosswalk who is about to be run down by a truck will be more likely to read MACK than to tell others about the neighborhood. By the same token, in meeting strangers or interacting in highly controlled social situations only selective parts of others are perceived. A second part of this reality is that, besides being selective in seeing others, we choose what we see according to *our* needs or experience.

The value of the perceptual vantage point for board leaders is to acknowledge and utilize the fact that they will *always be seen selectively* by others. Further, it is predictable that others will see them according to the situation in which they find themselves and the needs of the moment. The board member who understands this and can "read" the situation or anticipate needs has an edge in projecting an image of leadership that will be selected by others as "appropriate." This enlightenment corresponds directly with research that increasingly defines leadership in terms of transactions initiated by the leader.

Establishing Image

Every day individuals in human organizations send messages and signals to one another at the subconscious level. While there is normal verbal interaction among these individuals, some very strong communication occurs as a result of appearances and the context of appearances. We are all constantly sending and receiving signals that contribute or detract from a desired image. To understand that this subtle communication exists, and to capitalize upon it to establish a leadership image that can be perceived by others is the topic of this section. While there are many lenses that might be used to relate this topic, we shall concentrate on three: physical appearance, environmental images, and roles that convey images.

Physical appearance or image is made up of two major categories: our dressing pattern and our body language. Both are critical to the success or failure of a board member. While each individual must "work with what they've got" in terms of looks, it is possible to dress up the image of any individual.

Men and women serving on boards today are generally appearance-conscious. Gone are the days of the sloppy dresser. Still, all of us will acknowledge that some members look the role while others lack "pizzazz." Some observations on dress follow:

Hair length is generally a good indicator of personality, at least in terms of uptightness or easygoingness. Hair that is loose (not plastered) and medium long (not out of control) suggests a growing, open personality in the school administrator.

Eye glasses can be useful in projecting an image. Large and heavy glasses can mask youthfulness. Tortoise shell or rimless glasses suggest a studious or intellectual person. By the same token, tinted or colored eyeglasses suggest playful or shy personalities.

The use of *jewelry* for men and women, and ties for men and printed scarves for women, is an opportunity to promote visual values. As college professors have for years used the Phi Beta Kappa key to send a message to their colleagues, it is possible to speak quite clearly with symbolic ties or printed scarves, medallions, bracelets, and so forth. The assorted pieces of jewelry together have importance in establishing social contact and initiating communication with strangers.

In general dress, *color* is extremely important. Color speaks a universal language that everyone understands, and people respond to color even before symbols (for instance, stop signs). Additionally, we live in a color-coded world. Color is used to cue us, warn us, and encourage us. In the color spectrum there are three primary colors, red, blue, and yellow, and these are the most easily grasped visually. They are also the least intriguing and easily forgotten. Color is important in choosing dress to fit an occasion. White shirts, for instance, conjure up an image of tidiness. Yellow is a transitory color, used in society to warn or caution. Blue is a softer, less alert color.

Dress, for the board member, sets an initial impression of the role image. The member who anticipates the type of day she or he will have (budget sessions all afternoon) and dresses accordingly (conservative brown or gray suit, white shirt, solid or print tie of soft color) will find her or his image matching the role task. Or, for a special meeting with an important group, the choice of a symbol-projecting device such as a "sail" tie or special medallion can ease initial conversation and establish common values beyond the immediate meeting.

The reader may wish to review the contrasting images below and attempt to visualize dressing specifically to reinforce the image:

Aggressive	Retiring
Changeable	Constant
Secure	Insecure
Bold	Timid
Articulate	Inarticulate
Careless	Particular
Serious	Frivolous
Overconfident	Hesitant

Even more important than the clothes is the way in which they're worn and the general body language communicated to others. Years of investigation in the social sciences have led to a sub-specialization labeled kinesics—the study of movement and gesture. So powerful is this science in interpreting facial gestures, walking, and body posture that it is used regularly by professional labor negotiators to assess openness, defensiveness, readiness, suspicion, confidence, nervousness, and a host of other telltale traits in communication. Board members can use a knowledge of kinesics to both project an image and interpret the behaviors of others.

Over 135 distinct gestures and expressions of the face, head, and body have been recorded in American society. With so many cues, discovering the meaning of gestures may prove a difficult task. However, as Edward T. Hall has observed in his classic book, *The Silent Language*, "Man is constantly striving to discover the meaning of relationships between individuals and groups of individuals. The professional scholar soon learns to disregard the immediate explicit meaning of the obvious and to look for a pattern." Gestures, then, come in clusters, and by watching we can understand more clearly what is being expressed verbally. By the same token, the board member can use such gestures and posturing to reinforce what he or she wishes to communicate.

Through nonverbal feedback the board member can learn whether what he or she is saying is being received or rejected. Nonverbal behaviors can indicate a need to change the subject, withdraw, or try something different to facilitate the communication that the speaker wishes to come about. An old Cantonese proverb warns, "watch out for the man whose stomach doesn't move when he laughs." An Apache adage states, "speak with your deeds, listen with your eyes."

In general, the openness or tightness of the body limbs tell a lot about the person being studied. Crossed arms or legs, limbs pulled tightly against the body, tucked chins, and so forth are sure signs of discomfort. A reception cluster, by contrast, might involve an individual unbuttoning a coat, uncrossing their legs, leaning forward toward you, or otherwise not "blocking" you off from their body trunk.

Eyes and the face tell a great deal about the individual being studied. Ralph Waldo Emerson once observed, "The eyes of men converse as much as their tongues, with the advantage that the ocular dialect needs no dictionary, but is understood the world over." Studies, such as those conducted by Argyle and reported in *The Psychology of Interpersonal Behavior*, reveal that the amount of eye contact is significant. Normally, when two individuals are talking they look at each other about 60 percent of the time. Eye contact greater than 60 percent indicates an interest in the other person beyond what is being said.

By the opposite token, eye aversion in face-to-face communication is generally taken to be a sign of disinterest or avoidance behavior in the United States. Read with other signs, such aversion indicates poor communication. A tightening jaw muscle or pursed lips can indicate antagonism. A frown can mean confusion or, in some cases, disapproval. Raised eyebrows often indicate envy or disbelief.

Gestures add another dimension to the ability to read a person or send a person a nonverbal message. Classic evaluation or judging gestures are a finger pointing to the temple, or a finger alongside the nose, a stroking of the chin or beard, a slight quizzical tilt of the head. Frustration may be indicated by clenched hands or the wringing of hands. A pointing finger is a powerful message. As the Jamaican proverb observes, "a pointing finger never says 'look here,' it always says 'look there.'"

A person who speaks to you through a hand in front of the mouth, as children often do, or through clenched teeth, often reveals a lack of certainty about what he or she is saying. By the same cultural cues, a person who scratches behind his ear or wipes his eye with the back of his knuckles is signaling disbelief.

Communication, then, is influenced by both the dress of the board member and the body language translated by the board member. Careful study of these phenomena will help in assessing the intent or actions of others, allow the reinforcement of communication to others, and project an image appropriate to the occasion.

The environmental image of the individual board member is an image that can be created even without the benefit of poise or contributing physical appearance. Environmental image consists of on-the-job things that others recognize as a style. Examples of environmental image might be the way a board member's office is ordered, the means by which he or she uses media for communicating, the way that he/she manipulates and uses time, and the associations the person maintains.

The office of a board member reveals a great deal about the individual's personality, role image, work habits, and aspirations. Even in a sterile government office, with government-issued furniture, wall plaques, and name plates, individuality is evident. The board member who is aware of this can "dress the office" to improve an image.*

Another contributor to an environmental image is the careful choice of an appropriate communication medium. Most individuals regularly use the type of communication medium that they feel most comfortable with, be it a telephone, letter/memo, or personal visit. The error in this way of doing things is not to consider the receiver of your message in choosing the medium. Like school children, we are either better readers, or listeners, or prefer to be shown. The board member who understands this can begin to deliver the message in the *receiver's* favorite medium. As Marshall McLuhan has observed, "the medium can be the message." McLuhan continues, "The first item in the press to which all men turn is the one about which they already know. Why? The answer is central to any understanding of the media ... Experience translated into a new medium literally bestows a delightful playback of earlier awareness."

The board member contemplating a message to be sent must think of the purpose of the message. Is the message to expedite communication or to store information? Do you want to communicate exactly, or leave just an impression? Is this a public-type communication or does it contain some degree of confidentiality? Answers to the above questions might determine whether a memo will suffice or whether a face-to-face meeting is needed.

Two other observations might be made about communication in general and specifically in organizations. First, before communicating it is necessary to get the attention of the receiver. Everyone has heard the story about the man who got the donkey's attention by cracking it over the head with a two-by-four. While this degree of force is not called for, it is important to intersect the receiver's "frame of reference" or experience. This is why platform speakers use jokes to warm up audiences or casual conversations begin with banal observations about the weather. Finding common values or experiences helps the listener focus on your communication, whatever the medium.

A second observation is a true phenomenon which simply exists: most people respond to a telephone more readily than to a live person. Again McLuhan observes, "Anybody can walk into any manager's

---

*The office of a board member can refer to an office provided in the district office or his or her own business or home office.

office by telephone. The telephone is an irresistible intruder in time or place. In its nature the telephone is an intensely personal form that ignores all the claims of visual privacy." If a board member needs access to the chairman or superintendent in a hurry, thirty seconds on the phone can open the door for thirty minutes.

Like the office image and the way the board member uses the various communication media, the uses of time establish an image or symbolic identification. Each occupation has a "time sense" which results from the nature of the work. The scientist, for instance, is as a rule a precise person who jealously guards that precious commodity, time. Bankers are punctual by nature. Board members also have a time sense, but it differs from situation to situation. The board member who can assess the relationship between the use of time and the organizational mission can use time to create an image.

The modern board member may find himself or herself "meeting to death." There may be just too many things to attend to and the job may become overwhelming. For that reason, the member who wishes to appear anything but the image of "Chicken Little" must learn to make selective responses to demands on time. This notion is known as "managing time" or otherwise described as bunching up related events.

Because meaningless meetings and discussions may tend to fritter away time, the efficient board member (many of whom have great responsibilities at work or at home) must recognize how his or her time is allocated from day to day. Some sort of time-diagnosis like keeping a week's log of how time is spent might be very revealing. The board member who is always "too busy" won't last very long in office.

Another contribution to the overall environmental image of the board member is his or her associations. It is the pattern of associations in work, not a position title, that tends to define the job. The board member must give thought to the question, "How do I wish to be seen?"

In general, he or she will wish to be seen as someone who is in association with the "right" people in the district. The persons with whom he or she works, is seen, eats lunch, or stops to chat, add to that member's image. Those "attending behaviors" need to be addressed toward constituents that can be of use to the board member or, at least, not be harmful to his or her image.

ASSUMING ROLES AND TASKS

The final symbolic identifications that contribute to the image of the board member are the roles and tasks that are assumed. There are, of course, numerous roles available to the board member, and the emphasis given to roles or tasks establishes a projected pattern. Such behaviors are usually enacted through regular functions on a day-to-day basis and can be thought of in terms of combinations. For example, one useful role in an organization is the identification of concerns (listening, diagnosing, storing, reporting). Another useful role is diagnosing situations (evaluating, judging, deciding). A third might be the consideration of alternative actions (retrieving, planning, managing). A fourth might be directing changes (producing, legitimizing, telling, validating). The roles and tasks selected by the board member should be those that will appear harmonious to the arena.

Roles are critical due to their influence on the human systems found in school settings. Figure 10.2 suggests a number of roles that one might assume in identifying, selecting, and solving common problems.

Figure 10.2 Roles We Assume

Roles in Groups Attempting to Identify, Select, and Solve Common Problems

A. Group Task Roles. Facilitation and coordination of group problem-solving activities.

1. *Initiator contributor.* Offers new ideas or changed ways of regarding group problem. Suggests solutions. How to handle group difficulty. New procedure for group. New organization for group.

2. *Information seeker.* Seeks clarification of suggestions in terms of factual adequacy and/or authoritative information and pertinent facts.

3. *Opinion seeker.* Seeks clarification of values pertinent to what group is undertaking or values involved in suggestions made.

4. *Information giver.* Offers facts or generalizations that are "authoritative" or relates own experience *pertinently* to group problem.

5. *Opinion giver.* States belief or opinion pertinently to suggestions. Emphasis on his proposal of what should become group's views of pertinent values.

6. *Elaborator.* Gives examples or develops meanings, offers rationale for suggestions made before, and tries to deduce how ideas might work out.

7. *Coordinator.* Clarifies relationships among ideas and suggestions, pulls ideas and suggestions together, or tries to coordinate activities of members of subgroups.

8. *Orienter.* Defines position of group with respect to goals. Summarizes. Shows departures from agreed directions or goals. Questions directions of discussion.

9. *Evaluator.* Subjects accomplishment of group to "standards" of group functioning. May evaluate or question "practicability," "logic," "facts," or "procedure" of a suggestion or of some unit of group discussion.

10. *Energizer.* Prods group to action or decision. Tries to stimulate group to "greater" or higher quality decision.

11. *Procedural technician.*   Performs routine tasks (distributes materials, etc.) or manipulates objects for group (rearranging chairs, etc.)

12. *Recorder.*   Writes down suggestions, group decision, or products of discussion. "Group memory."

B. Group Growing and Vitalizing Roles.   Building group-centered attitudes and orientation.

13. *Encourager.*   Praises, agrees with, and accepts others' ideas. Indicates warmth and solidarity in attitude toward members.

14. *Harmonizer.*   Mediates intragroup scraps. Relieves tension.

15. *Compromiser.*   Operates from within a conflict in which his ideas or position is involved. May yield status, admit error, discipline himself, come halfway.

16. *Gatekeeper and expediter.*   Encourages and facilitates participation of others. Let's hear . . . Why not limit length of contributions so all can react to problem?

17. *Standard-setter or ego ideal.*   Expresses standards for group to attempt to achieve in its functioning or applies standards in evaluating the quality of group processes.

18. *Group observer and commentator.*   Keeps records of group processes and contributes these data with proposed interpretations into group's evaluation of its own procedures.

19. *Follower.*   Goes along somewhat passively. Is friendly audience.

C. Antigroup Roles.   Tries to meet felt individual needs at expense of group health rather than through cooperation with group.

20. *Aggressor.*   Deflates status of others. Expresses disapproval of values, acts, or feelings of others. Attacks group or problem. Jokes aggressively, shows envy by trying to take credit for other's ideas.

21. *Blocker.*   Negativistic. Stubbornly and unreasoningly resistant. Tries to bring back issue group intentionally rejected or bypassed.

22. *Recognition-seeker.*   Tries to call attention to himself. May boast, report on personal achievements, and in unusual ways struggle to prevent being placed in "inferior" position.

23. *Self-confessor.*   Uses group to express personal, non-group-oriented "feeling," "insight," ideology."

24. *Playboy.*   Displays lack of involvement in group's work. Actions may take form of cynicism, nonchalance, horseplay, or other more or less studies of "field behavior."

25. *Dominator.*   Tries to assert authority in manipulating group or some individuals in group. May be flattery, assertion of superior status or right to attention, giving of directions authoritatively, interrupting contributions of others.

26. *Help-seeker.*   Tries to get "sympathy" response from others through expressions of insecurity, personal confusion, or depreciation of himself beyond "reason."

27. *Special-interest pleader.* Verbally for "small businessman," "grass roots," community, housewife, "labor." Actually speaking own prejudices or biases on stereotype which best fits his individual need.

Adaptation of the concept of group roles as developed by Benne and Sheets.

Projective Tasks for Board Members

There are a number of generic leadership tasks in service on a school board that provide opportunity for visibility and image projection:

1. Developing an operating theory. Conceptualizing tasks and communicating those tasks to others in an organization. An operating theory is drawn from tasks identified and responses to those tasks. Image: resident thinker or model-builder.
2. Developing a response organization. Certain tasks are often nonpermanent responses to need. The way in which people, ideas, and resources are organized is often left to the leader. Structures are built or rebuilt to respond to those needs. Image: manager, coordinator.
3. Setting organizational standards. Because board problems often involve diverse groups of individuals with different needs and perceptions, an important task is to set standards and other expectations that will affect the resolution of problems. Such standards may include work habits, communications procedures, time limitations, or a host of related planning areas. Image: pace-setter or quality-control leader.
4. Using authority to establish an organizational climate. A board member is able to structure organizations by suggesting changes, allocating resources, and initiating policies. By concentrating on a uniform pattern or structure, it is possible to give the organization a tone or climate that results from the collective perceptions of people in the organization. Image: program builder, architect for process.
5. Establishing effective interpersonal relations. Since service on a board is a product of human exchanges or transactions within an organization, the establishment of interpersonal patterns can change the way in which an organization works. Image: good guy, friend, confidant, team-builder.
6. Planning and initiating action. Knowing when it is necessary to use authority to initiate change is a major leadership skill. Failure to lead planning or to act when action is required can undermine other board functions. Image: powerhouse, person who will take risks.

The leadership roles and tasks available to the board member on an everyday basis, then, provide another possibility to create an image that is favorable to the organization. The selection of the correct set of roles and tasks is dependent on the needs of the individuals being led and the flow of events within the structure of the organization itself.

In summary, leadership needs are changing. Unlike the previous decades, the 1980s and 1990s will call for a steady performance by open and responsive board members in school districts.

It is important that board members understand the nature of leadership. A large body of literature and extensive research tells us that successful leadership is the result of three factors: a set of skills or traits possessed by the leader; a correct environment or situation for the application of those skills; and the followers' perception that the leader is the one who can meet their needs.

By far the most difficult part of leading for board members in an era of declining resources will be being perceived as the leader. Understanding leadership "styles" and how to project an image that can be received by followers will be an important skill for all school board members in the coming decades. Using this knowledge of image to carry out tasks that are "projective" in nature can be beneficial to a successful tenure on the board.

PUBLIC RELATIONS

Public relations is a by-product of all school activity. Boards must develop a public relations policy that will (1) promote public interest and participation in the operation of the school system, (2) gather activities and reactions about the school system and report them to the superintendent and board, (3) provide a continuous flow of information about policies, procedures, problems, and progress of the school district, and (4) develop a climate that will attract good teachers and administrators and encourage school staffs to strive for excellence in the educational program.

Working with Parents and the Community

The school is often the center of community activities. It serves as a polling place, meeting place for community groups, location for school board meetings, and as a center for recreational activities. Where schools exist as community schools, the school building may be open long hours with a variety of activities scheduled for all ages. Adult education, community college classes, and university extension courses may also be housed on the elementary, middle, or high school campuses. Schools belong to the people and active participation of citizens in school activities helps insure continued community support.

LISTENING AND GROUP SKILLS

Practicing Active Listening

Communication among individuals in an organization is often a delicate art requiring a cooperative spirit and a degree of self-discipline. Nowhere is that more important than on a school board where it seems natural for one person to do the talking while others listen. A critical skill for the new board member, then, is to learn to actively listen to others.

Here are some guides to improving your listening skills which are worthy of review: focus on areas of interest in the speaker's message; judge the content of the message and not the delivery; learn to hold your fire and not reveal your bias; focus on central ideas and the flow of the message; take notes only for specifics, not for an outline; give the learner your conscious attention and fight back distractions; tune out distractions over which you have no immediate control; keep your mind open by avoiding blind spots and personal prejudices; and capitalize on thought speed—we think four times faster than we talk.

Board members should make a conscious effort to anticipate what the speaker will say based on what has already been said. They should mentally summarize what the person is saying. While listening, the board member should ask clarifying questions mentally and read between the lines. Finally, it should become regular practice for the board member to "feed back" what the speaker has said to insure that clear communication has occurred.

Small Group Conferencing

Board members may be involved in small group conferencing during teacher dismissal hearings, board retreats, in briefing sessions with administrators, and in board committee action dealing with problem solving, e.g., a board facilities committee deciding on after-school use of building by community groups. The process of conferencing can lead to the solution of a problem through something other than an executive decision. Involved in such a process is a clear definition of a problem, an analysis of factors important to a solution, and activities carried out by group members. In short, new board members will quickly find that conferencing is an excellent way of involving others in seeking answers to problems.

Working in Group Settings

Board members perform in a variety of group settings to accomplish tasks that are important to the operation of schools. Among these group tasks are: initiating activities, suggesting new ideas, defining problems, proposing solutions, coordinating activities, and evaluating results. The board members should also be aware that in a conference or small group session some behaviors will prove unproductive. Examples of such unproductive actions are: being aggressive and showing hostility toward other persons; blocking or otherwise interfering with a group process by speaking tangentially; competing to gain favor or to win recognition; and withdrawing by acting indifferent or being purposely passive.

Board members should periodically evaluate the effectiveness of their conferences and group sessions by reviewing sessions with some critical questions: Did this conference or group session have a clear purpose? Did everyone contribute or speak? Did I practice active listening to learn the positions of others? Did we agree on action steps? Does everyone involved understand his/her role?

Managing Committee Meetings

In larger meetings, such as standing committees of the board, the board member will be placed in a more directing role because of status leadership. Such a role can help the group to be more productive if the board member will concentrate on six parts common to any committee meeting. First, the leader must present topics so that their general importance is understood and that a pathway for discussion is clear and obvious. Second, the leader must initiate discussion by providing some advance thinking for the group. An analogy, case study, or even a misstated position can be used for this purpose. Third, the leader keeps the discussion on track by paraphrasing and providing transition statements from one topic to the next. Fourth, the board leader controls the flow of the discussion by keeping the group aware of time constraints. Fifth, the leader is responsible to the group for preventing sidetracking (such as restraining a talkative person) and for guaranteeing access to all who wish to participate. Finally, the leader summarizes the discussion by reviewing high points and illuminating decisions.

The board member must always remember that, because he or she is the official leader, the group will expect all meetings to be run in a professional manner.

Communicating through the News Media

Working effectively with the news media has been a difficult task for many board members. Often, an adversary relationship exists between boards and the media that does not have to exist. Board members may feel they are misquoted or that the press tries to sensationalize things. Media persons may feel board members are trying to manipulate the news, holding out the real news, or trying to hide information.

Probably, both groups are responsible for the situation. How then can board members do their part to communicate effectively through the news media? The following suggestions may help:

1. Except on personal matters requiring confidentiality, make sure all meetings are open to the press. Where sunshine laws exist, open meetings will occur as a matter of course.
2. Don't "play up to the press" or attempt to "play the press." Be honest and candid—take a position and talk straight to the press. Talk slowly and ask the reporter to read back what you have said. If interviews are live on television, remember that what you say for three to four minutes will be edited down to 15 to 20 seconds for airing. Be precise, don't ramble and be quoted out of context.
3. Set up meetings with the press to talk of ways to facilitate press conferences. Install t.v. lights, set up microphones, have copies of agenda and reports available for the press, provide them with tables on which to write, and give them access to phones to call in their stories.
4. Set up board meetings with the editor(s) of the local paper(s) and radio and television news directors. Ask them to send veteran reporters to cover board meetings if possible. "Rookie" reporters often bungle stories.
5. Appoint a press liaison person not to speak for the district, but to be a liaison with the press. Since the superintendent is charged with interpreting the school's program to the public, he or she must authorize any statements that speak for the school district. The board also speaks as a whole so any board statements must be cleared by the whole board.

Establishing the Position of Director of Public Relations

In smaller districts a separate position of Director of Public Relations may not be possible, but in larger districts such a position should be established. A Director of Public Relations can do much to keep the public informed through a variety of publications.

Obtaining Feedback from the Community

Feedback may be obtained from the community from many sources. Citizens Advisory Committees are found in many districts today. Parents, nonparents, and others may serve on such committees. Surveys may also be used to solicit citizen reactions to certain issues. Many boards use newspapers to ask the public for viewpoints and even to help grade schools on performance. Meetings with civic and church groups can also be used to obtain feedback from the community and also to help "sell the schools" to the public. Of course, we can't forget one of the oldest channels for two-way communication is the local PTA.

Communicating in Times of Controversy and Crisis

As more and more special-interest groups arise (many of them are ad hoc or temporary groups), strikes and other crises occur, it is important that boards have an effective communication program. Preventing flare-ups and handling rumors are important parts of an effective communication plan. In Chapter 4 we discussed ways of communicating during work stoppages.

Student disruptions today may arise out of the closing of schools or cutbacks in programs. Dealing with student disruptions will require instant responses on the part of the school administrator and board. If good communication lines have already been established with students, confrontations can be headed off and solutions to student problems or concerns can be discussed.

Communicating with Your Legislators

As more and more decisions about schools move to state legislatures, board members are finding themselves advocating beneficial legislation or trying to prevent legislation that will adversely affect the local school district. Boards may also participate with local groups in letter writing campaigns to state representatives. The following suggestions may be useful in getting your letters read by legislators:

Appeal to his home district loyalty by letting him know how an issue/ bill affects you and your locality.
Be as concise and specific as you can. Write concerning one bill or issue only.

Courteous letters will be appreciated. Legislators are people, too, and will be more likely to see your point if you provide helpful information rather than threats and criticisms.

Don't use form letters or mimeographed materials. Let your legislator know you can think for yourself. Do use plain or personal stationery or the letterhead of the group you represent.

Early in the game is the best time to write. If you write before a bill is out of committee, it will give your legislator time to act before final action has been taken.

Follow through with a thank-you note.

Give your legislator time to study the bill/issue, before asking him to commit himself on it.

"Honorable" is the correct title for all legislators. Use "The Honorable" before his full name on the envelope and the inside address. But in the salutation use "Dear Mr. or Ms." for representatives and "Dear Senator Smith" for senators.

Impact is what you will make when you write to your own representative. Legislators are more concerned with their own constituents.

Just because one letter is good doesn't mean hundreds of letters are better. Laws have been passed or killed because of a single, well-written letter. Many letters from you may make you a constant correspondent and a less effective one.

Know your legislator's full name. Spell it correctly. Write for a Legislative Directory.

Let your legislators know the facts and reasons behind your opinion. This is the crucial element of an influential letter.

Mail your letter first class.

Numbers and names are important. Thousands of bills are introduced each year. To avoid confusion, include the name of the bill's sponsor and the bill's number.

HOW PARENTS FEEL ABOUT SCHOOLS

Parents of school children are the primary supporters of our schools. We can benefit from the research about how parents feel about schools. What may seem to be common-sense strategies in getting through to parents are often ignored. The following observations may prove useful to the board member when he or she is trying to understand why parents support or don't support schools:

Why Are Some Parents Positive about Our Schools?

Parents have positive feelings about and support their local schools because:

1. The school has fostered good communication.
2. The parent feels welcome in the school.
3. The parent sees that his or her child is making progress in his/her academic subjects.
4. The parent sees school personnel as truly caring people.
5. The parent reflects family goals, values, and attitudes toward education.
6. The parent sees education as a step toward success.
7. The parent is involved in school decisions.
8. The parent is himself well educated.
9. The parent is an educator or former educator.
10. The parent has confidence in the school.

Why Are Some Parents Negative about Our Schools? (and what might we do about it?)

Parents may have negative feelings or are indifferent toward local schools because:

1. Their child is not succeeding in school.
    a. Include the parent in a staffing to evaluate progress and seek the reason for school problems and offer suggestions toward solution.
    b. Offer the school and district resources that might be helpful, i.e., psychological services, specialists, etc.
    c. Send home supplementary materials on a regular basis.
    d. Regularly schedule conferences with the teacher so the parent is kept aware of even minimal progress.
    e. Lists of activities which may be pursued could be sent home regularly.
    f. Information regarding summer programs, tutoring, etc. should be sent home to parents.
    g. Surplus workbooks or worksheets could be offered the child.
    h. Evaluate the child for special placement, i.e., Title I, Specific Learning Disabilities Program, Emotionally Handicapped Program, Language, Speech and Hearing Program, etc.
2. The parents have a lack of understanding of what the school is doing or attempting to do.
    a. Schedule a Parent Night – Open House with general presentations of school programs, materials, etc.
    b. Plan Parent Information Night in grade-level teams to discuss specific programs.
    c. Make available afternoon and evening conference time for working parents.

    d. Send a regular newsletter to parents, including information about specific school programs.

    e. Schedule Parent-Teacher group meetings.

3. The parents feel uneasy with the school situation, as they were not successful academically in their own school years.

    a. Use no educational jargon during conferences. Promote a feeling of comfort and ease within the parent.

    b. Share all information that is pertinent with the parent.

    c. State positive aspects of the child's schoolwork and behavior.

    d. Hold peer-group meetings with other parents.

    e. Show all parents the same respect. Do not talk down to parents that are less well educated than others.

    f. Invite parents to become involved in school affairs, i.e., volunteer programs, health room, field trip chaperone, etc.

4. The parent has a lack of trust in the school.

    a. Send regular newsletters home. Highlight events, specific recognition, etc.

    b. Schedule a conference to share information. Impress the parents with how much the school cares for the child.

    c. Follow through on all reasonable parent requests. Answer notes and telephone calls as soon as possible.

    d. Send schoolwork home on a regular basis.

    e. There should be a constant communication from the teacher regarding progress, class activities, etc. Telephone calls are most helpful.

5. Decisions regarding the child are made without consulting the parent.

    a. Information regarding the general school program should be sent home regularly.

    b. Information should be sent home regularly regarding specific aspects of the child's progress.

    c. Hold parent-teacher conferences with other staff people brought in if it is appropriate.

    d. Printouts for reading or math tests, state assessment tests, Metropolitan tests, etc., should be sent home with an accompanying letter of information from the school or the teacher.

    e. Regular telephone calls from the teacher.

6. The parent has a literacy problem or does not understand school jargon.

    a. All communication that goes home should be written in clear, concise language.

    b. Non-English-speaking parents should receive school communication in a language that they can understand.

    c. Explanatory notes should be sent along with any "official" type of school communication.

    d. Regular telephone calls from the teacher or someone who can communicate in the language of the parent.

7. The parent is swayed by friends or neighbors who have negative feelings about the school.

    a. Information regarding the general school program should be sent home regularly.

    b. Schoolwork that has been graded should be sent home on a regular basis.

    c. Telephone calls from the teacher should point out good as well as bad situations.

    d. Send regular newsletters home showing the achievements of the school and of specific individual students.

    e. Promote a feeling that the school is always open to the parent.

8. The parent is swayed by reading local or national publicity that is adverse to the public schools: Why Johnny Can't Read, etc.

    a. Send information regarding the school programs regularly to the parents.

    b. Send newsletters to the home showing the progress that the school is making.

    c. Build confidence in the school. Highlight progress that has been made both by the school as a whole and the child as an individual. Compare school scores with state and local norms. Compare this year's scores with those of past years.

9. The parent has many problems and no time or energy to devote to the child and his schoolwork after the day is over. The parent is raising the child alone, with a lack of money, in an unstable family situation, etc.

    a. Offer conferences at a time convenient to the parent.

    b. Investigate the possibility of before and after school care for primary department or young intermediate age youngsters.

    c. Investigate the possibility of holding a breakfast program.

    d. Investigate the possibility of using school vehicles to transport children to the Boys' Club, Girls' Club, or YMCA after school.

    e. Allow youngsters to remain in a study situation to complete homework after school.

    f. Offer self-help counseling sessions for single parents, or other such groups.

    g. Schedule small group counseling for specific youngsters who seem in need of such help.

    h. Allow the children to seek counseling when they feel they need to talk to someone.

    i. The teacher should telephone the parent as soon as a problem situation is noticed.

Reading The School Board Primer *indicates you have a strong desire to learn and improve your performance as a school board member. It is hoped that* The School Board Primer *will help you focus your energies to become the best board member possible. Good luck.*

Index

DATE DUE

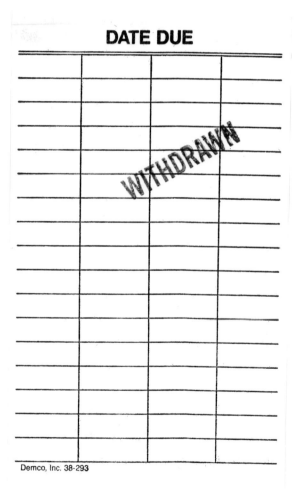

Demco, Inc. 38-293